Choosing to be Free

Choosing to be Free

The life story of Rick Turner

Billy Keniston

First published by Jacana Media (Pty) Ltd in 2013

10 Orange Street
Sunnyside
Auckland Park 2092
South Africa
+2711 628 3200
www.jacana.co.za

ISBN 978-1-4314-0831-3

Cover design by publicide
Set in Stempel Garamond 10/15pt
Printed by Ultra Litho (Pty) Ltd, Johannesburg
Job no. 002075

See a complete list of Jacana titles at www.jacana.co.za

Contents

Acknowledgements

Even though I have had to write this without you, I have still
written it for you, because of you. You persuaded me that this story
is worth telling, and then you taught me to tell stories in a new way.
You reminded me of the art that is within me, and insisted – against
all my protests – that I already have all I need to thrive. You taught
me that art must be beautiful, but also ferocious. Words must come
from a place of love, but spit fire.

WHATEVER ITS OTHER BENEFITS, writing is a lonely craft.

Surely I am not unusual in having relied on the friendship and support of dozens of people over these last years in order to bring this project to fruition. I can't imagine it otherwise.

For those few dear friends and loved ones who have stood by me, through all the different layers and phases of this project, spanning nearly half a decade, a book is hardly adequate compensation for all of the gifts I have received. And yet, ironically, more profound than any assistance with editing, layout, money or space to write (all of which was substantial), what I often needed most was simple reassurance that a book is, in and of itself, a beautiful contribution to our world. Perhaps no one taught me this lesson more clearly than Andy Trull, who believed in the project from the start, and consistently provided me with physical, intellectual and emotional refuge at his beautiful hermit lab, nestled in the woods of rural Ontario.

This project was very much a journey for me; I have had a great many homes over these last years. Gregory Jenkins, in Baltimore, Eva Gyurovszky, in Budapest, Simone Haysom, in London, Mandisi Majavu and Tony Morphet, in Cape Town, Cindy and Rodney Bloom, in Eugene, Brendan and Carey Moran, in Hillcrest, and S-fire Miria, in Virginia, all shared their homes with me during my long wandering months of research and writing.

Through it all, Libby Loft never stopped believing in me, and was again and again home for me – allowing me space to be nurtured when small, and to focus and be productive while thriving.

Although he fears that he is a member of a trade forever forgotten by the march of progress, I remain indebted to my father, Kenny Trainor, for showing me that writing is an admirable pursuit, and for staying committed to the essential task of protecting the integrity of the language. Josh MacPhee, Bec Young and Kassak Lajos, both through their own craft and with their respect for mine, have helped me to relax into the fact that what I do is, indeed, art.

My deep thanks to Gerry Maré for his generous assistance in translating a large number of documents from Afrikaans.

Beyond this extensive 'economy of friendship' that sustained me over these years, I also relied on a number of other avenues of support. The Institute for Anarchist Studies provided a grant, in order to produce a short essay on Rick Turner. Nearly fifty different people funded me through Kickstarter, in order to begin the work involved in transforming my initial research and writing into a book. To mention only some of the most notable contributions, I must thank: Shannon Walsh, Frithjof and Ingrid Wodarg, Claudia, Robbie and Sylvie, Mark Enslin, Aaron Winborn, Loraine Perlman, Brian Dominick, Linda Moore, Fran Welland, Andrew Nash, Jay Gillen, Bill Wetzel Sr., Wendy Johnson, David Biles and Johanna Hulick. Omar Badsha gave me direct support, both through Kickstarter and by enabling me to participate in a conference about the Durban Moment, in Grahamstown, in 2013. Furthermore, Bill Leigh's continuing support and respect for my choices goes above and beyond any reasonable expectation of kindness.

Additionally, I was fortunate enough to have space to write at a number of writing residencies, including: the Hermit Lab (Hermitlab.ca), the Stonehouse Residency for the Contemporary Arts (Stonehouseresidency.org), the Virginia Center for the Creative Arts (Vcca.com), and Instituto Sacatar (Sacatar.org).

Finally – and fundamentally – I must thank Georgia Phillips-Amos, whose companionship and assistance was absolutely crucial for completing this project. When we met, I was wavering and wobbly. Remarkably, she has steadied me, insisting that I carry on through repeated waves of difficulty, step by step (from Marakesh to Medellin to Brooklyn) until the end.

Introduction

WHAT'S IN A LIFE?

'Human beings can choose. They can stand back and look at alternatives. Theoretically, they can choose about anything. They can choose whether to live or to die; they can choose celibacy or promiscuity, voluntary poverty or the pursuit of wealth, ice-cream or jelly. Obviously they can't always get what they choose, but that is a different question.'[1]

– RICK TURNER

WHAT IS IN A LIFE?

How can a life be understood, as one continues to make meaning along the way?

Stories. Hints. Scraps. Little bits of evidence that lead in possible directions.

Our lives are made up of all the choices that we make, or do not make. Choices made visible, but not chosen. Choices made, but not understood, or not re-evaluated later, or regretted and carried like a weight.

The work of studying history is – whatever else historians might claim – quite simply the study of human choices. We learn from other people's life choices so that we can choose how to live.

Our lives are all quite messy, and perhaps even more so if we are living in opposition to an established order, against armies and ideas that try to constrain us. We don't really live our lives 'in order', so the attempt to make a clean chronology from the outside is futile and pointless. We live our lives more in the form of a collage – or multiple collages layered on top of each other – rather than in a simple linear progression from birth to death. We are constantly connected to ideas and people and places and memories and dreams and plans, in an endless web that has a coherent logic only if enough of the connecting threads are visible at once.

The life and work of Rick Turner is an anomaly; his choices are hard to translate across the three decades since his death. He was a white anti-apartheid activist; an atheist who wrote of the 'Christian human model' of 'loving people over things' and converted to Islam in order to marry an Indian woman; a socialist who spoke out against the Soviet Union and its satellite states; a non-pacifist who criticised the use of armed struggle against apartheid; and, most importantly, a man who stressed 'the impracticality of realism' and 'the necessity of Utopian thinking'. How could a man think and act like this in the repressive atmosphere of South Africa during the 1960s and 1970s?

Murdered in his home at the age of 36, Rick Turner lived a short life. The window in which he was able to make an impact on his society was very narrow. Nonetheless, for those who came into contact with them, his ideas had a profound effect on their imaginations about what was possible. Since his death, his legacy has yet to take proper shape. In the severely compromised political climate following the end of apartheid, there is little room for the idealist vision that Rick Turner lived and died for.

IN HIS OWN WORDS

I first encountered Rick Turner in a course on 'The Liberation Struggle in South Africa',[2] where I was assigned to read a short essay entitled 'The Present as History'. The essay was included as the postscript to Turner's 1972 book *The Eye of the Needle: Towards Participatory Democracy in South Africa*.[3] The postscript was intended to address some of the practical problems involved in bringing to life the Utopian society that Turner outlined in the bulk of his book.

Inevitably, much of 'The Present as History' centres on the role of white people. Turner felt strongly that the intransigence of the white population in South Africa must be opposed not so much through force, but through organised initiatives of conscious whites and through black pressure, in whatever ways available to them. He took a firm stance against the timidity and lack of vision among white opponents of apartheid at the time: 'It has to be concluded that white liberals remain white first, and liberals second. They are offended by the barbarities of South African society, but not sufficiently outraged to be willing to risk sacrificing their own privileged positions. This is not merely a question of cowardice; it also represents both a lack of imagination and ignorance.'[4]

'The Present as History' sparked my interest tremendously. Having myself been involved in efforts (in the United States) to confront the 'lack of imagination and ignorance' of white liberals and leftists, I found it inspiring to encounter a white South African who had spoken out against these attitudes already in 1972. Furthermore, I admired Turner greatly for his ability to calmly address the practicalities of overthrowing apartheid, despite the devastating climate of repression at the time.

I soon read the rest of *The Eye of the Needle,* and my inspiration increased, as I saw that Turner's overall vision for social change was very much in line with my own desires: a decentralised and cooperative economic and political structure, in which hierarchy is obliterated as much as possible and autonomy is maximised. While many of Turner's peers were committed to either moderate proposals for reform or dogmatic revolutionary programmes, Turner advocated a radical transformation of both the structures and the values of society, without the arrogance or rigidity of a party platform. The enduring emphasis in Turner's writing was on the idea that people ought to be able to determine the shape of their society, granted that they are given the necessary space to be full participants in their own lives.[5]

CASSETTE

'It is a curious experience for one who did not know Turner to talk to those who did. Whether they knew him well or only slightly, he made an almost inexplicably powerful impression on them ... In speaking of him today, as in speaking at his graveside before, many of them have testified abundantly to the extraordinariness of Richard Turner.'[6]

– ANDREW NASH

Motivated by Turner's ideas, and intrigued by my growing sense of his impact on the movement of the time, I began considering writing about him. I didn't think of myself as someone who would write a biography of any kind; I thought of myself as either a revolutionary or a historian, or both, and, either way, as someone focused on broader social questions than the life of one man. In order to get a better sense of the possible project, I decided to contact Rick's daughter Jann to ask for her support. She immediately agreed, and began putting me in contact with others who were close to her father. If I had any previous doubts about studying Turner, these early conversations wiped them all away. Across the board, everyone I contacted responded to me favourably and with great enthusiasm.

I remember quite vividly my first phone call to Fatima Meer. Meer had spent her lifetime dedicated to struggling for social justice. She was also a close friend of Rick Turner, a colleague at the University of Natal, a fellow banned person, and the host of his marriage to Foszia Fisher. I was incredibly nervous to speak with her. I could only get out the sentence fragment 'I'm working on a thesis about Rick Turner ...', to which she immediately replied, 'I'll help you. How much help do you need from me? Shall we meet once, or do you need multiple meetings? I loved Rick Turner, and I'm happy to help anyone get his story out.'

Fatima was 80 years old when I interviewed her, and living at home with full-time nursing help to take care of her physical needs, but her mind remained impressively sharp. She spoke with eloquence, every sentence carefully constructed. We sat together for many hours, while she recounted her memories of Rick and answered my questions patiently and thoroughly.

Everyone whom I interviewed spoke of Turner with great fondness, while simultaneously impressing upon me the great sense of loss they have felt in the years since his death, not only on a personal level but also in terms of the spirit that he brought to thinking about radical social change.

I soon came to feel as if my connections to Rick Turner's loved ones were the most rewarding part of the project. In the years that it has taken me to complete this book, I have only grown closer to everyone I have interviewed, and my gratitude for them has only increased. My relationship with Turner's friends and family has developed a much richer quality than the formal arrangement of an interview tends to allow. Jann Turner, who welcomed me into her Johannesburg home to read through her boxes of papers related to her father, told me that I'm the only person who has met so many of the different people that knew Rick well, and so in my writing I have the ability to allow these various people to speak to one another. Indeed, the process of learning all of these stories, from so many different voices, has been like a long and deeply engaged conversation, slowly reaching further depths, day by day. Even more so, it has felt like becoming part of an extended family.

If I have succeeded in my aims, then this book will be a gift, first and foremost, to all those who shared their stories with me in order to write this. While some people I've spoken to will not be around to read it,[7] and while many other people were crucial in helping me succeed in writing it, nonetheless the book remains fundamentally the product of the conversations I've shared with Turner's loved ones.

I have tried to develop a structure for the book that gives the stories gleaned from these conversations as prominent a place in the narrative as possible. Rather than merely quoting from the transcripts, I have chosen instead to present their words as full-length narrations, standing alone. It is my hope that the different voices that I encountered in this process are able to speak fully within this text, for themselves and in dialogue with one another. These sections are often grouped together in twos and threes, my intention being to increase awareness of multiple different perspectives on any given point, and to heighten the conversational feel of the narrative.

This is neither a trivial nor a merely aesthetic issue. Indeed, the decision to spotlight the stories of those who knew Turner well is a fundamental concept behind this book. I do not claim to be the only authority on Rick Turner, but rather take my place as one of many voices that can contribute something to make sense of Turner's life and the context in which he lived and which he helped to shape.

SEEING LIKE A STATE

'Love is a continual interrogation. I don't know of a better definition of love. (In that case, my friend Hubl would have pointed out to me, no one loves us more than the police.) That's true. Just as every height has its symmetrical depth, so love's interest has as its negative the police's curiosity.'[8]

— MILAN KUNDERA

I feel as though I ask many of the same questions as the security police.

Just like the police, I want to believe that Rick Turner was a revolutionary and that he dedicated most of his waking hours to this task. I want to believe, as they did, that both his ideas and his projects were a threat to the continuation of a system of racial and economic privilege. And I do not think that either of us are insane for holding this belief. Turner was involved in a large number of activities, prolific in his writings and speeches and public dialogues, in his stubborn dedication to a new society. But the police and I have very different reasons for wanting to study his thoughts and actions.

For the police – and the infiltrators and social scientists whom they hired – the goal of all investigations was to establish a case against him. In other words, the police always intended to prove a hypothesis about him which they had already concocted, from a distance. For over a decade, Turner's public appearances, his friendships, both his private and his published writings, his telephone calls and his interactions with friends and family were all scrutinised carefully.

In everything Turner did, the state saw the *rooigevaar*, the communist threat, which was one of the principal justifications for its repressive measures. It understood enough to see that he had 'a marked ability to influence people', and that 'In an era of racial and labour conflicts, conditions are ideal for [Turner] … to promote the idea of a social and economic change in the Republic of South Africa'. This analysis would eventually persuade the police to kill him. As Turner had written in *The Eye of the Needle*, 'dissent anywhere may be contagious, and hence fatal.'

Nonetheless, it is important to remember that those who attempted to neutralise Turner failed to understand fully the nature of his particular role within the political culture of South Africa. They couldn't see, as Rick's close friend Tony Morphet did, that he was 'constitutionally incapable of playing the stereotypical role of a revolutionary leader'. What was most dangerous about Rick Turner – and what remains vital to be understood – was the aspects of his life and politics that failed to fit neatly within the dominant narrative of South Africa's liberation from apartheid. Turner never was a member of the African National Congress, the Communist Party or any trade union or political party of any kind. His vision for transformation in South Africa was independent and radical in a way that the vision of the 'stereotypical revolutionary' never can be.

The security forces kept extensive records of their surveillance of Turner's activities and ideas. It is only now, years after his death and after the fall of apartheid, that some of the secret surveillance documents have become publicly available at all. Most of them were created anonymously, based on information supplied to the police from 'delicate sources', who had infiltrated closely enough into Turner's life to spy on him. In some instances, these files are impressive in their accuracy, the careful attention to details of when Turner was where, with whom, and what he said. In other moments, the police descriptions are laughable in their gross inaccuracies, in the ways in which their fear of Turner caused them to exaggerate and distort reality.

In either case, understanding how the state saw Turner is an important part of understanding who he was. Turner lived the bulk of his life in extended conflict with the government of South Africa. As a result, he unavoidably gained a shadow that would not leave. His ideas and choices were of course his own, but as a subject of constant surveillance he lived a parallel life within the imagination of the functionaries and murderers who were responsible for understanding and neutralising any potential threats.

WHAT'S IN A LIFE STORY?

'In the conventional biography, the presentation of lives was presumed to be objective, truthful and factually correct ... The resultant linear biographical product stood as "the truth" about the "real" individual's life.'[9]

– CIRAJ RASSOOL

This book rejects any attempt to make a rational, linear ordering of life, of history.

My project is to tell the story of Rick Turner's life: not only to tell the story, but to tell it with grace, to tell it beautifully, to honour his contribution to the world. The story needs to breathe, to call out in passionate prose and poetry: 'A man lived here, and this is what he made of his life!'

Rather than unfolding as a dry chronology from birth to death, the structure of this book is intended to give the reader the feeling of being drawn in, bit by bit, allowing curiosity to build in layers. Instead of handing the definitive story of Rick Turner's life – something that I frankly doubt could possibly exist – I invite the reader to join me in the project of making meaning out of all the disparate perspectives and incomplete answers that together comprise an image of a brief, but powerful, life.

In sum, this book is a collage, a scrapbook, a recording of stories spoken by friends and family, a photo album full of portraits taken from various angles, a protest march attended by thousands of passionate protesters, a letter written lovingly by hand, sent from a dear friend.

WHY RICK TURNER?

'People came from everywhere to see him, to discuss their projects, to clarify their thinking, to raise troubling issues. He mobilized individuals; directed them towards action, away from despair and cynicism.'[10]

– TONY MORPHET

There was no way to do this without having it consume me.

I couldn't make sense of another man's life without having my own life overtaken by his story. The story is in me, has infused itself inside me. I have to tell this story now, because I can no longer carry it on my own.

In the years I've spent working on this project, I am often asked, 'Why Rick Turner?' I can of course answer this question on a number of levels. Of course, there are relatively rational motivations, which have to do with my desire to see the kinds of transformation in society that Turner dreamed of and advocated. I could also say that I am concerned about the way that 'heroes' are made in the story of South Africa's liberation, and I'm concerned that men and women like Turner – those outside the dominant parties in contemporary South Africa – will be marginalised or forgotten. True enough. But there is something deeper, something far more significant.

I find myself consumed, more than anything, by an incessant question: How is it that we make meaning in our lives?

This is why I am so centrally fixated on Rick Turner's choices. Why and how did Rick Turner make the choices that he did? What was he responding to, hoping for and battling against? This questioning must be done with unflinching honesty, but also deep empathy. It is necessary to dig deep into the details of his life – bit by bit, story by story – to begin to assemble together a feeling for the world as Rick Turner saw it. I ask all of this not merely for curiosity's sake, or for the benefit of historical memory, but quite crucially for myself. Because I am alive, and am struggling to live a life with dignity, making ethical choices in the direction of an ideally possible society.

The work of studying history is – whatever else historians might claim – quite simply the study of human choices. We learn from other people's life choices so that we can choose how to live.

* * *

Rick Turner, I have been your student. I have lived among your friends and family. I have seen their admiration for you, their appreciation for every moment spent with you, and I have seen them grieving. I have carried the nightmare that came with your death. I can feel your absence, the weight of it, even though we never had the chance to meet. You were gone before I was born, so I have had to build my image of you through the scraps that remain, shared with me by those who cherished you.

There is something about your will, your determination, that I have struggled intensely to understand. In moments, I can see myself in you. I recognise myself in your choices. In other moments, I see myself living under far more desirable circumstances, and yet battling against a nagging cynicism, a failure of will. At times, I become blinded by the weight of the present tense, as if the society as it is now – this system of permanent warfare – will not possibly give way to something else, something better. How were you able to be so at ease with your sense that the system couldn't possibly last?

Reading your words, watching your actions, shakes me out of my stuck places, reminds me to find new reservoirs of courage inside myself.

Prologue

Interview with Jann Turner on Radio
South Africa, 28 April 1993
(edited transcript)

Jann: It's essentially a personal journey to come back and discover as much as I can about who killed him, and really to raise the question again. And also, in a sort of lighter sense, and it's been quite wonderful, being here, is talking to his friends and people that knew him, and finding out about who my dad was, because I was 13 when he was killed, and I didn't know him as an adult.

Q: Have you found that there's been any progress in the investigation?

J: We know almost nothing, which is what we knew, really, on 9 January 1978. There's been no development at all. It's impossible to say. There's nothing which we can use to point a finger towards anybody. It was clearly a political murder. He was banned at the time. He had been harassed by the security police and by BOSS [Bureau of State Security] and by right-wing terrorists throughout his banning.

We're talking about a very different time. 1978 was a very different time to now. In 1993, we don't see quite the same level of vilification of somebody who has a different point of view. I mean, my dad was openly a Marxist, and that made him very vulnerable. He was very open about his politics, and his politics were essentially threatening to the state as it then was.

All we know is rumour, stuff that's essentially come up without it being substantiated. There's very little on it, which is very strange, given that this is an excellent police force that's been able to solve all sorts of murders. This is a white man murdered in a white suburb in 1978, and it's completely unsolved. It's a complete mystery, which suggests that it was not supposed to be solved, that the people that did it, did it with an enormous amount of care.

I know that the murder file is still open. I'm here to appeal for any information that anybody has about who might have done it.

Q: *What if somebody phoned you and said 'I killed your father', how would you react to that?*

J: *I would like to meet with them and ask them what they did and why. I'd simply like to understand why they went there that night to kill him and that's all. I'd like them to explain it to me. I simply need to understand.*

Q: *Do you see it as a mission in your life to try to find the person who killed your father?*

J: *I think in the process of coming to terms with a loss like that, which is a continuing process, I'll never rest until I know. Part of me will always need to know; I have to have that piece of the picture filled in. My father didn't die of Aids or cancer or of illness or old age. Somebody came up to our house that night, and shot him dead. I need to understand that as part of the process of coming to terms with it at all. I mean, it's difficult because in some respects you never come to terms with something like that, you never stop grieving. And in a sense, one becomes sadder as one becomes older. I mean, the sadness of his absence is more profound. And that's why I'll always be looking.*

In another sense, and this is the other part of my journey here, one comes to realise that he is alive, that somebody who lives a life in the way that my father did, with such a searching commitment to who they are and what their country is about, can't ever be killed by an assassin's bullet because their ideas can't die.

The one thing that one can draw comfort from is that when somebody lives their life like that, like Chris Hani or David Webster, or my dad, you can't ever kill their ideas, and they're very much alive right now in South Africa, which has for me been the wonderful thing about being here and learning about my dad and how much he is alive.

Q: *When you were 13, did you understand what had happened, could you grasp what had happened?*

J: Yes. I mean, in a 13-year-old way, but very clearly, because my whole life had been (I mean, up until 13, which isn't very long, but nevertheless) had been lived in the context of this politics, and of my dad's political involvement. I mean, from the age of two-and-a-half I can remember going up and talking to the policeman who was sitting at the end of our garden, listening in to my dad's conversations, and my mom pulling me away. All of these things function to make you begin to understand. I knew about our house being bugged and our telephone being bugged and about being followed. When my father was banned, I understood that quite clearly, although simply because I was eight when he was banned.

If, when you spend time with your dad, and he has to get permission from the minister to go and spend twelve hours in a game reserve with his kids, and you have to report to a police station in every couple of towns that you pass, and you get followed as you're going around the game reserve, I mean, you understand, in a very particular way, what's going on. You get a very deep sense of the fact that these people, for some reason, think he's very dangerous or something, or that his ideas must have so much influence that they can do that, that they can follow us around a game reserve, when he's just spending time with his kids. So you understand a lot because it's there, it's the world as it presents itself to you.

It is now 35 years since Rick Turner was murdered. At this point, it seems certain that we will never know the full story of the assassination.

The Durban police were from the first moment of their investigation so blasé, so careless and so cursory, that it soon became obvious to those who cared about Turner that the police had no intention of solving the case. Successive waves of investigation into the death have been initiated by the Turner family over the years, but nothing conclusive has come to the surface. In the absence of the truth, various theories have been thrown into the debate, from all angles; all of them just rumours and guesses based on what information there is available.

The process of trying to apprehend Turner's assassin has been similar to having dust thrown in your eyes, repeatedly. Each new dead-end stings a bit more, as the frustration with the situation builds. As Jann Turner put it so eloquently in 1993, Rick Turner's murder 'was not supposed to be solved ... the people that did it, did it with an enormous amount of care'.

Now in the cold dawn
Jann Turner

The man with the gun walks free away
    soft across the wet grass
between the policemen who smiled
and turned to cover you with their blanket.
'He's dead' I said
but they said nothing ...
we are not alone in our hurting, our incomprehension
we are not alone in our anger
we are bound, we burn together with strength
with our wild fury
and so I, scarred with my father's blood,
I know what I must fight.

Whoever was responsible for Turner's death has either already died or has successfully weaselled himself into a safe hiding spot for a long, long time. In all likelihood, whoever fired the fatal shot did so on orders from above, and whoever gave the orders has also escaped justice for decades.

While Turner's killer has yet to be brought to justice – and probably never will be – some pieces are clear enough, and slowly the whole picture can come into view.

Rick Turner had been a target of the South African government for over a decade prior to his death. The security police subjected Turner to endless surveillance, tapping his telephone, infiltrating the political organisations in which he participated, gathering information from his neighbours – poking into the most intimate details of his daily life. Rick Turner spent the last five years of his life under a type of house arrest known as a 'banning order', which effectively cut him off from all possibility of teaching, writing or political organising and also severely limited his relationship with his children.

The apartheid state made itself clear: it intended to silence Turner.

* * *

'If a man happened to be 36 years old, as I happen to be, and some
truth stands before the door of his life; some great opportunity to
stand up for that which is right and that which is just, and he refuses
to stand up because he wants to live longer, or he is afraid his home
will get bombed, or he is afraid that he will lose his job, or he is
afraid that he will get shot, he may go on and live until he is 80 …
and the cessation of breath is merely the belated announcement of
an earlier death of the spirit. A man dies when he refuses to stand
up for that which is right. A man dies when he refuses to stand up
for that which is true. So, we are going to stand up right here …
letting the world know that we are determined to be free.'
– MARTIN LUTHER KING, JR.

Speaking at their father's funeral, young Jann Turner, aged 13, and her
9-year-old sister, Kim, read this quotation from Martin Luther King,
Jr. because, in their words, 'it shows how our father lived, and what he
believed in'.

Rick Turner happened to be 36 years old at the time of his death, the
same age as Martin Luther King. Both men lived, at some level, constantly
aware of the potential danger facing them as a result of their convictions.
They each carried on living out their hopeful and defiant values – in spite
of all the hardships and risks – because, as Turner put it, 'you can either
be cowed or you can choose to be free. I've chosen to be free and I accept
the consequences.' All the same, the assassination of Turner – like that of
King – came as a devastating shock to all who knew him and highlighted
the extent to which viciousness is necessary in order to maintain a deeply
unjust society.

At least this much is clear: no matter who pulled the trigger, in the
final analysis the system as a whole, the entire structure and mentality of
apartheid, was to blame for Turner's death.

It's no mystery that apartheid was a brutal system, with tens of thousands
of casualties. In the end, not only Turner's death, but that of thousands

more will never be properly accounted for. More often than not, the petty bureaucrats, politicians and psychotic assassins who kept apartheid afloat have been able to avoid taking responsibility for their crimes.

In this climate of immunity, the real question is not 'Who killed Rick Turner?' but rather 'What is the weight of his absence?'

PART ONE

The Farm

ONE

Space to Be

'My entire life is based on this contingent and absurd choice.'[1]

– RICHARD TURNER

HOME

RICHARD TURNER WAS BORN ON 25 September 1941 in Cape Town. As a white male South African at the time, Richard was more or less guaranteed to have a life of relative comfort, materially and socially. That he would be well cared for, given a decent education and would pursue a stable career was a given. There was nothing particularly remarkable about his origins or, at least, nothing that would indicate his later aversion to the morals and habits of the community that raised him.

Richard was the only child of Jane and Owen (Paddy) Turner, who had emigrated from England. As a young man, Paddy had come to South Africa as a soldier in the British Army in the Anglo-Boer War. Jane had been raised in the working-class East End of London. When she met Owen, he was already twenty years her senior and had been widowed. After Jane and Paddy married, she agreed to move to Africa with him, in search of a better life. At first they settled in what was then known as the Gold Coast (now Ghana), where Owen became co-owner of a construction company. According to Tony Morphet, when Jane fell pregnant, 'it was decided that Mrs Turner should travel south for the birth of the baby because the local medical facilities were inadequate ... and Cape Town was the obvious choice. It offered excellent medical facilities,

3

it was sufficiently British in general orientation and it was attractively safe from war-time hazard.'[2]

Using the money they'd earned in the Gold Coast, Jane and Paddy established themselves by purchasing a small-holding outside Stellenbosch. The farm, which was known as Welcarmas,[3] while modest by South African standards, included a hundred or so acres of land, two cottages, and a house with a grapevine-covered veranda that for many years (until 1960) served as a country tearoom. The land was set on the steep slopes of Helshoogte (Hell's Heights) mountain pass, overlooking the Stellenbosch valley below. Welcarmas was primarily a fruit farm. In addition to growing and selling fruit, the Turners ran a packing operation called Simonsberg Fruit Supply, which packed fruit from neighbouring farms in the area for export overseas. Bought at the end of the 1930s, the farm was obtained relatively cheaply, but as the economy recovered after World War II and overseas markets became accessible again, fruit farms such as the Turners' became much more valuable. While the family never amassed a fortune from farming, they nonetheless lived comfortably. Relatively speaking, they lived a life without luxury, but at the same time they always had all they needed.

Welcarmas became a central feature of Richard's life. Not only did he spend his childhood years there, but he remained a frequent visitor to the farm during his days as an undergraduate student at the University of Cape Town, and he returned to live on the farm again after finishing his doctoral studies in Paris. The first twenty-eight of his thirty-six years alive were spent orbiting around this same patch of land at the top of Helshoogte. Over the years, Richard's relationship with the farm took many forms, though he was rarely, in fact, involved in actually working the land. As Jane was soon widowed, she ran the farm more or less alone, with the help of about a half-dozen workers. There was a coloured family who lived on the land, the Louws, and Jane also hired African migrant labourers from the Eastern Cape. While Richard did help out with various tasks around the farm, such as pruning and helping take produce to the market when he was a young adult, in the main he was allowed ample time to focus on his school work and on playing with his friends.

During his university days, Richard would often drive out from Cape Town – about fifty kilometres away – at the weekend, and bring his friends or his girlfriend, Barbara Hubbard, with him. For three years, Richard and Barbara lived together on the farm, running it together so as to allow Richard's mother the chance to take a break. But even during these years, the business of the farm was less prominent in Richard's life than his relations with radical students and intellectuals from UCT and Stellenbosch. So, in essence, Welcarmas was primarily a space for Turner to develop himself – a space in which he felt at home and able to devote time to shaping his ideas through reading and conversation, his two favourite pastimes.

That Richard was able to thrive at Welcarmas was due in no small part to his mother Jane. Throughout Richard's life, Jane Turner was a powerful presence, providing deep and unflinching support and care for her son. Richard's father Paddy was an alcoholic, which greatly limited his capacity to be present for young Richard. None of Turner's childhood friends can recall Richard ever mentioning his father; it seems that the two had virtually no relationship to speak of. Further, drinking contributed to Paddy's early death, when Richard was only 13. Paddy's absence – first through alcoholism and later after his death – was an important and abiding loss for Richard. Although he did choose sobriety as an adult (no doubt influenced by his father's choices), he otherwise showed no signs of being damaged by his father's addiction. In essence, Richard was his mother's son – and an only son, at that. Jane more than compensated for the loss of her husband.

Jane Turner showed her deep love in her own particular way, which was rarely sentimental. She had a fierce temper, and Richard would have had to learn early on not to cross any of her boundaries. At the same time, Jane was relatively permissive, in the sense that she allowed Richard considerable room to be autonomous and make his own decisions. She believed that he ought to be able to learn from his own mistakes. Further, Jane consistently indulged her son's wishes, from playing cricket with him as a small boy and buying him the magazines that caught his fancy to hosting his friends and allowing him to spend his teenage days absorbed in thought. Jane's indulgence of her son's voracious desire to grapple with ideas allowed him a nurturing foundation to trust his innate intelligence and pursue a lifetime's vocation as a thinker and teacher. Jane remained proud of her son and supportive of his thinking even when his ideas led him deeper and deeper into a head-on collision with the apartheid state.

If anything, Jane was protective of her son to a fault. Her deep love for him caused her to struggle at moments with making room for Richard to have other fulfilling relationships in his life, especially with his girlfriend and later wife, Barbara Hubbard. Jane is remembered often by family friends for her hard edges, for her capacity to be cold or fierce. But whatever her faults, Jane's support for Richard during his youth was very special. She created space for him to simply *be,* to grow into himself without pressure to follow any particular course in his life.

All things considered, Richard Turner was well raised. All his material needs were more than suitably met and he was afforded plenty of leisure time. Even if only by one parent, he was well loved and imbued with a deep sense of confidence in himself. Perhaps it was a bit of a lonely childhood, with no siblings and with having to spend years away at boarding school. Richard quickly matured into a rather unworldly young man, absorbed in quiet, creative pursuits, inside himself; he devoured books and began his lifelong love affair with rational thought in his early teenage years.

A colonial product
Mike Hubbard

Richard was a colonial product in some sense, but not in the stereotypical sense. It's a passing culture, the British in Africa. Whatever background you came from, as a European in Africa you could in some quirky way rise up. Jane, his mom, was very much like that. She was from a very tough generation.

A story could easily be written about Jane, how she went from a poor background in eastern London to be running a farm. Very much a self-made person. Jane was, oftentimes, rude. She was a tough and difficult person, very vulnerable in some ways and quite easily hurt. At the same time, she could be very kind.

The first time I went out to the farm was when I

was 11 or 12. I biked out there with my friend from Koelenhof, near Stellenbosch. It was about a five- to seven-mile ride. We struggled up the pass and we got up there around one. We cycled up and there was Jane, who was in her early fifties and quite glamorous.

In any case, she was surprised and amused to see us, so she said, 'Let me get you some lunch.' So we went back to the house and we didn't need our packed lunches. Jane provided a nice lunch for us and we went on our way. That was quite an adventure.

Space to be ourselves
John Clare

Richard and I went to St George's Grammar School, a private high school run by the Anglican Church. Both our parents had enough smarts to let us escape the South African state system. Nonetheless, ours was a rather dim little school. At school they didn't ask the best and brightest to talk about ideas. I don't think you can imagine what an intellectual desert South Africa was.

I think we both felt we were outsiders, so we sort of clung to each other. And we both thought that apartheid was essentially ludicrous right from the start. It was the one immediate common ground that we had. We didn't know anyone else who thought apartheid was totally ludicrous. We were both completely bemused and outraged by apartheid. It seemed natural to both of us to feel this way and we couldn't understand why the rest of the world around us was clearly off its rocker.

We lived in a white world with black servants, and there were all sorts of things that blacks couldn't do. They couldn't sit on the same park benches, they couldn't sit in the same buses, they couldn't stand in the same queue. You had to be pretty bloody stupid not to notice, but yet everyone else presumably *did* notice but had grown accustomed to it or believed their superiority was dependent on being accustomed to it. We couldn't get over how absurd it was. And also, how disgusting it was.

But they weren't the things that we talked about. I'm surprised, looking back, how little time Richard and I spent talking about these issues in our youth. We were both going through a normal adolescence, I guess.

I spent all my summer holidays with him, at the farm. There was this large rambling bungalow at the top of the pass, and just below it there was another bungalow. And that, for Richard and me, was our haven. It was surrounded by eucalyptus trees and very private. Jane just turned over the bungalow to him. She never pried, never interfered, never poked around. We were free to do there exactly what we wanted. And what we did was we talked most of the night and we slept most of the day. What a liberation for young people of our age in this period! In this strict, critical society, to be free together to do what we want.

Jane may have been difficult. She had this brisk attitude and she was determined beyond sentimental. For example, she ran a tearoom for a while, but she hated it. Jane wasn't a very sociable sort of person and she wasn't one to smile broadly if she didn't know you. I think people found going to the tearoom a bit of an endurance, so fewer and fewer of them went. Eventually she just shut it down.

But Jane was a rare woman for her time. She was interested in ideas. I had never met a woman of her age, of her generation, who was. All my parents' friends were numbskulls. They played golf and bridge and didn't talk about apartheid. Jane was utterly non-racist in her views (but she also tiptoed around the situation in which all people who worked for her were black and she didn't pay them very much).

Jane was always very good with me. Most remarkably, she made those liberated summers possible. She recognised Richard needed his freedom and she recognised that he got something from me. She was as charming as she was capable of being. She didn't ask us to do anything. She just let us go. That was a really magical time. And if you ever have children, do the same. It is the greatest gift you can give a child at that age – 13 or 14. Just give them space to be themselves and not be bothered by adults from the outside world. It's unbeatable.

A NORMAL ADOLESCENCE

'The child is not only learning how to understand the world, he is also working out a value system. And it is a system and not just a haphazard collection of independent principles.

(This does not, however, mean that it constitutes a logically satisfactory system.)'[4]

– RICHARD TURNER

Richard had a relatively normal upbringing within a profoundly abnormal society. In 1948, when he was seven, the National Party won enough seats in the whites-only parliament to take office as the government and proceeded to implement its new policy of apartheid. This entrenched the system of segregation that had long marked South Africa and extended it into every area of social and individual life. As a result the physical and social landscape of the country was significantly reshaped, and every effort was made to silence any possible dissent or protest.

The 1960s were known as the 'golden age' of apartheid, when the brutal methods of state repression allowed the economy to grow 'faster than almost any other capitalist country'. White South Africans began increasingly to enjoy an excessively high standard of living, a 'collective white consumer orgy … uninterrupted by black resistance to apartheid'.[5] But the decade began with an escalating campaign of protest against the system. The African National Congress (ANC) declared 1960 'the year of the pass', to focus attention on the much hated passbooks, which Africans were obliged to carry with them as proof of their entitlement to live and work in the 'white' cities of the country. But the campaign was pre-empted by an initiative of the rival Pan Africanist Congress (PAC), which had broken away from the ANC the previous year. On 21 March 1960, in the small township of Sharpeville south of Johannesburg, thousands of protesters responded to a PAC call and gathered outside the police station to defy the law and demonstrate non-violently.

All participants arrived without their pass and offered themselves for arrest. In the stand-off that followed, the crowd of some five thousand or more sang freedom songs and shouted slogans while the police slowly gathered reinforcements. Finally, in a moment of tension (the police would later claim they had been assaulted by stones and that the crowd was becoming unruly) they opened fire. When it was all over, the police had killed 69 people and injured 180. It was the most horrific expression to date of the determination of the apartheid state to defend the system. Images taken by journalists of dozens of bodies splayed all over the ground spread across the globe, spurring an international outcry. Many within South Africa regarded the Sharpeville massacre as a crucial moment of awakening.

It was in the context of these turbulent times that Richard Turner grew up and reached the age of entering university. While all of the events of repression and resistance certainly had a profound effect on Turner's later choices, he nonetheless made it through his undergraduate studies largely uninvolved in politics. Richard entered university believing that perhaps someday he would be an aeroplane pilot. He loved pop music and cricket, and going to the (whites-only) beach. In spite of the absurdity of the unequal and segregated society surrounding him, Richard Turner experienced a surprisingly normal adolescence.

He's here! He's here!

Michael Hubbard

It was 1959 and we were living in a residential hotel in Sea Point in Cape Town. It was exciting because Barbara (she was 16) had been to a party and met this boy, Richard, and they were going out on a date. And so I (being 11 years old) was hanging around in the hotel room to see what sort of person could be so crazy and have such bad taste as to want to go out with my older sister.

I remember very clearly I was sitting at the top of the first flight of stairs and this young man with red hair, wearing a tweed sports jacket, came in and asked me, 'Could you tell me where Barbara Hubbard's room is?' And I said, 'Yes, yes!' I raced along and rapped eagerly on the door saying, 'He's here, he's here!'

I was actually taken along on the date. We went to the Odeon Cinema to see a film called *Ice Cold in Alex*. That was my first meeting with him.

I think he regarded me, as one would if 17 and interested in the older sister, as a complete nuisance to be avoided at all costs. There was certainly some of that. But at the same time I enjoyed his company. I enjoyed firing questions at him because he would always try to answer them. He wouldn't say, 'I don't know about that,' or 'I couldn't care less,' or 'Shut up,' or something like that. However engaged he was in courting my sister, he felt somehow internally motivated to answer my questions.

Richard would be around quite a lot. We went out to the beach together. He had a canoe and took us down to Camps Bay. He had a keen interest in cricket. And I remember him coming along to the hotel and he always wanted to listen to the Hit Parade on the radio,[6] which

11

was very important in those days in teen culture. His favourite was Little Richard.

Barbara and Richard seemed to fit very well together at that point in their lives. I would say Richard was her lifeline almost.

It's important to understand the environment that we had grown up in. Our dad's alcoholism and our being poor forced us to grow up early at one level. But it also means you don't have too much confidence in who you are or where you're coming from. You want to find a way out of this hole that you find yourself in with your family. We were really looking for, somehow, emotional support beyond the family, anything to get us out of that place. Richard was our lifeline in that way. He was exciting and thoughtful. He was different.

Manna from heaven
John Clare

Richard met Barbara Hubbard at a party when he spilled his orange juice over her. One thing that brought them immediately together is that they were both awkward – outsiders, not really belonging. Barbara was a very literate, erudite girl. All the mainstream girls he approached ran a mile because he was not immediately presentable. He dressed in a very scruffy manner. He didn't have time for the niceties of social chit-chat. So Barbara was manna from heaven for him because Barbara was charming and pretty and seemed willing to build her life around him.

She later in her life became a much more forceful, independent woman. But at the time she met Richard she fawned on him, she adored him, and she made him the centre of her life. I think that, for a while, Richard liked that and it was much in the way he had grown up with his mother, who absolutely doted on him. Tough nut though she was, as mental as she was, it was plain to absolutely everyone, including Richard, that his mother adored him. He was the centre of her life.

I think Barbara gave him the same sort of feeling. That was the nature of the relationship between them initially.

Right from the word go
Barbara Hubbard

We got along right from the word go. And he slowly became the centre of my life – and certainly I think I did for him. From the time I was 16 until we got married when I was 21, we really were very close – as close as you could possibly be with friends, with everything.

I think the first thing that we did is listen to Little Richard because he was tone deaf, absolutely tone deaf. I tried to teach him to sing – or to hear – the differences in 'Row, row, row your boat' and he couldn't even sing that tune. He couldn't sing, but he liked and enjoyed pop music. He particularly liked Little Richard, because a lot of it was shrieking. He liked dancing to it. Again, because he couldn't hear the beat, he was quite a disjointed dancer, but he had fun. He was fun.

He was incredibly conventional in those days, which I'm not and I never was. I look more conventional than Richard, but at that time he still believed in God, while I refused to be confirmed. He was quite shocked by my refusal, he asked why and I said, 'I just don't buy into it.'

He was always didactic, even at that stage when he was fairly shaky about what he was being didactic about. He would say, 'I think you should read this,' and 'We must read that,' and then we would discuss it. So it was quite an intellectual relationship as well. He could make something clear in a way that very few people can. When I had a very knotty philosophical or political problem, I would often ring him up and he would say something that would make me think about it quite differently, or see a possibility through it.

QUESTION OR REJECT

'I am responsible for my values not in that I am aware of having selected them, but in that I could possibly question or reject them through reflection.'[7]

– RICHARD TURNER

When Turner began at the University of Cape Town in 1959, he first studied towards an engineering degree, following in the footsteps of his late father. But whatever Richard's initial goals at university, his time as a student gave him room to begin considering where he felt he fitted in society, and where his passions lay. Tony Morphet describes the climate at UCT at the time – in the context of the broader society for white South Africans – as offering 'a field of experience which differed considerably from the narrow cultural and intellectual life of the conventional school system. It was common for students to find themselves engaged in preparing new definitions of both self and society ... and the integration of the general cultural experience of university life with the specifically political dimensions of the 1960s period caused many students to examine their own situations with more penetrating critical knowledge. Turner was one such student.'[8]

UCT presented Richard with a refreshing departure from his previous education and exposed him to a whole new terrain of thought. A university that imagines itself as an open space founded on principles of academic freedom tolerates a certain level of criticism of the reigning politics of the time. In such an atmosphere, it's not surprising, then, that Richard quickly matured into a determined opponent of apartheid and began to search out forums and organisations in which to act on this discontent.

Richard joined the National Union of South African Students (Nusas), the main liberal, non-racial organisation for students. In addition, in his free time he worked as a teacher in adult literacy classes in the black townships of Cape Town. After his first year of studies, he moved into an apartment with friends in Vredehoek, close to the city centre. In his new home, he found himself in the company of other young whites who shared his frustration with the injustices of the system. These were important first steps in the process of redefining his values, however inherently limited they might have been.

Writing in his adulthood, Turner described the difficulties of young whites attempting to transform their values from a racist mentality to a liberal one:

> His school and home background fills him with racialism. He starts with certain ideas about the mental and social inferiority of blacks, certain emotional reactions to blacks, reactions which go beyond his intellect into his reflexes, and certain habitual ways of behaving towards blacks. One day he discovers, perhaps at university, that it is factually incorrect to believe in the biological inferiority of blacks. He begins to think that after all, 'they' are at least potentially educated, civilized and intelligent, like 'us'; that 'they' are not irreducibly different, but can become like 'us'. This is, of course, great progress in comparison with his old position, but it is only relative progress. He still assumes that everybody essentially wants to be like him. He still sees history through 'white' eyes, as whites civilizing the rest. His emotional and behavioural reactions to race are still there.
>
> Very often, when he has made the first step, he thinks he has gone the whole way. He is still very confused about race, but thinks that he is not. He therefore behaves with a mixture of arrogant paternalism – deriving from his view of history – and of over-polite timidity – deriving from his emotional confusion – towards blacks he meets. This is the situation of many liberal white students.[9]

But the political situation was changing fast, and it would soon transform Richard's circle of white liberals enormously. The liberal values espoused by UCT were unable to provide a real alternative to the increasingly repressive climate in South Africa.

Fruitless opposition
John Clare

At the time we were closest, the university had a night school for Africans in one of the townships. I ran the night school almost from the time we arrived and Richard taught there. And that was something we both thought was worth doing. Neither of us thought liberal politics as they were practised had much future. We didn't think there was any point sitting around a table talking about things. We were both much more concerned to do what we could to alleviate the suffering of the majority of the population.

Richard was good at that. He was always a good teacher, always had a way with the people he was teaching. We all deserve teachers like Richard and we're lucky if we come across them at any stage of our education. Someone who is willing to engage you at the point where you're starting and will lead you on and ask you the questions that will make you explore the ways forward for you. That was Richard's gift.

Richard's relationship with Nusas [the National Union of South African Students] while we were at university was negligible and that was part of his rejection of what seemed to us to be fruitless opposition. Not that the liberal opposition to apartheid was wrong, but that it was fruitless. Of course there was some point in it; you have to keep the spirit of opposition, you have to keep the flame flickering in some way. But neither of us thought it was a very effective way.

We were both sceptical of mainstream left-wing politics, a scepticism I think Richard retained throughout his political life. He had his own – you know what an idealist he was – he was a socialist idealist. At that time in South Africa, and I guess it's still true now, there wasn't much time or patience for socialist ideas.

A SECOND CHOICE

'Although there is no real first choice, a genuine second choice is a possibility.'[10]

– RICHARD TURNER

Richard Turner's fascination with being an engineer didn't last long. After his first year of studies at UCT, he made a radical shift and began studying philosophy. Very quickly, he threw himself into the study of ideas, thoughts and values. His passion for philosophy would last a lifetime and prove to be one of his greatest strengths.

One cannot understand this decision simply as 'switching majors'. His philosophical studies had to do much more profoundly with questions such as 'who am I?' and 'how can I live as fully as possible a liberated existence?' rather than the much more superficial question 'what will I do to make a living?'

Intrigued with French philosophy and particularly the work of Jean-Paul Sartre, Turner applied to study philosophy at the Sorbonne, in Paris. While Turner's studies at UCT had exposed him to the work of Sartre, according to Tony Morphet, it had been 'unconvincingly taught and he was determined to go to the source, to meet Sartre himself'.[11] Given that one of UCT's philosophy professors later testified against him as an expert witness for the state on the topic of communism, it is understandable that Turner found his instruction at UCT to be lacking.

For a young white undergraduate in the South Africa of the 1960s, going away to France to study for a postgraduate degree would have been an unusual and difficult choice. Most bright and ambitious students of the time who sought to leave behind the rather narrow confines of a semi-colonial upbringing would almost inevitably end up in England, the imperial metropolis. (The ties with Britain were still quite strong; South Africa had only become a republic and left the Commonwealth in 1961.) Furthermore, as Morphet explains, 'France and existential philosophy were difficult choices for someone who had yet to learn French and who had been trained in the philosophic traditions of empiricism. England would have been in every way a more reasonable choice.'[12] But this was precisely the brilliance and power behind Turner's decision: he was consciously and ambitiously choosing an *unreasonable* path, in order to break out of the limitations of his upbringing.

For Turner, choosing to go to the Sorbonne and study the philosophical work of Jean-Paul Sartre was probably the single most influential decision of his lifetime. His doctoral research on Sartre, and the political and intellectual culture in France at the time, were to have a profound effect on him. The years in France set him on a permanent course of radical confrontation with the social system in which he had been raised.

TWO

A Thrilling Time

Leaving for Paris

Barbara Hubbard

WE LEFT FOR PARIS on 27 December 1963 on a boat, immediately after our wedding.

Initially we weren't going to get married, because he didn't believe in it. But then we changed our minds because I wanted to go with him to Paris, and it was impossible without being his wife. Believe it or not, I couldn't get a passport. I couldn't get anybody to sign my passport application.

'Why would you want one?' they would ask me.

I'd say, 'I want to go to Paris with my boyfriend.'

They'd say, 'Are you going to marry him?'

When I said I was not going to marry, they would say, 'Then I won't sign it.'

In the end I said to Richard, 'I can't go with you. I won't go with you. I'll fund myself part-time through art school and we'll perhaps catch up later.'

He initially agreed, and then one day he just arrived at my parents' home and said, 'Will you marry me?' and I said yes.

We got married in John Clare's garden in Vredehoek, and John's mother gave us a Christmas cake and gave me my first camera, for which I was very grateful.

Richard's mother didn't attend. She was going to
attend, and we went and spent our last night at the farm
and she vanished during the night. That was the kind of
thing she would pull. His mother did not like me at all,
but that was quite standard with her for anyone whom
Richard liked. She was feisty; she was to be reckoned
with. Jane made several attempts to get between us, as
she did with a lot of people. It's sad. It wasn't worthy
of her. It was a real waste, because she was clever. But
towards the end of her life, I think partially because
she was suffering from dementia, she became very
dependent on me and apologised to me. I don't think
it was necessary for her to apologise as I became very
fond of her.

I asked him whether we should call the marriage
off because she wasn't in attendance, and he said, 'No,
let's go.'

But she then cut him off and wouldn't give him any
money for his studies in France, which in turn torpedoed
my desires to go to art school, as I had to work.

We lived quite a meagre existence, but we didn't
much mind because we were focused on something else
entirely than material comforts.

I IMAGINE THEY RATHER LIKED THAT

Richard Turner's years in Paris are, for the most part, a great mystery.
Barbara is the only person alive today who can speak with any real
knowledge about what she and Richard experienced together in France.
For those who knew Turner before and after his time at the Sorbonne, the
journey has a rather magical quality in their minds. As Michael Hubbard
says, 'They had to live very, very simply. I imagine they rather liked that.
The image of an intellectual living in a loft somewhere in Paris is not
unappealing. There is a long tradition of intellectuals doing that from
other countries. I think it was a thrilling time.'

Everyone agrees that Paris was a transformative experience, something quite fundamental to Turner's life choices and to the contribution he was able to make to the South African situation. Tony Morphet, for example, goes as far as to say: 'It is this period (1964–66) which in my view constitutes the point of Turner's major life choice, in which he conceived of his life as a total project. Until then he had developed within the limits of the given traditions of his particular milieu ... but decisive changes were made during the period in France and through the process of philosophic study.'[1] And yet no one can give much substance to this observation. In order to understand precisely *why* Paris was transformative, a lot more would have to be known about Richard's time there.

But the information is scarce, and so people tend to resort to their imaginations; they try to guess what *must have happened* in Paris. As a result one gains the impression of a romantic life spent as an intellectual in the alluring city of Paris, which has long been the home of artists and thinkers living in exile. One gets the impression too that France was a politically more open environment than South Africa, and that Turner was exposed to radicals and socialists of various stripes. The upheavals in France in May 1968 must surely have had a longer period of gestation and the revolutionary ideas that emerged then must have been brewing for years beforehand, while Turner was studying there. This is all, however, just conjecture.

What is known for sure is that Turner went to the Sorbonne in order to study Jean-Paul Sartre and existentialist philosophy, and succeeded in producing a doctoral thesis on this topic. But the thesis was written in French,[2] and few of his South African peers read it or took a significant interest in Sartre's ideas. Many questions still remain. What was the real nature of his studies? Did Turner live among and engage with a number of like-minded philosophers and develop his political consciousness through extensive debate with them? Or did he live a rather solitary life, absorbed in thick, dense philosophical texts? How close was Turner able to get to the well-known and controversial Sartre, and what kind of a man was he? What was the social and political climate in France during those years? Some attempt must be made to answer these questions if we are to understand Turner's lengthy love affair with the ideas of Jean-Paul Sartre.

'EVERYTHING THAT SEEMED A LITTLE FOR ORDER'[3]

To study Sartre, truly and with passion, meant not only to grapple with difficult theoretical concepts, but also, quite profoundly, to come to understand an incredible, unique human being. Sartre was a prolific writer, one of the most well-known intellectuals in France for decades. He wrote more than a dozen books as well as a number of plays and started two newspapers. From the beginning of his career in the 1930s until his death in 1980, when 50,000 people attended his funeral procession, Sartre maintained a powerful influence within French society.

Sartre was a public intellectual, a dynamic, explosive personality, and he constantly pushed the limits of thought and behaviour. Despite his frequent and repeated clashes with the Communist Party, Sartre was a committed socialist. He spoke out bitterly against the French occupation of Algeria and in defence of the use of violence by Algerians (and all oppressed peoples) to liberate themselves. Sartre spent his life in an open marriage, maintaining multiple love affairs simultaneously with his deep commitment to Simone de Beauvoir. Through all of Sartre's choices, what seems most consistent was his persistent longing for freedom, his deep craving to understand the exact nature of liberty, and maximise human autonomy, both on an individual and a social level.

> Sartre was, then, fundamentally a libertarian and disrespectful personage, who situated himself ... within the debates over modes of daily life that brought together major currents from libertarianism and Anarcho-Syndicalism. He would never depart from this primacy, and ... would not support any party, detesting the hierarchical relations between master and pupil, not acknowledging a debt to anyone, never setting up any dialogue with his contemporaries, enunciating his truth in violent and subversive discourse, and recreating from scratch a new and radically deviant functioning for daily lifestyles ... Sartre remains constant from the start right up to the end of his trajectory, even if he does not cease asserting that he is changing all the time.[4]

As a result of his urgency, his stubborn, fierce desire, Sartre's search for freedom – whether in his personal life, his political participation or his theoretical contributions – involved many contradictions, missteps and failures. In regards to this seeming weakness, 'he would say something wonderful. He would say, "I think against myself." You have to think against everything that has been given to you by education. You have to criticise every single thing which is being given to you.'[5] At the heart of Sartre's life and thought was this constant, profound provocation. 'In general, it always comes back to not having gone as far as possible in my radicalism. Naturally in the course of my life I have made a lot of mistakes, large and small, for one reason or another. But at the heart of it all, every time I made a mistake it was because I was not radical enough.'[6]

When Richard Turner went to Paris to study the philosophy of Jean-Paul Sartre, this didn't mean that he and Barbara were able to live the same kind of open and provocative lifestyle as Sartre did. In fact, their time in Paris was a relatively quiet, isolated and hard-working period. Although Turner was generally quite a social person, who thrived on discussion and debate, his postgraduate studies provided limited opportunities for this kind of learning. The demands of his studies (which required both a disciplined approach to philosophy and the need to learn the French language), combined with a shortage of money, meant that the young couple spent the bulk of their time working, reading and writing. In addition, soon after their arrival in Paris, Barbara became pregnant, and so the years to come were also very much focused on taking care of young Jann Turner.

Boy, were we poor

Barbara Hubbard

Once in Paris, I worked at the Berlitz School of Language teaching English as a second language. Richard worked as well, when he wasn't studying. Boy, were we poor. But it was good for him. We lived on chicken soup and baguettes and cooked on an alcohol stove in a fifth-floor walk-up in Paris. Very romantic, but very cold. I can't tell you how cold it was.

And also, I got pregnant. For someone with an A in biology, I decided that the new pills that I was on didn't suit me, and I thought I wasn't going to have any children, so I stopped taking them. Surprise, one month later I was pregnant. And we decided we would keep the baby. Richard was particularly pleased. I had said I would never have children, but anyway Jann was born.

After the first year, we left Paris, because we were really broke, and Richard got a job in a place called Nogent-le-Rotrou. There, we had a nice flat and we had enough money to eat properly. In those days the French state set a goal to increase the population up to 100 million French people. So, when you got pregnant you got something called the Book of Maternity, and it had vouchers in it that you tore off every time you went for an examination. You'd get a cash bonus, and you'd get cash for the pram. We actually did very well.

We were there for three years. On the long summer holidays we went to places like Corsica, we went to nudist camps. We bought a car, a two-seater, and we had a tent and we had long, long days. We travelled during that time to Yugoslavia. We were going to travel to Kiev, which turned out to be not so easy, travelling with a six-month-old child.

In 1965, we went back to live in Paris. We lived in the south of Paris (in the only communist ward – we didn't choose it for that reason, we chose it because it was cheap) and we had two rooms divided by the main corridor in a three-storey house. On the third storey lived the local prostitute. And we all had one loo, and we had to clean the house and loo. Everybody had to do it on alternate days. It was quite the place to live. The prostitute was a character who could swear like a trooper in French. And Jann at this stage was really young. She could just about walk – about a year old.

But Richard settled into the Sorbonne and loved it. I helped him a great deal, in the traditional way that women did in those days. He wasn't a good typist; I was fairly good. I translated a lot of what he did because my French was somewhat better, my grammatical French. I helped him write his thesis. The ideas are his – none are mine. I helped him to type it. We worked on the thesis, really very closely. I know an awful lot about philosophy (which I have never used) because of those years. I read the whole *Being and Nothingness* and *Critique of Dialectical Reason*. I think I deserve a medal for having read that in French, but I did.

THE BURDEN OF FREEDOM

According to Turner, the bedrock of Sartre's philosophy is the idea that 'There is no human nature and no necessary values for man. Man creates himself, and this fact gives him the possibility of performing a total reflection ... which, therefore, will permit him to realise his absolute freedom.'[7] Sartre was an advocate of absolute liberty, of the refusal to submit to any power, in heaven or on earth, that would limit people's capacity to decide their own destiny. Once freed from the constraints of destiny or God, we are left the exhilarating and terrifying task of constantly crafting our own course, our own vision for the world.

A repeated emphasis throughout all of Sartre's philosophy is on the notion of choice. Turner wrote, 'Although there is no real first choice, a genuine second choice is a possibility.'[8] With this formulation, Turner made two very important points at once. First, he acknowledged that our initial set of values is not something we can choose. We are born into a society, and we adopt its behaviours and values; we come to be the person that makes sense within that context. But at the same time, we are not doomed to accept the world-view we developed through our upbringing. We have the capacity to decide who we are, what values we believe, and the structure of relationships that we want to be part of. But this is not a simple process, and it is reliant on our desire and capacity to reflect on our values and choose something else.

Turner explains: 'Empirically, most people seem to behave in terms of roughly the same set of values throughout their lives, without ever questioning them and so becoming aware that they are not absolutes.'[9] The values we live by seem to be impossible to change, because they give us a certain essential coherency within the world in which we find ourselves. In other words, no matter how unpleasant our values or the life that comes with them, they make sense.

To those who know only one reality, it can seem as if 'A new choice is not a possibility; it is a threat.'[10] This fear of making 'a genuine second choice' is explained in gripping detail by Sartre: 'Thus we are perpetually threatened by the annihilation of our present choice, and perpetually threatened with choosing ourselves, and in consequence becoming other than we are ... the absolute change which threatens us from our birth to our death remains perpetually unpredictable and incomprehensible.'[11]

The risk of change is that we shall lose all previous coherency. While there is the potential of liberation in reinventing oneself, there is always also the cliff edge of disequilibrium, the deep awareness of being lost and alone. Some people are not, in Turner's words, 'morally strong enough to stand up to the anguish involved in accepting this total responsibility'.

Moreover, 'Even though each individual's frame of reference is unique, it will not necessarily differ very greatly from other people's, since they are in the same society and will tend to encounter the same ready-made behaviour patterns.'[12] Both Turner and Sartre assume a fundamental equality among human beings, in that all of us have the same capacity to be free, to choose our circumstances, our values, our basic concepts of ourselves. But both also acknowledge that an awareness of this freedom is quite rare. As Turner reminds us, 'To invent is much more difficult, and requires much more favourable conditions than to learn, so in general we just learn.'[13]

Without taking time to reflect on the nature of the choices that lie beneath all our values, we remain imprisoned within the logic of our upbringing and our society. In short, we may not even be aware of the fact that the framework that we live within – our conception of our self and the world – is a choice. Nonetheless, according to Turner, we are still 'responsible' for our values and for the society that shapes those values. 'I am responsible for my values not in that I am aware of having selected them, but in that I could possibly question or reject them through reflection.'[14] Again there is the stress on *possibility*; the core of Sartre's philosophy is not that people 'must' or 'will absolutely' do any particular thing at all, but rather that they could do anything.

In essence, Sartre's understanding of freedom places humanity into a valueless universe. Stripped of all higher powers and moralising ideologies, we are left with a meaningless existence. Though the existence of a God may well imply that human beings are not free, nonetheless the great majority of people remain loyal to churches and mosques, rabbis and gurus, because having faith reduces the difficulties involved in being alive. People voluntarily surrender themselves to religion and to other authoritarian structures out of a desire to be released from what Sartre calls the 'anguish' of freedom.

The only release from meaninglessness, from the nothingness that we are born into, comes from our decisions. In this sense, we are, Sartre says, 'condemned to be free; because once thrown into the world, [we] are responsible for everything [we do]'.[15]

In Turner's articulation, 'freedom is a human being putting the past out of play'. Or, in another formulation, 'to be free you must be able to separate yourself from a causal chain'.[16] That is, in every moment in which we are able to recognise that our past does not dominate our present and we are able to make a new decision, we are free. However, becoming aware of this freedom causes anguish.

The anguish of freedom that Sartre describes does not require a person to have reached the state of feeling that the whole of human existence has no meaning whatsoever. In Sartre's words, 'Anguish, then, is the *reflective* apprehension of freedom by itself.'[17] If we are not bound to our past, then our future is not a given, either. In Sartre's framing of what it means to be human, there is no set coherency, no essential continuum in our lives. As Turner says, 'it depends on me for there to be a continuum.'[18]

The very structure of most of our activities excludes anguish. For the most part, life appears to be a causal chain. We all crave a certain sense of coherency to our lives; a feeling that our efforts have a direction or a momentum that is tangible and satisfying. We write stories to make sense of our past experiences, and we imagine ourselves into the future.

But, 'precisely because it's my choice, I am aware that nothing can compel me to adopt that conduct'.[19] Just because we make a particular choice in this moment doesn't in any way guarantee that we will not change our minds in the future. Turner gives the example of a man standing at a cliff. 'I do feel anguish. Though I don't want to jump off the cliff, I don't know that in five minutes I won't want to jump off the cliff.'[20]

The exhilarating aspects of Sartre's philosophy are clear: once the constraints that most people take for granted are removed, everything is suddenly possible. Of course there are elaborate systems in place to mangle and confine human brilliance, as well as all the moral messaging that tries to limit people's inherent longing to dream. But none of this matters, because it is all the design of human beings, and so it can also be destroyed and re-imagined by human beings at any moment.

Turner wrote: 'When the frame cannot contain a new fact, the frame itself will change.'[21] This describes a process in one's life in which values that have previously felt essential suddenly appear to be completely inadequate. While this can be a frightening experience, it can also be a genuinely hopeful moment, when the framework we have chosen fails us and therefore allows for transformation.

Turner saw clearly, both at a personal level and on a broader scale, that the framework for his life could not possibly contain the basic understandings about human freedom that had become dear to him. The framework for South African society generally – and for whites in particular – could not possibly allow for a fulfilled and meaningful life. So, the framework itself needed to change.

While Sartre's philosophy necessarily relates to the very personal choices that human beings make – about their own conceptions of themselves and their values – it is also very much a philosophy of radical social change. Our freedom as individuals implies that we have also the capacity to make fundamentally different choices about the nature of our society. In large part, what made Sartre inspiring to Turner was the notion that 'a social institution is certainly not a solid existing thing like a mountain or an ocean. It may have certain material substrata – written rules and regulations, or a school building to house it in – but ultimately an institution is nothing but a set of behaviour patterns'.[22] In confronting the seeming permanence of racialism and gross inequality in South Africa, Sartre's philosophy offered a deeply liberating perspective.

By the time Turner arrived in Paris, Sartre was nearly sixty years old and lived a relatively private and busy life. The two men met on only one occasion, towards the end of Turner's time in Paris. Although the engagement was pleasant and amicable, Sartre made it clear that he was not interested in playing any kind of mentoring role for Rick. Sartre refused to read Rick's doctoral thesis, not even to comment on it. Sartre once said: 'In my opinion a disciple is someone who adopts another man's thinking without adding anything new or important, without enriching it, developing it, or advancing it ... I can't think of anyone at the moment who is thinking in a new way by using me as a starting point.'

Nonetheless, Sartre's philosophy was to play an important role in Turner's later curriculum as a university professor, and Sartre's ideas would also figure prominently in Turner's political writings and speeches. The most profound example of Turner's capacity to bring Sartre's philosophy to life in fresh form was his book *The Eye of the Needle*. This work is deeply rooted in Sartre's notions of human freedom, of the essential capacity to choose one's values and behaviours. Written in delightfully clear, simple prose, *The Eye of the Needle* outlines the ways in which people are socialised into a particular model of society, and yet are able at any moment to make a second choice, to adopt a new set of values. Turner confronted the stubbornly pragmatic liberalism of white South Africans, provoking them to 'explore the absolute limits of possibility, by sketching an ideally just society'.[23] In Turner's last years, while restricted by a banning order to his home in Durban, he again returned to the study of Sartre's philosophy. Producing what is arguably his most ambitious philosophical work, Turner wrote nearly 500 pages of a manuscript, summarising Sartre's essential contributions, and linking his philosophy to that of earlier thinkers like Rousseau, Kant, Hegel and Marx.

Turner not only absorbed the basic premises of Sartre's philosophy; he assimilated them into his experience as a white South African and made Sartre's theories viable within the political context in his own country. Given the two men's limited contact, the similarities between their life choices are quite remarkable. They were both utterly uninterested in the normal markers of success in present society. Neither Sartre nor Turner aspired towards wealth, and both valued people over things. Both attempted to make their intellectual work as accessible as possible, particularly to oppressed people. Furthermore, both refused – to the extent that they were able – any position of undue power over anyone else. As professors, they both sought to create a classroom environment that maximised participation and minimised the distinction between teacher and taught.

At the same time there were some important differences between the two. Politically, Turner was a much gentler person that Sartre; he presented his ideas calmly and reasonably, whenever possible. Turner also never shared Sartre's strong belief in the validity of armed struggle. As for his private life, Turner's approach to romantic relationships was by no means as open and daring as Sartre's. Nonetheless, he shared Sartre's longing to have deep, authentic connections with his partners, on the basis of equality.

In spite of any differences, philosophical and practical, Turner mirrored Sartre in a great many ways, and remained dedicated to Sartre's philosophy throughout his lifetime. It is generally true that while we of course learn the curriculum presented by our teachers, we learn our teachers even more so.

* * *

Perhaps the most important aspect of Turner's doctoral education was Paris itself – in the daily life that was available to him there. While his years in France were necessarily consumed to a large extent by his challenging intellectual work and his domestic life with Barbara (and then Jann, as well), Turner was nonetheless affected by certain essential features of French society. Having come from a deeply isolated and repressive society, he was exposed in France to a great deal more information and thinking to greater possibilities than he would ever have encountered at home.

The simple fact of having access to news media that weren't heavily censored by the government would have been a profound shift for

Richard. Not only was the print, radio and TV news in France more 'free' in comparison with that in South Africa, but he also had access to a wealth of periodicals of various sorts, such as *Les Temps Modernes*.[24] Throughout his life, Turner was an avid reader, with an insatiable appetite for information to understand contemporary events. He would have taken full advantage of the French media, not only to be aware of European realities, but also to maintain a level of contact with the situation at home.

It should also be remembered that Turner came of age in a society in which all forms of communist or socialist activity and organisation were forbidden by law. His years in France, then, would have been his first opportunity to consider seriously any kinds of arguments or proposals for an alternative economic system to capitalism. Not only was there an active and open Communist Party in France, but precisely at that moment the structure and ideology of the party were being challenged by various voices within the Left.

Sartre, for example, had an extended and conflicted flirtation with the Communist Party. While he was never a fully fledged member, he was often what was then called a 'fellow traveller'. Reflecting on those years, Sartre saw his work with the party as deeply limited:

> I was dealing with men who only considered people of their party as comrades, men who were covered with orders and prohibitions, who judged me as a provisional fellow traveller, and who placed themselves in advance in the future moment when I'd disappear from the melee, taken back by the forces of the right. For them I wasn't a whole man; I was a dead man on reprieve. No kind of reciprocity is possible with men like that; nor any mutual criticism, which would have been something to hope for ... It was putrid, and we were never sure that they weren't in the process of slandering us somewhere.[25]

Over time, Sartre began to take a critical stand against authoritarianism, attempting to distance himself from the Soviet Union and the Communist Party structure in general.

Fortunately, Turner was spared the long, arduous ordeal with the party that Sartre had endured in the 1950s. He never went so far as to become a 'fellow traveller' of any party. The existence of anti-authoritarian and idealist socialist tendencies in France (such as Existentialism and Anarchism) provided him with room to develop a socialist politics without feeling fettered to the Soviet Union. As a student in Paris, Turner was also exposed to the New Left student movement that was taking form in France. The storm of protest, confrontation and utopian ideas that exploded in May 1968 had been steadily brewing during Turner's years in France.

Overall, the social and political atmosphere in France suited Turner quite well. Had he chosen so, he could very likely have stayed on in Europe for a great deal longer than he did. Having finished a French doctorate, he might have been able to find a teaching position in France. At the same time, he was British by heritage, and his British passport would have allowed him to establish himself in England where his quality of life could have been considerably higher than in South Africa. As Tony Morphet has said:

> At a step Turner placed himself outside familiar constructs of South African reality and instead located his thought within radical European traditions. Such steps have been taken before and since by South African intellectuals but in the great majority of cases the decision has been accompanied by a choice to remain in Europe. Two factors make Turner's case unusual. The first is his decision to return to South Africa and the second is his refusal, or perhaps inability is a better description, to compromise the insights won in the philosophic study when faced with the South African reality. It was these factors which led to his active commitment, to his writing *The Eye of the Needle* and indeed to his subsequent death. From this point on the life project gains consistently in unity, coherence and depth.[26]

It was a difficult choice, at best, to return to South Africa at the end of his studies in Paris, and a source of contention with Barbara. Still, Turner was certain that he wanted to go home, and he embraced the risks involved as well as he could understand them at the time.

THREE

Coming Home

'*We must realize that love and truth are more important than possessions. We must do this to be human ... We can learn to live differently as individuals, and we can also learn to live differently in small groups by experimenting with types of communal living based on the sharing of property. Only if the new culture is embodied in the process of moving toward the new society will that society work when we get to it.*'[1]

– Rick Turner

IN THE MEANTIME

Meanwhile, back in South Africa, conditions had deteriorated greatly. In light of the brutality of the Sharpeville massacre, and the subsequent banning of the ANC and PAC, many South Africans felt that they had no alternative but to turn to armed struggle. While the ANC and PAC leadership began preparations for sabotage attacks on government installations, a small group of whites, many of them members of the multi-racial Liberal Party, also turned towards violent means.

The African Resistance Movement (ARM), as the group came to be known, was never a very large organisation, only ever swelling to a membership of a few dozen. Over three years, ARM carried out relatively few attacks (including more than one failure). The most sensational action was the bombing of the Johannesburg train station, which injured 22, killed an elderly woman, and forever soured the reputation of the ARM.

In the end, the group was easily smashed by the state. In 1964, while Turner was away in Paris, the government arrested the majority of its members in less than 96 hours, and eventually hanged John Harris, for planting the bomb at the train station.

In spite of their brief – and tarnished – career, the ARM made a notable mark, particularly on young white opponents of apartheid. The organisation made a particular impact on Rick Turner, as he happened to befriend a number of members of the group during his time studying at UCT. While it is unclear precisely how much he knew about the actual workings of the ARM, it is certain that he took a keen interest in the group, and particularly in their eventual demise.

Properly secretive

John Clare

The members of the African Resistance Movement were properly secretive. The reason the organisation was broken so quickly wasn't that internal security was weak. The state was able to shut down the ARM because they arrested a man named Adrian Leftwich, the only member of the organisation who knew who all the members were. So within a matter of weeks the entire organisation was rounded up.

If Richard knew, I don't know, but I didn't know Alan Brooks was a member until he was arrested; and Stephanie Kemp, I was not aware she was a member.

Even my wife at the time, Sheila, only told me she had been a member after she had been arrested. She had joined under the mistaken impression that this was some sort of offshoot of the Liberal Party and intended to do good things. She was taken within a few days of being recruited to a tutorial atop Table Mountain and she was given a revolver and sticks of dynamite. And I think she quit on the spot. She didn't realise it was a sabotage organisation and she certainly wasn't into violence of any kind. But she had been in long enough to know who the members of her cell were, and that was why the police wanted her, too.

The police told Sheila that she had to give evidence against two other ARM members. And that was insupportable, so she had to leave. We smuggled her out.

Soon afterwards, I left too.

Greatly hardened
Mike Hubbard

If you're going to understand Rick's political position, you've got to understand the ARM. Richard was on the periphery of the ARM. Richard had been sharing a flat with Alan Brooks. I always enjoyed his company. A quiet person, lots of merry humour twinkling in him, wonderful chess player, and full of silly stories. I was always thrilled when he came around.

Richard was always non-violent, so he kept himself out of that, but he was friends with these people. I don't know how much he knew, but certainly if Barbara knew what was going on, he would have known more about what was going on. Nonetheless, Barbara was getting more and more tense around that group. I remember, one Sunday evening, Barbara was upset, worrying out loud, 'Where is Richard? Where is Richard?' It was a very tense time. I didn't understand that exactly at the time. But I understood, in retrospect. Suddenly the papers were full of Richard's friends getting arrested … Alan and the others. Alan and Stephanie were tortured. I did see Alan once after that; he was greatly hardened by the experience.

As events unfolded and Turner saw the fruits of the ARM – both its attempts at sabotage and the repression that followed – his vision for an effective means of resistance started to take form. Looking back over a decade later, Turner summarised the lesson of ARM as follows: 'In fact the ARM episode, in which disillusioned students tried sabotage, shattered their own and others' lives and did great damage to the cause they were fighting for, made me acutely aware of the danger of students turning to violence.'2

Kenneth Hughes, a white liberal active at the time, describes ARM as 'both a crime and blunder, and my generation spent several years having to pay for it and pick up the pieces … the impact on the apartheid state was paltry; but the damage done to Liberal causes was immense.'3 The fact that the ARM included many white university students meant that the crackdown on the organisation led to a corresponding crackdown on the student movement. Prime Minister Vorster demanded that university authorities 'clean out their stables' of any left-leaning students within Nusas, as well as any staff members who may have supported their cause.

The combination of the collapse of the ARM and the imprisonment of much of the ANC leadership had a great impact on the South African political situation. While the ANC was able to set up a permanent infrastructure in exile, focused on military training and international diplomacy, for those remaining in South Africa the organised left virtually disappeared. All forms of radical thought and action were severely curtailed.

In spite of all the unpleasant aspects of the ARM episode, Rick Turner nonetheless felt motivated by the news of ARM's demise to return to South Africa. Perhaps the tragedy that befell his friends in the ARM served to highlight the necessity of focusing his life's energy on more effective means of confronting the system.

Our friends were in uproar

Barbara Hubbard

Around the time that Jann was born, the news of the ARM arrests came through, and Richard and I were devastated. I just remember him breaking down and crying when the news came through that Alan had been arrested and tortured, and tortured quite badly. That really affected Alan for the rest of his life. And Stephanie Kemp had been arrested, and tortured as well. And then John Clare had to leave because the police were hunting for his wife and she left with their daughter, who is about eight months older than Jann.

So our friends were in uproar. There were trials, there were things happening, and our focus began to shift back to South Africa.

In addition, we had re-established contact with Richard's mother; once Jann was on the way, she began to write again. Jane wanted to go and travel. She had started sending Richard little itsy bits of money, and putting pressure on him to come home and help her operate the farm.

But there was a huge debate about whether to go back to South Africa or not. I was very mixed about it. I would have preferred to stay in Britain or in France. He could have taught. He got a good degree from the Sorbonne. He met Sartre, and he got to know some of the other great philosophers of the day. Also, we had got very involved in the student protests in France at the time. The main uprising was in '68, but there were a lot of smaller ones beforehand. From about '65 there were a lot of things happening in Paris. So, I wasn't all that keen on going back. But Richard was.

Unwisely, I'm sure

Michael Hubbard

I remember at one point Barbara saying to Richard, 'If you go back to South Africa you're going to get killed. With the aspirations you have in South Africa I don't want to go back.' Then it all revolved around, 'Well, when my mother retires who is going to run the farm?' Unwisely, I'm sure, Richard decided he would go back and run the farm. So in August 1966, they returned and moved into the main farmhouse, and Jane moved into the cottage.

BEARING FRUIT

GEHEIM/SECRET

During his stay out of country, Turner visited Yugoslavia during August 1965. During this period one Peter Hammond contacts him. It appears that Hammond at that time was teaching in Red China and that Turner himself was interested in such a post. Turner went to the Red Chinese mission in London for further information. However, nothing came of this and on 12 August 1966, Turner is back in Cape Town.

— From the security police files

In disembarking in Cape Town on 12 August 1966, Rick Turner was returning to the country of his birth, the city where he had gone to university and, most importantly, the farm where he had spent his childhood. He was then 25 years old, a newly graduated doctor of philosophy, a husband and father. His wife Barbara was returning to her home town as well, and their young daughter, Jann, was setting foot on African soil for the first time in her life.

Having spent nearly three years away, Turner came home with a whole body of experiences and thoughts that none of those he had left behind could easily relate to or make sense of. It was not simply the fact that he had studied abroad and could read and speak a foreign language. There was something deeper, less tangible and more thoroughgoing that suddenly separated Turner from his country and his peers.

And yet, despite the tremendous broadening of his horizons while away, Turner came home with his small family, not to start a revolution, but to grow fruit. Richard's mother Jane wanted to get away, travel the world a bit and let go of some of her responsibilities on the farm. So she asked her only son to come and tend the farm for a while. Perhaps she even hoped that he would some day take over the management of the farm entirely.

While Rick Turner's skills management of the farm quickly soured, his return to Welcarmas did bear fruit of some kind. In establishing himself in the Cape Town area after his return from Paris and inviting others to join him in a series of provocative discussions, Turner found his footing as a radical educator within the liberal and left-wing student movement. With the farm as a sort of 'free university' space, Turner began opening up new avenues for critical thought and action. As his confidence grew, he became increasingly influential, at least among small pockets of people. Turner's bluntly radical stances – rooted in an awareness of realities abroad and expressed freely and without fear – gained him respect, and also the unwanted attention of the apartheid government. Using infiltrators – 'delicate sources' who wrote secret reports on his activities – the security forces took an increasing interest in a man whom they began thinking of as quite dangerous.

YEAR OF UPHEAVALS

That Turner was able to find sympathetic allies in this climate points to his remarkable capacity to engage with people, regardless of the fact that his ideas went far beyond the dominant politics of the time. Turner found likeminded friends and associates within both the University of Stellenbosch and the University of Cape Town. Despite the generally conservative atmosphere at Stellenbosch, there were nonetheless a handful of professors and students sympathetic to Turner. Most notably, Johann Degenaar, the Socratic head of the philosophy department, and his younger colleague André du Toit ran a discussion group called 'The Circle' in which Turner participated regularly. Degenaar and Turner became friends. In addition, Augustine Schutte at the Dominican Priory in Stellenbosch (who later became a professor of philosophy at UCT after leaving religious life) became close to Turner and made regular visits to the farm.

Though the English-speaking UCT was more liberal in its outlook than Stellenbosch, the intellectual climate there had been stifled by the general political repression and by the exodus of its more radical members of faculty; and the liberalism which the university espoused was both limited and cautious. Among students there were a number of small radical groups, including the Radical Society and the Modern World Society. Both had a dozen or so members and were primarily spaces for shared reading and discussion. Turner was friendly with both groups and contributed, through writing and conversation, the ideas and texts of the New Left, including such thinkers as Sartre, Marcuse and Gramsci.

So, while things were relatively quiet politically upon his return, Turner nonetheless found himself absorbed in a network of radical thought that proved sustaining. Furthermore, the great wave of upheavals that spread across the globe in 1968 reached South Africa in small ripples, enough to shake up the defensive and embattled atmosphere and begin to create room for a more radical theory and practice.

The various social movements that have come to be thought of as characterising the sixties achieved a kind of climax in 1968. Despite the fact that many of them ultimately failed or were violently suppressed, they nonetheless communicated a certain spirit of tenacity and hope that is rare in human history.

In May 1968 students at the Sorbonne in Paris took over their university and transformed it into a fully public space for learning and living. Teachers, students, workers and community members all participated in classes, discussions and the management of the place. They set up barricades around the campus and tore up paving stones in order to fight off the police and maintain control of their 'free university'. The occupation of the Sorbonne soon spread to other universities throughout France. Sympathetic wildcat strikes, involving millions of workers, swept the country. The uprising was characterised by an unprecedented utopianism. Hostile to organised political parties and trade unions, the rebel students and workers broadcast slogans such as 'Live without dead time', 'Beneath the paving stones, the beach' and 'We don't want a world where freedom from dying from hunger comes at the risk of dying of boredom'.

This spirit of rebellion arrived in South Africa, as well, but slowly and in a much more muted form. Without television, and with print media and radio carefully censored, news filtered through narrow channels and spread among a small group of South Africans.

The most notable expression of the spirit of '68 occurred at UCT. In May of that year the anthropologist Archie Mafeje, who had trained at both UCT and Cambridge University, was appointed as a lecturer in the university's anthropology department. While the euphemistically named Extension of University Access Act had recently closed UCT and similar institutions of higher learning to black students, it said nothing about the employment of black staff. In practice, however, very few blacks had ever been appointed to positions at universities like UCT, and on the few occasions when this happened, it was in African languages departments. The head of UCT's anthropology department, Monica Wilson, who had championed Mafeje, saw his appointment 'as a natural extension of this precedent – one would be appointing an African sociologist to teach about African societies'.[4] But the government was not persuaded by any reasoning of this sort and began pressuring the UCT administration to reverse their decision. UCT caved in and withdrew its invitation to Mafeje to join the faculty.

In response, student organisations demanded that Mafeje be hired and negotiations began between representatives of the university and student groups. Towards the end of July, Raphael Kaplinsky, a leader of the Radical Society, presented the university with an ultimatum, and threatened a sit-in protest if the students' demand was not met for Mafeje's reappointment.

On 9 August, after a mass meeting was held in Jameson Hall with nearly a thousand students in attendance, hundreds of people responded to the call for a sit-in and proceeded to occupy the Bremner administration building. At that time university policy required students to wear a jacket and tie if they wished to enter the building. In a symbolic expression of shaking off old customs, Kaplinsky made a speech outside, proclaiming, 'We'll stay inside until our demands are met. The only rules are that we don't wear jackets and ties.'[5] While no one – even the leadership – really expected the sit-in to last very long, the students ended up occupying the administration building for nine days, living, eating, talking, learning, playing and sleeping in some of the rooms, in the hallways and on the stairs.

What do you do then?
Michael Hubbard

It's a story with some tragedy in it.

We thought there would be a few of us going down to the administration building to occupy it, and it turned out that practically the whole meeting came down ... nearly a thousand students. We could hardly fit into the building.

We went into the Senate chamber, which was the biggest room in the building, and we all sat down. The question then, as in any similar situation, is 'What do you do then?' No doubt the administration, that had simply opened the doors and let us walk in, felt the same. They must have thought, 'they'll be gone in a few hours.'

Some students would go in and out. Some would go to classes, some would go home, some got so involved they didn't want to leave. There were many seminars, lectures, as well as endless discussions in the evenings on 'What do we do now?'

Were we a disorderly bunch? No, we were intent that

we shouldn't get in the way of the administration. We were very orderly.[6] We even had a security service. The UCT staff continued to go about their jobs during those nine days. The UCT administration didn't shut down.

The sit-in at UCT was a far cry from the militant clashes of Paris. It was not – as the police said afterwards – a 'riot'. Also, unlike other protests at the Sorbonne or Columbia University, the UCT sit-in didn't call for a full student strike. No attempt was made to stop students from attending classes and meeting whatever other obligations they might have at the university.

At the same time, some fundamentally radical notions behind sit-in protests were carried out at UCT. The most important task of such a protest is to demonstrate a tangible alternative to the university as it currently exists. This alternative can take many forms, but at the very least it must create a different learning environment. During the UCT sit-in, 'lectures, tutorials and teach-ins were held on a range of topics, from student power and academic freedom to homosexuality, and political discussions went on through the night, often dominated by charismatic speakers such as Kaplinsky and Turner'.[7] The essential feature of these 'free university' classes was not only the subjects taught, but the way that learning happened, which was fundamentally more cooperative and equal than the usual university class.

In addition, the protesters created cooperative structures to manage the daily affairs of the group. Decisions about strategy and management of the space were made in large, democratic meetings. Various tasks were divided among smaller committees, so as to provide food communally, keep the building clean, secure the space from any outside threats, as well as produce an unofficial newspaper.

While the UCT administration responded relatively calmly to the sit-in and in general tolerated the students' presence for over a week, it was not in the slightest degree moved to change its mind. As far as having their basic demand met, the students were defeated. In fact, the administration didn't need to force the students to leave Bremmer Building. A contingent of Afrikaans students from the University of Stellenbosch arrived at UCT and threatened to storm the building. Coupled with the presence of police, this had the effect of persuading the UCT students to leave willingly, so as to avoid both violence and arrest.

While the end of the sit-in was far from a resounding victory, many of the young people who participated left with a different awareness of what was possible, and remember the experience fondly decades later. Andrew Colman, who participated in the sit-in, summarised its significance in his eyes: 'The sit-in went far beyond our small group of radical youth. It included people who were just slightly liberal, who simply felt it was unfair and racist that the university didn't give Mafeje this job. Many of them said they weren't very political when they went in, but they all said they were very political when they came out. It was a huge educative experience for most of those people. It wasn't an overwhelming defeat. We weren't expecting the sit-in to be successful.' Echoing this sentiment, Michael Hubbard said: 'It had a big effect on us, even if in terms of South African history it doesn't make any noise. We had a good reason to feel our protest was in response to an important issue. I don't think any of us regret that at all. But how it fits into South Africa more broadly, I guess it doesn't really.'

In some small way, the sit-in marked an important shift in the energy and momentum of the opposition to apartheid, particularly among white students. While many whites still attempted to be reasonable and make respectful demands of the government, at least the possibility of more radical thought and action was once again visible.

* * *

GEHEIM/SECRET

During the weekend of 1.10.1968 he met in a big tent on his farm Welcarmas with students of both sexes from the University of Cape Town. He invited them to his farm after the riots by the Cape university against the decision of the Minister of Education not to appoint a non-white, Archie Mafeje, as lecturer. Turner played a leading role during the riots.

Rick Turner (with, on occasion, his daughter Jann) was among the thousands of visitors and supporters who participated in the sit-in. He contributed to the mass meetings where decisions about the protest were made, as well as to some of the 'free university' classes held in the administration building. While he was not one of the key leaders of the sit-in, he had a broader grasp of its significance than many others. Having been at the Sorbonne himself and having followed the news from France in May, Turner understood that the real goal of students occupying their university was not merely to force concessions, but rather to call into question the entire structure of the university, the economy and the society as a whole.

Throughout his lifetime as a university lecturer, Turner was consistently involved in efforts to create room for critical thought outside and counter to the logic and structure of the academy. In a speech he delivered years later about the sit-in and similar protests internationally,[8] he explained his critique of the university system as follows:

> Students want to live in a culture that is engaged in something more than simple descriptions. They don't want universities to train them to be technicians for servicing the present social machine. They want universities to be involved in the creative task of evaluating the present social machine, of exploring different ways of organizing the society, of trying to discover new ways of living that are not just based on habit and tradition, of judging in terms of what is *possible*, not in terms of what *is*.
>
> Today's students' complaint against the establishment is not that the members of the establishment don't have the right answers, it is that they don't even seem to realize *that there are any questions*. All they want to be able to do is to be able to be part of a society which actually looks for questions and answers, a society which isn't smug, whether its smugness be that of the old Czech Stalinist bureaucracy, the American influence-peddling party machine, or the white South African oligarchy.
>
> So white South African students should try a little hard thinking about their values and about their society. Thinking, provided that it is done honestly, and provided that you do something about your thoughts, is far more revolutionary and dangerous than mere rioting!

THE LONG HAIR TYPES

GEHEIM/SECRET

On 7.9.1968 Turner was one of the speakers who addressed students of the University of Cape Town on Czechoslovakia from the steps in front of Jameson Hall ...

On 4.11.1968 a trustworthy source reports as follows: 'I want to warn you against this man Turner. He's not only a Marxist but definitely a revolutionary. I came to this conclusion out of conversations that I've had with him during the past year and I'm convinced that he will also try to influence others to his perspective. Richard Turner is a Mao Tse-tung man and a hardened supporter of everything that goes along with that.'

On 13.1.1969, a reliable source reports that he distributed soft-cover books that deal with the activities of Rudi Dutchke, student-agitator in Europe, and Che Quevara (*sic*), a Cuban revolutionary, among students at the University of Stellenbosch ...

Demanding their attention
Mike Hubbard

Rick was very much in a pivotal position, particularly in that period. What Richard brought was something unique to him. Maybe someone else could have gone over to France and studied existentialism and written extensively about it, but really no one else had. And, in any case, to be influential requires someone who wants to live out his ideas, live out his philosophy, and there certainly aren't many who try to do that; someone who seems to *have* to do that, who seems inspired by the forces around him.

I can remember a group of philosophy students coming down to my house – Mike Morris, Jeremy Cronin, Bernard Holiday. Rich was at my house that afternoon. They said, 'You're promoting Plato.' Richard thought there was an enormous amount one could learn from Plato. I can remember they were challenging him. In response, Richard said, 'OK, let's just start with the basics.' By the end of the afternoon they were all going off saying, 'Hmm. Maybe Plato does have something useful to say.' He had a way of thinking very clearly and simply – not so much in the rest of his life, but certainly in terms of philosophy and engagement.

Even as early as '67 Richard was starting to give talks, particularly around the city and out on the farm. I remember he organised a teach-in on the Vietnam War at UCT, and in other ways helped to raise awareness of more global issues, such as the student movements in Paris and Berlin. After the sit-ins at UCT in 1968, Richard starting inviting groups of people who were at the sit-in to seminars out at the farm. He was particularly interested in raising discussions on education and especially the ideas of Ivan Illich.

Over time, there was a growing awareness among the security police that they had someone living in Stellenbosch who was quite unusual. So Richard started to demand their attention, and they started monitoring him.

Not only were the police monitoring him, also some of the student activists distrusted him at first. I remember even Raphael Kaplinsky, the head of the Radical Society, saying at the time, 'I think he's somehow linked to the security police. He's a phenomenon; you don't get someone like this speaking so openly.' You have to remember that this was at the height of the Cold War. In South Africa the way the Cold War was presented was by saying, 'We are the bastion in Africa against communism.' And here's a guy who's talking openly about Marxist ideas and socialism. After the Communist Party had been banned, most people spoke very carefully, but he didn't. He shared his ideas very openly.

GEHEIM/SECRET

On the evening of 21.9.1968 Turner organised a party on his farm 'Welcarmss Cottage'. There were a great number of students present and a trustworthy source reported on this as follows: 'several long hair type students were already under the influence of alcohol and drugs that they could not speak properly. Other than the excessive use of strong drink, some of them openly smoked dagga. Turner moved around among the students and it was clear that he had an exceptional influence over them. Other than that he spoke about the so-called victory that the students had with their "sit-in". Turner frequently elicited a conversation about Marxism and then persuasively told of his experiences at the Sorbonne University in Paris and showed the advantages of student agitation according to Marxist principles.'

* * *

'If you haven't been through it, you can't imagine the desert that we lived through during apartheid. Hitler and Mussolini were fascists, with grandiose delusions, on a global scale. The apartheid bastards had not even the slightest hint of anything grand; they were fascists, but in the dullest, most provincial way.'

— DAN O'MEARA

Apartheid provided little room to breathe. In addition to the imposing infrastructure used to control the black majority and the military and police apparatus used to spy on, detain and torture people, there was also the stifling cultural atmosphere of an authoritarian society. All forms of art and media were heavily censored, leaving people with limited room to express themselves or be exposed to information and creativity from abroad. While the idea of a counter-culture spread through the Western world during the 1960s – with new styles of dress, new music, new models of living together, new ways of speaking, and experimentation with sex and drugs – this was, in the main, still only a rumour inside South Africa. Neither the government nor the young people who might have embraced such a counter-culture had a very thorough idea of what it meant.

But whether or not the authorities sufficiently understood the new attitudes, they were certainly sure they hated them. They were constantly on the lookout for any signs of deviancy among young people. In particular, the government sought to draw links between self-identified radicals and transgressive behaviours such as excessive drinking or smoking dope; in this way it hoped to smear the reputation of anyone involved in left-wing political circles.

Richard Turner, the son of an alcoholic, lived a sober lifestyle and actively expressed his objection to being intoxicated. In particular, he prized the strength of his own mind – and of rational thought generally – and saw no reason to intentionally cloud one's thinking. If social events happened at Welcarmas, organised by him, the main activity of the gathering was certainly not on getting drunk or smoking *dagga* (marijuana). For Turner, the central emphasis of any gathering of this kind – no matter how informal and relaxed the setting – would have been engaged, critical conversation. More than anything, Richard loved a good discussion. He would have found the company of people too much 'under the influence' to speak properly, absolutely boring.

This is not to imply that Turner was narrow-minded and prim, or opposed to counter-cultural attitudes. Far from it. He was very much intrigued by the idea of trying to embody a radically different set of cultural values, within the process of opposing the dominant culture. He believed strongly in breaking down the established roles of men and women, teachers and students, whites and blacks. He was also inspired by the idea of sharing property to the maximum extent, of creating social structures that maximised autonomy and love.

In fact, Turner's interest in counter-cultural experimentation became a major source of conflict with his wife. His curiosity with the concept of 'free love' led him to have an affair, which put additional strain on an already taxed marriage. Furthermore, while his mother tolerated his frequent guests and the various political conversations, she most certainly wouldn't have permitted turning the farm over completely to the fulfilment of some utopian vision of rural socialism. So, while Welcarmas was the site of numerous social gatherings for the Turner family and their friends, these were neither as transgressive as the police would have liked to believe, nor as revolutionary as Turner himself might have desired.

In the months that followed the sit-in at UCT, Turner played a crucial role in continuing the radical political discussions that had begun in the hallways and offices of Bremner Building. At Welcarmas he hosted a number of gatherings, giving people space to deepen their political analysis and consciously link their efforts to the overall spirit of upheaval that was spreading internationally at the time.

Much more serious

Andrew Colman

South Africa was the back end of the world.
   Rick was a very charismatic character without being a demagogue. He was the opposite of a demagogue. He had a very small voice, literally and metaphorically. He was a quiet-spoken, polite, not aggressive and not at

all pushy man. All of those qualities sound the opposite of charismatic, but they all constituted his special kind of charisma. It was what made him so persuasive, really. Because he wasn't shouting from the rooftops and he was so rational and cool. He was just a great guy and in a different way from everybody else.

Rick was absolutely the key in opening us up to new ideas and news from abroad. First of all, he had been living in France and was heavily influenced by the precursors to the Paris student uprisings. Quite simply, he could understand French, which to us was just magic. None of us spoke a foreign language in those days, and that was the language of the day to speak if you wanted to know what was going on. So, yes, he was absolutely a key conduit of modern thought, young people's modern political thought in the outside world, which we were very hungry for.

I have very distinct memories of sitting with him bent over a shortwave radio on his farm listening to French broadcasts. He kept saying there are thousands of them in the square now, and he was giving a running translation of the uprising. He thought there was going to be a revolution in France, or that there might be. Looking back on it, that sounds like an exaggerated interpretation, but at the time a lot of people believed that.

I was running the Modern World Society, which had a publication called *Modern World*. Our group was sort of Marxist. I mean, we weren't really Marxist, but we liked the label because it sounded more radical.

There were various other groups like that, and Rick was one who floated between all these groups. He was very ecumenical in his political views, even then. He was very radical, but not a communist. Like many of us, he was very anti-state, particularly anti-Soviet. In this way I think he might have been influenced by French and US students. He was the most anti-authoritarian of all of us.

Rick kept open house, out at the farm. I guess I shouldn't say open house because it was quite a long drive from Cape Town. But there were very frequent meetings. The meetings I went to were just informal – I doubt if there was ever an agenda – but serious. It wasn't for chit-chat; always serious political discussions. Usually between half a dozen and twenty people and we used to sit around, sometimes outside, sometimes in his lounge, and discuss the events of the day, such as the student uprisings in Europe, or just local issues. Sometimes very theoretical. Sometimes people would actually do readings and talk about interpreting passages in Marx or articles that had been written.

It was mostly white, English-speaking people. Were there some Afrikaners or so-called coloured people? I can't remember any. Many of us were Jewish.

I wouldn't describe the gatherings at Welcarmas as being a party atmosphere. There may have been occasions when we would have had a barbeque. That would have just been secondary. And as for the stereotyping by the police that Rick's farm was some kind of hippie, free love space, it's just not true. It wouldn't have happened at Rick's farm. It's true at that time, in the mid- to late '60s, there was a huge amount of free love and lots of casual sex going on. But not at the farm. I went there plenty of times and it wouldn't have felt like an appropriate venue for it because Rick wasn't like that. Even more so, Rick's mother wasn't like that at all.

Why we were together at the farm was always because we wanted to discuss issues of the day. It was much more serious than any of us are today, I would think.

CERTAINLY WASN'T IN A VERY BAD WAY

While Richard Turner's return to his childhood farm afforded him a number of opportunities to engage with the growing radical opposition in the Western Cape, other aspects of his life quickly started to fall apart.

In spite of his deep love for his mother, Turner had little hope of succeeding at the task of running the farm. He was a voracious reader, a great lover of intelligent conversations and a natural educator – not a farmer. Turner conceived of Welcarmas as a social gathering space, a place to share good company, ideas and values, much more than an enterprise or occupation. With this attitude, the farm began to flounder as a business under Turner's management. In fact, his management skills were so lacking that Jane eventually decided to sell off portions of the land, to reduce her own burden. In addition, the demands of the farming lifestyle led to increasing levels of strain in his marriage to Barbara, and when he eventually moved away from Cape Town in 1969, he left his wife and family behind.

Some order in my life

Barbara Hubbard

We made an attempt to take over the farm for Jane, as we had promised, but it just didn't work.

What didn't work is that Richard was terribly bad at running the business. I didn't get involved in running the books initially and I should have, because he lost a lot of money. He didn't do the things his mother had done, like going to the market or opening the little fruit store, because he didn't think he had to do that. In the meantime he had increased his wages. The concept of a profit and loss account sort of passed him by.

One day I said, 'What are all these things in this drawer?' He said, 'They are all the invoices I have to take to the accountant.' So, I took them and it turned out he was losing money. His mother was incredibly angry with him about it and basically took back the running of the farm, although I helped her with it.

We lived there then with my mother and his mother, which was difficult. Although they were in separate little houses, it was still difficult and definitely contributed to the bust-up of our marriage.

In addition, we had some conflicts over his attitudes and behaviour towards me as a woman. I spent much of my childhood attempting not to be a girl and dressing up like a boy. I was very conscious of the limitations that women were under. So, I would say to Richard and his male friends, 'I don't know how you can talk about liberating people when you guys still behave like white South African men, expecting women to make you tea, drop your clothes on the way to the bathroom and expect someone to pick it up.'

That certainly was a big element of conflict in our relationship – probably our only real disagreement. He did change, and began to lose that 'I'm here to be waited on' attitude. When he went to live with Foszia, he had really changed quite a bit.

Even worse than the other strains, it was a time of free love and Richard decided we should have an open marriage and I decided we shouldn't. I attempted to make it work for about two months and then I left him. I left him and he was always cross with me about it.

I remember once Richard said, very angrily, 'Barbara left me because she wanted some order in her life.' But he was right, I did. I don't want disorder.

GEHEIM/SECRET

```
On 2.9.1969, he accepts service at Rhodes
University at Grahamstown as lecturer in
Political Science. On the same date, he
attends the 'Free Universities' first lecture
and gives a lecture about 'Jean-Paul Sartre'
a philosopher who propagates change through
violence.
```

After the collapse of Richard's relationship with Barbara, he left the farm and moved in 1969 to Grahamstown, where his friend Andrew Colman found him a job in the politics department at Rhodes University.

I think we just ignored it

Andrew Colman

It was either December '68 or January '69 that I moved to Grahamstown, and later that year Rick contacted me and he wanted a job. I called a colleague, who was a politics lecturer. It was possible in those days to fix a job for people, and we kind of fixed a job for Rick. And he turned up very gracefully on his own and it was then obvious that his marriage had broken up. I wouldn't know what happened to get to that point. I suppose I wasn't interested at the time, although his marriage must have been deteriorating.

I don't recall having the kind of conversation I would have now with somebody who turned up without his wife. I might have done, but I don't think either of us ever asked him, 'What happened or how do you feel?' It must be awful. I think we just ignored it and slipped back into the same kind of discourse we had had before. He certainly wasn't in a very bad way. He must have been. I've subsequently gone through as amicable a divorce as it's possible to have, and it was horrible. So it must have been bad for him, but it wasn't apparent. He was an extremely cool character. He was very, very relaxed, and I suppose well adjusted. He certainly wasn't in a broken-down state.

The move to Grahamstown was temporary. Although he didn't allow people around him to know it, Turner was undergoing a time of adjustment, a process of transition, which must have been difficult for him. He had to adapt to life as a single man, in a town that was unfamiliar to him. Though Grahamstown is like Stellenbosch in being dominated by a university, it is also very different: a frontier town, a colonial outpost, with the memory of wars of conquest hanging in the air.

Very quickly he entered into a close friendship with Ann Oosthuizen, an English lecturer at the university who had recently lost her husband, a highly regarded professor of philosophy. She was older than Turner, 'an extremely interesting and attractive woman' in the words of Andrew Colman, though according to Ann her relationship with Rick was not a romantic engagement. With Ann, Andrew and a handful of others, Turner built up a new intellectual and political peer group. He settled in easily to teaching and involved himself in the few incidents of student protest that arose at Rhodes at the time.

But his stay was short-lived. After about six months at Rhodes, Turner left and at the start of 1970 transferred to the University of Natal, in Durban. There he would truly thrive, intellectually, politically and emotionally, and come into his own.

PART TWO

The Durban Moment

FOUR

Whites First, Liberals Second

'The stereotypical reaction of white to black is only the most obvious expression of a society in which all relationships, from courtship to commuting, become stereotyped. All relations become rituals. The paradigm for human relationships in white South Africa is the tea party in which the white ladies coo properly over the maid's cakes and circulate pre-digested opinions about 'the servant problem'. Not an idea, not a moment of communication, troubles the smooth, empty atmosphere. The excitement of self-discovery, the excitement of shattered certainties, and the thrill of freedom: these are experiences that are closed to white South Africans. The price of control is conformity.'[1]

– RICK TURNER

'THE ONLY VEHICLE FOR CHANGE'

WHILE THE SIT-IN AT UCT WAS an inspiring moment of student protest, student politics as a whole went through an intense transition in the late 1960s. The National Union of South African Students (Nusas), which had always been a racially integrated and liberal organisation, came under steady criticism from its black members for being dominated by white people and white (liberal, Western) values. In 1967, when black students at the Nusas national convention, held at Rhodes University, were made to sleep in separate accommodation from the white student delegates, they were enraged. The acceptance of apartheid divisions was held up as yet another example of what seemed like a spurious commitment to integration on the part of white students. Black delegates felt that integration, as evidenced by the behaviour of their white peers, did not mean genuine equality in social relationships, nor were they likely to take equal risks in advancing social change, as evidenced by their unwillingness to stand up to the Rhodes University authorities. Steve Biko, a medical student at the University of Natal and a charismatic student leader, condemned what he termed artificial integration, which he called 'a one-way course, with the whites doing all the talking and the blacks the listening'.[2]

In essence, what Biko and his colleagues were calling for was a fundamental shift in the relations between white liberals and blacks. The old dynamic, in Sartre's words, had come to an end. 'A new generation came on the scene, which changed the issue. With unbelievable patience, its writers and poets tried to explain to us that our values and the true facts of their lives did not hang together ... By and large, what they were saying was this: "You are making us into monstrosities; your humanism claims we are at one with the rest of humanity but your racist methods set us apart."'[3]

Working in collaboration with other radical black students, Biko began articulating a new politics for South Africa, which came to be known as Black Consciousness. This was concerned primarily with fostering an autonomous and unified black viewpoint. Inspired by the Black Power movement in the United States and the writing of Frantz Fanon and others, Black Consciousness encouraged black people to separate themselves from white people, no matter how well-meaning, and establish their own structures for empowerment and self-defence in terms of a 'black' political identity.

Black Consciousness encouraged black people to be proud of themselves, and aspire to be strong. According to Biko, 'the black man has become a shell, a shadow of a man, completely defeated, drowning in his own misery, a slave, an ox bearing the yoke of oppression with sheepish timidity.' Biko then used this analysis to put forward an intriguing paradox. 'This is the first truth, bitter as it may seem, that we have to acknowledge before we can start on any programme of changing the status quo ... The only vehicle for change are these people who have lost their personality.'[4] By naming blacks as the 'only vehicle for change', Biko articulated both a strategic and a moral programme. Strategically speaking, he felt strongly that no genuine change in South Africa would be possible without a strong and assertive black movement. But perhaps more fundamentally, the moral message was that black people had to place themselves at the centre of efforts for social transformation, because the process of assertion and revolt itself would be healing. For not only were oppressed people potentially agents of their liberation, but they were also (and necessarily) agents of their own subjugation. In relation to white liberals, this meant that their paternalism and tutelage had to be shunned because it crippled black people, keeping them trapped within their own inferior sense of themselves. It was precisely this acute attention to moments of complicity that gave Black Consciousness its explosive power.

Having developed the Black Consciousness viewpoint, a group of black university students split off from Nusas in 1969 to form the South African Students' Organisation (Saso). The Saso manifesto explains the decision as follows: 'Saso accepts the premise that before black people should join the open society, they should first close their ranks, to form themselves into a solid group to oppose the definite racism that is meted out by the white society, to work out their direction clearly and bargain from a position of strength. Saso believes that a truly open society can only be achieved by blacks.'[5] In Biko's words, the goal was 'to remove [the white man] from our table, strip the table of all trappings put on it by him, decorate it in true African style, settle down and then invite him to join us on our own terms if he liked'.[6] This bold assertion of black autonomy forced white student activists to reconsider their role in the process of social change.

Looking closer at the substance of Black Consciousness thought, one sees that it is more an invitation than a threat. Black Consciousness invited whites to reconfigure themselves as neither innocents nor as saviours, as neither entitled to their present status nor excluded from human interactions with the black majority of South Africa. As Biko put it, 'If they are true liberals they must realize that they themselves are oppressed, and that they must fight for their own freedom and not that of the nebulous "they" with whom they can hardly claim identification.'[7] Rick Turner immediately understood this point, writing, 'The refusal of blacks to want to be "like whites" is not racism. It is good taste.'[8]

Nonetheless, there were many struggles among liberals and within the white left about how best to respond to the challenge of Black Consciousness. Many were resentful of or confused by its message. Some felt that it was 'racist' to call on blacks to work only among themselves or that Black Consciousness somehow went against the long-term goal of a non-racial society. Furthermore, it was unclear for many whites, particularly students, how they might engage in politics in a majority black society, but in all-white organisations.

'WE HAD TO FIND OUR OWN ROLE'

The developing strength of the Black Consciousness viewpoint forced a growing handful of whites to adapt their own politics in response. During its early years, Black Consciousness flowered rapidly throughout the country. Its advocates were very articulate and assertive, and their influence spread fast. Beyers Naudé, the director of the Christian Institute, summarised the implications of Black Consciousness in this way: 'Organisations usually described as "white liberal" or "white-controlled" will face a period of temporary estrangement ... until the black community feels that it is strong enough to move back as equals or until these organisations adapt rapidly and creatively to black pressures. Reconciliation will become increasingly difficult. To meet black anger with duplicity or delay is dangerous. To try to meet it with brute force is fatal. To talk about goodwill and tolerance without concerted action is futile.'[9]

However, the necessary shift in values among whites didn't tend to come easily or quickly. On the contrary, many people within the white opposition to apartheid remained deeply stuck in the old ways of thinking, and appeared torpid and listless in the face of the challenge of Black Consciousness. A persistently cautious approach, combined with deep ignorance, characterised much of the white liberal politics that Turner encountered in the late 1960s and early 1970s. Liberals and leftists had been so thoroughly intimidated by the apartheid state that what passed as proposals for change were frequently so mildly stated that a reader looking back now would find it difficult to grasp the courage that often lay behind the words.[10] Michael Nupen, professor of the politics department at the University of Natal, which Turner joined in 1970, summarised the political climate at the time in this way: 'Opposition to the racist ideology of South African domination was conducted at the time Turner wrote either as etiolated liberalism or as a dogmatic mechanistic marxism. Both were philosophically impoverished to the point of incoherence. They were also politically bankrupt having been thoroughly defeated.'[11] In this context, Turner's writings and talks must have struck like lightning into the heart of white liberal thought – leaving liberalism exposed, exploded, surpassed.

Rick Turner described white liberals as being 'white first, and liberal second'. By this he meant that their capacity to envision any fundamental change to their way of life or their values was profoundly limited and compromised by their daily participation in a racist social, political and economic system. 'They are offended by the barbarities of South African society but not sufficiently outraged to be willing to risk sacrificing their own privileged positions. This is not merely a question of cowardice; it also represents both a lack of imagination and ignorance.'[12] Turner saw white people as being trapped within a social structure – which was of their own making – that persistently and severely constrained the capacity of human beings to have any kind of genuine interaction with each other. Turner understood quite clearly just how stuck and confused white people were at the time:

> White South Africans do take their rights to exploit blacks for granted, but their psychic and cultural makeup is much more complex than that. They are very ignorant of how their society works; they are ignorant of history and of the nature of social relationships; they are very insecure, and underlying their apparent arrogance is often a deep fear both of blacks and of any pattern of behaviour that threatens their perceptions of the naturalness of ... their right to exploit. Thus we cannot assume that they will necessarily react rationally to any form of challenge.[13]

Turner saw the moral concern and commitment to action among whites at the time to be so tepid and ineffective, that he sought to shock them out of what he called 'the impracticality of realism'. His rejection of reformist politics was rooted in a deep-seated morality, an unshakeable belief that oppressive systems cannot be reasonably 'reformed', but instead must be done away with altogether, to make way for dignified and meaningful human relationships.

Turner saw that 'mentally the white public is kept in a continuous state of war-readiness ... The whites are prepared for a fight and would probably fight if they had to. With the balance of forces as it is at present, they would certainly win in any straight black–white civil war.'[14] He felt strongly, therefore, that the intransigence of the white population must be opposed not so much through force, but through organised initiatives of whites and through black pressure in whatever ways were available to them. Turner spoke out strongly against any attitude among whites that they were irrelevant merely because blacks had to take a proactive role in the struggle:

> It is said that change will come from the blacks and therefore any processes of change that happen to be occurring within the white group are essentially irrelevant. It seems to me that this is a very serious mistake to make. I certainly agree that the major factor in bringing about political change in South Africa will be black action ... [but] political activity directed at and within the white group in an attempt to create at least a group within white society who would be more willing to envisage change is very important.[15]

Towards these ends, Turner involved himself crucially in the process of re-examining the old liberal structures and in helping build a new organisational format for white people. In taking a sympathetic stance towards Black Consciousness, he also played a crucial role in helping whites avoid feeling alienated or rejected and find a positive role for them in the struggle.

Turner's most powerful contribution to the debate around Black Consciousness was an article he wrote in 1972 entitled 'Black Consciousness and White Liberals'. In it he responded to the general impasse between Black Consciousness activists and white liberals by adding two new ideas, which shifted the whole discussion in important ways. First, Turner bluntly and emphatically declared that white people were profoundly in need of a different consciousness, a different culture, in order to become fully human:

> It is arguable that the main 'contribution' of western civilization to human history was the development of a new and higher level of ... exploitation of one's neighbours ... Whites are where they are in the world essentially through having developed a great capacity to wield force ruthlessly in pursuit of their own ends ... At present, white consciousness is cabbage consciousness – a mindless absorption of material from the environment ... Black consciousness is a rejection of the idea that the ideal for human kind is 'to be like the whites'. This should lead to the recognition that it is also bad for whites 'to be like the whites'. That is ... in an important sense both whites and blacks are oppressed, though in different ways, by a social system which perpetuates itself by creating white lords and black slaves, and no full human beings.[16]

Secondly, Turner rejected the ways in which both black and white activists characterised themselves as representing two antagonistic positions. Rather, he insisted that there were actually three different positions: racism, liberalism and radicalism. By defining Black Consciousness as a form of radicalism, Turner acknowledged that its politics were different from and antagonistic to liberalism, while nonetheless offering white people a clear and simple path out of their own irrelevance – to become radicals themselves. 'So far the argument has been formulated in terms of the categories "liberalism" and "racism", with resulting confusion on both sides. The introduction of the third category enables us to clear up these confusions, and to point to the real problem, which is the need for a new culture ... Radicals believe that "white" culture itself is at fault, and that both blacks and whites need to go beyond it and create a new culture.'[17]

At a most basic level, Turner insisted that white people sympathetic to the black movement must continue to seek out roles for themselves, regardless of the fact that black people were demanding their autonomy. His own role lay in exerting influence over the white left within the student movement, in particular within Nusas. Nusas had been greatly destabilied by the establishment of Saso and by the spread of Black Consciousness thought in general. The values that were fundamental to the organisation were being openly and directly challenged by people who would ideally have been natural allies. Without the support of black students, Nusas had considerably less credibility as a vehicle for expressing the concerns of South African students.

As a political science lecturer on an English-speaking university campus, it was relatively straightforward for Turner to influence the development of Nusas politics. Having himself been a member of Nusas as a student at UCT, Turner was well immersed in the issues and concerns of the student movement when he arrived in Durban in 1970. His influence spread well beyond the classroom. Turner often gave talks at various student forums and participated in student protests sponsored by Nusas on a regular basis. Only 28 years old at the time, he was able to relate easily to the students. He was well liked and respected by many of them, especially by those who were thinking through what radical opposition to the injustices of South African society meant.

What he does is to translate
Halton Cheadle

Rick's engagement with student politics was very important because it arose at the same time as Steve Biko. Steve Biko and Rick met together and shared their ideas with one another. Biko was articulating a Black Consciousness ideology, what he called a necessary separatism. Biko felt that in every organisation, whites come in and they take up leadership positions. In response to this problem, blacks have to overcome their own psychological inferiority issues and become leaders. What Rick does is to translate that viewpoint into what becomes effectively the vision and strategy for a white student movement. The viewpoint that Rick put forward in 1969–70 was that the appropriate role for white students was not in fact to lead and to make change but to prepare whites for change. The black student movement was to lead the revolution, with the assistance of whites. This was very much a strategic vision that Rick Turner gave the student movement. I think he defines exactly what happens to the student movement from 1970 onwards.

Rick becomes enormously important for the first serious attempt to try to respond to Black Consciousness in a constructive way. I mean, the ANC lambasted Black Consciousness; they saw everything as a bloody challenge to their party. But I think you need to realise that, despite what the ANC says, they just weren't an option at the time. I mean, the ANC got hammered in the '60s. They say they were deep underground in the '70s; my God, if they were, then they were so deep that no one knew about their existence. There were definitely links, but they were quite careful. But no one was organising. They certainly will try to present something different now, but my sense of it was that the ANC wasn't around. I suppose that's where Rick fits in; in a milieu in which there was no serious underground organisation. The university is a relatively safe place to teach politics. Radical ideas in a university setting have an incredible effect in a situation without an organisation.

We had to find our own role

Dan O'Meara

The kinds of people who ended up being influenced by Rick arrived at university at just the moment when there was no left-wing influence at all; no organised and no structured left-wing influence. Which meant that – by default – we were all swallowed up by the liberal establishment and we became, for a while, hugely concerned not to be described as 'communist' or to go beyond the bounds of the law. Our principal organisation was Nusas. Then, two things happened to change our position.

The first thing that came along was 1968, as a general cultural and political phenomenon. It had a huge impact on English-speaking campuses because it allowed us to defy parental authority and the state. It was a moment when we were suddenly given permission from elsewhere to question everything. We were influenced by what happened in Paris, Berlin, London, the Black Panthers, the demonstrations against the Vietnam War, it was everywhere around us. It enabled us to think that we were not totally isolated. The huge problem for whites on the left after the banning of the ANC and the Communist Party was that there was no home.

The second, and by far the most important, was the Black Consciousness Movement. It was a defining moment in South African history, and, for whites who ended up on the left, it essentially forced us, very starkly, to look at the limits of how far we were prepared to go.

It helped that Biko was enormously charismatic. It must be remembered that most white leftists had never met a black person on terms of equality, so dealing with Biko on those terms was really mind-shattering. Biko just refused absolutely any kind of 'you are better or more powerful because you're white' attitude; he forced people to meet him on grounds of absolute equality. In my case, I worked briefly with Biko in a Nusas conference for a week. I was 19 years old, and I've never in my life met anybody as impressive as that. I would say he's probably the most influential person I've ever met. In a week, he totally changed my world-view, and he shook me out of my comfortable little liberal existence.

But on the organisational level, the schism was

enormous. When Saso left Nusas, the old liberal moderate reformists were pissed off and they felt betrayed because they felt they'd done so much to defend black students in Nusas. The radical minority said, 'Yeah, they're absolutely right, but that puts us in a huge dilemma, because we support them but they don't need our support, so what the hell are we gonna do?'

After Saso broke away from Nusas, the white radicals decided to resign from Nusas for about a year and a half. We couldn't resign from it because you were a member by default, but we were no longer involved in it. So we were looking for a role, and along comes Rick. Rick's timing was crucial, because he started to influence Nusas at exactly the moment that we were ready to make a big shift. Had he come before, I don't think he would have had nearly the same impact.

We weren't running away from Black Consciousness; we couldn't have. It was very clear to everybody that I ever worked with that Black Consciousness was hugely important and progressive. But the point is that we couldn't run *towards* Black Consciousness. Biko and his compatriots had not an ounce of racism in them, but they just were not interested in working with whites. 'It doesn't bring us anything. You guys can't do anything for us. We've got to liberate ourselves. Change your own damn community, we're going to change ours.' That was the message.

A CONSTANT FINGER IN THE EYE

Rick Turner was committed to making his life choices consistent with his political philosophies. As a white person striving towards a non-racial society in apartheid South Africa, it was difficult to avoid moral compromise. The whole society was geared towards providing white people with material comfort and social privilege, at the expense of the majority. Every day would present dozens of small moments when this intense disparity would present itself – subtly to most, and starkly to those, like Turner, who were attentive to it.

To the extent that it was possible, Turner went out of his way to eat in restaurants that allowed a mixed-race clientèle, watch movies in theatres that didn't insist on segregated seating, and swim at the beach reserved for Indian South Africans. Furthermore, going against the deeply ingrained logic of his society, he refused absolutely to hire a (black) domestic servant. On a deeper level, Rick Turner worked hard to let go of the negative attitudes and behaviours that were often associated with white liberals. 'Rick didn't have all the trappings and arrogance of the white left. That also attracted him to a lot of the black activists. They had a great deal of respect for Rick. And so Biko and others didn't see him as a white person or treat him as a white person. His ideas and his approach were so different from the normal condescending attitudes of whites that we came across; and that makes a huge difference.'[18]

GEHEIM/SECRET

From 21–22.5.1971 he is present at the monthly, multiracial 'Workshop' at the Phoenix Estate in Durban of which he is the organiser. Here it is made public that he married an Indian woman, Fozia Fischer, in accordance with Muslim faith.

The most fundamental choice Turner made to break away from the stifling confines of racism was his second marriage, to Foszia Fisher. As Fisher was racially classified as 'coloured', the marriage broke a number of apartheid laws: the prohibition against inter-racial sex, marriage and cohabitation. As the law so severely forbade their relationship, Turner converted to Islam in order to marry Foszia according to Muslim rites. Tony Morphet explains the significance of the marriage in this way:

Unsympathetic critics saw the marriage as a provocative political act challenging the state but this was certainly not the case ... If he was to be liberal first and white second, then no compromise with irrational constraints, whether customary or legal, was possible at this point. The marriage was a great triumph for both people, yielding to them a personal growth and an emotional richness as well as serving to unify private experiences and public life. The marriage aptly symbolizes the barriers which Turner was prepared to break through in his quest for a life which unified consciousness, values and actions.[19]

Rick's relationship with Foszia represented a powerful bond that sustained them both through the many challenges of his last years. The two connected to each other immediately and deeply, and their lives became interwoven at all levels. They shared an interest in the study of philosophy, in particular Sartre's notions about the capacity of human beings to choose the circumstances of their own lives. During their seven years together, Rick and Foszia shared a home in Durban and a number of intellectual and political projects.

Although they were never explicitly punished for their violation of apartheid laws on racial mixing, many – both friends and critics – felt that the relationship contributed to the state's determination to get rid of Turner as a visible and outspoken opponent of racialism. After he was banned by the state, the burden of living in the most circumscribed way fell on both Rick and Foszia together, affecting the most intimate aspects of their lives, for a full five years. Through it all, the couple remained dedicated to the legitimacy of their love and committed to sustaining a hopeful vision for a society rooted in the celebration of human freedom.

GEHEIM/SECRET

On 6.5.1970 Turner addressed non-white students at the Alan Taylor Residence, Durban. The subject of discussion was 'Black Power' Movements in America. He presented the history of the Negroes in America, when they were oppressed and their struggle to attain freedom. He praised the role of Dr Martin Luther King.

Things that really spark a relationship
Foszia Fisher

My first encounter with Rick was at the medical school where he came to give a talk on Black Power. After he finished somebody got up and said, 'Well you are a white person, how can you know? How dare you come here and tell us about black folks?' And he said, 'Well, I would be happy to sit down and listen ... I have done some reading, but if somebody has got more information, hey, go ahead.'

He pretty much got my attention immediately, with what he was saying and how he was saying it. When the lecture was over, he came over and we talked for a while. When I had to go back home, Rick asked, 'Do you have a lift?' So we went back together. Rick was sitting in front and I was at the back. We talked. Rick discovered that I was studying Sartre, was passionate about Sartre. And then he said he was talking in a fortnight, and would I come? I said, 'Ja, sure.'

At the end of that second lecture, Mamphela Ramphele had decided she would throw a party and so we stayed for it. Rick and I got talking, we got to know each other and that's what started it. That's what drew us together, talking about the meaning of freedom, about reason, what it means to make choices – the kind of things that really spark a relationship.

At that point I didn't even know if Rick was married; it came out later. He thought I knew, and then we talked about it. He said that he had married Barbara for the wrong reasons and they were pretty

much going their own ways after '69. And at that point
I was committed to someone else, who was living in
Cape Town. I said I didn't believe in divorce, I thought
that if you have made a commitment you have to stick
with it. He replied that even though there had been
problems, he hoped that Barbara would come back and
live with him, because they had two kids. But in the
meantime, Rick got involved in lots of things and we
did things together.

When Rick came to Durban he didn't have a place
to stay. First, he stayed with some friends. Then, some
students had a house near the university, a condemned
house, but it did have electricity and water. Rick
moved in there for a couple of months. It was amazing,
I remember spending time there talking, planning
workshops, and having seminars. I was busy with my
studies and Rick was teaching. I would meet him at the
university; his colleagues would look at him and at me
with questions in their eyes, but not asking out loud.
We talked about the risks we were taking; we could get
arrested, things could happen, but we figured we could
deal with it.

When Rick bought the house in Bellair, Barbara
came down to look at it, but she soon decided that she
didn't want to move there. Then, at some point (she was
in a relationship with somebody else) she decided to stay
in Cape Town and in November 1970 she asked Rick for
a divorce. Soon after that, Rick said to me, 'Will you
marry me?' I answered, 'Yes, but how is it going to be
possible? And no, because I'm in love with somebody
else.' So I left Durban to marry this other person, but
soon after I got there I realised that I had changed, that
my relationship with this other man was no longer
possible. Also, Rick came down to Cape Town and he
said, 'I can't trust you to make the decision you need to
make without me being here.' So Rick made it difficult

and easy at the same time.

So what happens? Rick and I live together? How could that be possible? We thought we could make it work by not hiding it, and also not drawing attention to it, but just being together. So, coming back to Durban, we moved into the house on Dalton Avenue together.

One day he said to me, 'We have to make peace with your parents, because it's important.' He had come to my parents' house before, but they had no idea initially that we were in a relationship. So, after we moved in together, we went to my parents' house and we told them what we were doing. They went absolutely crazy. My father first refused and said to Rick, 'You know this is dangerous.' Rick said, 'I'm aware that it would be much harder for your daughter than me, because I'm white and I wouldn't be treated as badly as her. But it's something that we've talked about.' I think my father relaxed then, though my mother continued to refuse. Eventually they gave in.

We came back to Durban in January 1971. One day in May, we arrived home and found Fatima and Ismail Meer in our driveway. They said, 'Oh, you are getting married this afternoon! We've got the Imam waiting at our house, so get changed and come.' You see, we had wanted to get married, but nobody would marry us, none of the churches would do it, because of the law. But since Muslim marriages were not state marriages, the Imam was willing to help us. So we went to the Meers' house, with one other person, who was our witness.

The first part of the ceremony involved Rick's conversion to Islam, because we couldn't get married otherwise. Islam was important to my family and it was also expedient for the marriage, but Rick was genuine in his conversion, because he was genuinely curious about everything. He studied the Quran and Malcolm X's ideas. Was he Muslim? It depends how you define it.

Anyway, after that was done we got married. And then we had tea. I had a white sari on and Rick had a suit on.

We were due at a Nusas conference in Pietermaritzburg that night, so we went from the wedding straight there. It was obvious something had happened; within two minutes we were telling our friends. So that was our wedding day.

It was good how it happened. We figured it was stupid not to marry, because we wanted to make our commitment clear and open. We wanted to assert that it wasn't just about sex, some cliché like 'black is better' or that kind of stuff. What tended to happen, previously, was that people who had mixed-race relationships kept them hidden, and that made them almost sordid. But we felt strongly that just because what we were doing was illegal, it didn't make it sordid.

I would meet him at the university, and we'd have lunch together in the staff dining room. The white liberal university went into a tail-spin. Being well-mannered most of them, they would greet us and say hello, but they wouldn't talk to us.

Strangely, one group of friends that really struggled with my relationship with Rick were my friends in the Black Consciousness Movement. I had been close to a number of members of Saso through my university years, and involved in it to some extent, but after being with Rick I was less inclined to go. I would have been put into a position of having to defend Rick's whiteness. I believe that the individual is not the issue, it's the structure. I just thought it would be a waste of everybody's time for me to have to constantly argue that point.

The most fearless person

Dan O'Meara

Rick was the most fearless person that I've ever met. He'd invited my wife and me to dinner at his place. You know, he was living openly in a mixed marriage, and illegally. I said to him, 'Rick, why do you do this? I mean, Foszia is lovely and I can understand why you're in love with her, but you know you're going to get smashed, you know you're giving a finger to the government and they're not going to leave you alone. Why aren't you more circumspect?' And he said – and I will retain this till the day I die – 'Look, Dan, if you live in a fascist country like we do, you have two options: you can be cowed and you can internalise the rules of fascism and live by them, so you become a fascist to some extent, or you can choose to be free. I've chosen to be free and I accept the consequences.'

FIVE

An Un-training

'*There is no body of key facts that have to be learned in some special order. What has to be learned is a particular way of thinking, the ability to analyse, to think critically, and to think creatively. And if there were a body of key facts, children would not learn them in school.*'[1]

– RICK TURNER

HIS BASIC STYLE

RICK TURNER WAS A TEACHER; this was his profession and his passion. Nonetheless, he had an extremely unconventional attitude about schooling and about the role of teachers. At a fundamental level he was sceptical about the basic structure and values that govern the majority of schools, from kindergarten through to university. He understood that most of them are designed to sculpt people, to train them so that they passively accept the larger social system, no matter how unjust it might be.

In contrast, Turner saw his role as a teacher as fundamentally about un-training, of opening people up, giving them the room needed to re-evaluate their value systems and the kind of society they would like to be part of. His approach in the classroom was based on discussion; on raising questions, rather than providing answers. Duncan Greaves has described Turner's teaching style as 'emancipatory', because it placed students in control of their own learning process; 'the teacher is present as a facilitator rather than an instructor.'[2] Indeed, a longing for freedom permeated all Turner's efforts as an educator.

Turner's position in the politics department of the University of Natal allowed him to thrive as a teacher. Michael Nupen, the head of the department, was a dynamic individual and colourful character. A diligent and well-read philosopher, with strong Marxist sympathies, he respected Turner's work and gave him room to express his political views openly in class. While Nupen was by no means an activist, he didn't in any way attempt to hamper Turner's radical critique of apartheid society. In fact, the two grew to be close not only as colleagues, but as friends. Many of the students who were influenced by Turner also admired Nupen.

Still, the two could not have been more divergent in their approach to education. Nupen was deeply rooted in the patriarchal tradition of education. His lectures were precise, theatrical, grandiose. His presence in the classroom was imposing and forceful. Turner, on the other hand, was deeply critical of lecturing, and rarely did so. As he once explained:

The lecture system discourages thought in the following ways:

a. it makes the class passive consumers of information and inhibits questioning.

b. linked with the exam system it tends to encourage fact learning, rather than the acquisition of exploratory techniques.

c. it distances staff from students in a way which exaggerates the authority of staff and minimizes the potential of the students. This works in a vicious circle; passive students don't encourage or challenge staff to teach well, and vice versa.[3]

Rick Turner was an influential teacher precisely because he refused to conform to the standard role and practice of teaching.

His basic style
Tony Morphet

I suppose what was absolutely unique about Rick was that he didn't appear or you never thought that he was driving a particular argument. What he was very,

very good at is what was later called deconstruction. He would invite you into a dialogue by making some proposition, and you would then answer and he would deconstruct your position. Rick opened people up, so they experienced the exchanges as exceptionally enlivening. They took themselves really into completely new places. That was his basic style.

That's what Rick did, I think, in class as well. Michael Nupen was the exact opposite. Michael Nupen was like a cannon shot – *Bang! Bang!* – huge concepts launched at the students. Nupen was very, very powerful in constructing a group; a group with a common vocabulary, a common set of gestures, a common framework, which he dominated. Nupen was a huge guy, with an enormous head. And he would walk in with a Hegel book, in German. He'd crack the book open and begin reading in German and all the students would mutter, 'God! Look at this ...' Then he'd get out a translation and he would say, 'This is what it says; but you must hear it in German to really get it.' They admired him enormously.

With Rick it was rather different. Rick would sort of unfold, unfold, unfold and then produce a very simple, very clear description of a difficult concept. In addition, for Rick the classroom was not a strict boundary; there wasn't so much strict class identity. Some of his students would visit at Dalton Avenue independently. The students in the class would be pursuing rather different reading patterns and there seemed to be no common text. He would put out some propositions and get in this dialogic process and then say, 'Well, this book might interest you', 'You might be interested in this', and 'There is this guy and that guy'. So that the reading patterns of the class would be hard to follow from the outside.

Whereas with Nupen you had to do your Hegel,

and then you had to do Marx, and you had to study Stalin. Nupen was a great defender of Stalin, which was an unusual position to take up. And there were pretty strict reading requirements from Nupen – lots of it. So, Rick was very different from Nupen, but they got on extremely well, and a group of students coalesced around them both.

All of Rick's students were smart, and they still are, but they were changed forever by him. Some people were more intense than others with him. But I have never encountered anyone who was resistant to or rejected what Rick was trying to do.

The only people who rejected him were departmental colleagues, in a classic university way. Here was this guy who was obviously doing extraordinary things with students and having a very important influence, and other professors were losing influence. They were traditional historians and traditional political scientists, and they got very, very bitter. You know, something like 'He's not scholarly like us'. So there were some very intense moments in that department.

Never going through the syllabus
Foszia Fisher

Rick would start his class, and he would say, 'There are two things …' But it would never be two things, it would always be so much more. Rick very much used a Socratic method, asking the students lots of questions. I remember one of his students in his political science class saying, 'Dr Turner, I really resent the fact that you allow the class to be sidetracked. We are never going to go through the syllabus.' Rick replied, 'We're not being sidetracked. This is the syllabus.' But the student wanted notes, you know; he was ready to take notes, but he wasn't being given that, he was given discussion. Rick's style wasn't about giving notes for talking around a subject, or saying to people, 'Here is a bibliography – go read.' He didn't do that. Most of the class was discussion. So even in Politics I, Rick would lecture and there would be less debate, but it would be in a very conversational style and he would ask questions and develop it through the questions.

Rick disappointed those who wanted that model and excited those who hadn't realised there was a different way of doing it. With Rick, you were always on the same plane. And the whole meaning of 'educate' – to bring out from what's already there – Rick did that. Rick's teaching was a process of *un*-training the students, removing the restrictions that had been put on them during their upbringing, so that they could go and explore. He asked students to explain how they saw things, rather than feeding them words to swallow that don't actually interact with their system of meaning. What does it mean when you say, 'I believe in a democratic society?' What's a democratic society? What is nationalism? What's the sense of being a citizen? What does it all mean? For Rick, it wasn't important to simply prove that you had done the reading. When you're being asked what you actually believe, you can't just reply, 'Sorry, let me read this book and find out.' Regardless of whatever is in a book, what do *you* think?

SYMPATHETIC STUDENTS

A number of students took Turner's courses seriously and developed a relationship that went well beyond the traditional one of teacher and student. Turner had a 'special personal gift of entering the world of discourse of his students'.[4] Rather than insisting on maintaining a polite and formal distance, Turner allowed his students to be real about their thoughts and about their life choices. Likewise, Turner was open about his own life, and even hosted his honours seminars at his house. He often made himself available for conversations outside class and frequently participated in student activities and protests. Much more so than other university lecturers, Turner was a public presence on campus and attempted to engage quite directly with students and the issues they faced. Tony Morphet explains: 'Turner's age and his openly experimental lifestyle placed him at a level very similar to that of his students and his interactions with them were always conducted through their frames of reference. The complex new conceptual structure and techniques of thought he was introducing were handled with an utmost simplicity and clarity.'[5]

Turner's demeanour was highly unusual, compared with that of other lecturers. In the conservative and provincial climate of the time, his relaxed and conversational approach was, for a handful of students at least, a breath of fresh air. For them, Turner provided not only a dynamic new curriculum, but also a window into an entirely different way of life. According to Fatima Meer, 'Rick was an unusually popular lecturer, and would frequently have extra students sitting in on his classes. He exposed white students at the University of Natal Durban to the realities of apartheid and particularly encouraged them to begin to understand black resistance to the system. At that time, the university was very isolated from this information.'[6]

Working alongside Michael Nupen in the politics department, he helped to nurture a small group of students who were rigorous in their studies and thinking and also had a strong social consciousness. In Tony Morphet's words, Turner and Nupen 'drew to them, in the lecture halls, in the informal discussion sessions and outside in the variety of alternative learning situations, a group who were ready to issue challenges to the prevailing interpretations of South African reality'.[7]

Many of the young people who admired Turner were looking for ways to confront the injustices in their society. Turner helped to direct this longing for a better society towards a deeper critical analysis, as well as towards concrete action. Over time, activist-minded students came to rely on Rick Turner for advice and a number of them went on to have active and prominent careers in the struggle against apartheid.

They were just incredibly good

Dan O'Meara

Michael Nupen decided he didn't want to teach anymore. He had the financial wherewithal and he wanted to do his own things. So, I was hired to replace Michael briefly, in 1972. Rick was the person that I reported to. I was in awe of him, terrified of him, and I didn't understand what the hell was going on with him.

I came from a Johannesburg background, where I was on the so-called radical left. But going to teach at Natal was like going to a different country. I mean, Rick was doing things we hadn't even thought of. First of all, Rick was trained differently. He hadn't come to teaching social science through the anglophone world. No other anglophone intellectual in South Africa had been exposed to the ideas that Rick studied in France, and he had mastered the material. For example, the first class I had to teach was an honours political science, which included Halton Cheadle and others taught by Turner. They'd all had two or three years with Rick and they were just incredibly good. In each of Rick's classes, he would pick a few of the students that he found to be exceptional, and he would give them special attention: inviting them to his home, to seminars outside class, and so on. The students trained by Rick, the really good ones – these people knew how to think, they knew how to pontificate and they knew how to ask the right kinds of questions. His influence was extraordinary as a teacher.

People are embarrassed to say this now, but the English universities, and particularly a place like the University of Natal, were fifth-rate. The idea in a South African university at the time was still very patriarchal.

The professor would arrive, give a lecture, this would be the absolute truth, the students would take notes and go and learn those notes and reproduce them in an exam, and that was knowledge.

Rick broke with that absolutely. He was absolutely ruthless in terms of not allowing people to just sit embarrassed in the corner. Everybody had to speak. And this was very unsettling for a first-year student, but they loved him. Because he did it in a way which didn't make you feel stupid, which empowered them.

Rick had a certain kind of charisma. It was different from Biko's. With Rick you knew right away that this was a guy that was going to challenge you intellectually, and so you wanted to rise to the occasion. His emphasis was on involving people in the kinds of activities that would oblige them not to just ask questions, but ask questions about themselves and their own role. He had the ability and character to bring the best out of students.

The first thing is of course that he is a lecturer

Halton Cheadle

In my third year as Rick's student, I was in the honours course, and we would meet at his house. God, I mean it was absolutely amazing. He lived in a sort of run-down house, with unmade beds and what have you. I come from a background where I had to make my own bed and clean everything, wash dishes after supper and so on. I could never live like that. I remember Rick sitting in bed with crossed legs, with Foszia under the sheets. Rick and Foszia were wonderful, they were absolutely extraordinary. Anyway, I was listening recently to a recording of one of those honours seminars. The talk is on Sartre's *Being and Nothingness.* It's quite impressive how Rick expounded on the text, taking us through this unspeakably obscure book. My God!

Rick taught alongside another intriguing teacher, named Michael Nupen. Nupen would call himself an egalitarian; but he was an iconoclast. He just creatively destroyed all of the kind of undigested pieces of stuff that you accumulate at school and from your father. It was a brutal process. But he was brilliant. And we were very much ready for Rick, after studying with Nupen. Systematically, Rick would come in and lay the basis of how one ought to look at the world. That is to say, Nupen broke things down and Rick built them up. I've always thought the two of them together were absolutely magnificent.

Both of them were very critical of Stalinism and the Soviet Union. So all of us who studied closely under Turner and Nupen were quite influenced by their attitudes towards socialism. They helped us to make an important shift, away from just a generalised opposition to apartheid and increasingly towards a class-based way of seeing the world. But throughout our lives, we remained very wary of the South African Communist Party.

On the other hand, I would say that Rick was a Marxist. If you look at *The Eye of the Needle,* you'll see that it's an attempt to situate a Marxist vision within a Christian context. Rick's particular style of subversion is so subtle; he plays on a series of values that of course everyone shares but that they never work through. That's how Rick was. He would always take the principle of value and then drive it to conclusions that most people wouldn't have wanted to end up at.

As a teacher, Rick was quite rigorous, in the sense that he stated his ideas plainly and clearly, and yet always was ready to expound on them in depth. He expected his students to do the same. You didn't have to agree with Rick, but the one thing that happened after any kind of engagement with him – if you held your views during the conversation – is that you would have a much better basis for holding your views. In other words, he really did force you to articulate your position, to think it through thoroughly.

TEACHING TOWARDS FREEDOM

In a capitalist society, where social relationships are unequal, schooling teaches people passivity, acceptance of hierarchies, the toleration and defence of a society that does not meet basic human needs. This is a general phenomenon and, of course, begins at a very young age. Turner argued that, more so than the curriculum, the structure of schooling, 'the style of education and, in particular, the form of discipline get me used to certain types of relationships with other people, for example, deference to authority figures, bureaucratic order as a mode of life, etc.'[8] In other words, the most essential lessons about the world are conveyed to children subtly and persistently for over a dozen years even before university. According to Turner:

> Schooling prepares individuals not just for social living, but also for living out specific roles in a specific social structure. The social structure may be one of gross inequality, but if the socializing mechanisms are working effectively, independent, kicking children can be turned into passive, accepting adults at the bottom of the pile, who accept their role because they have been deprived of the capacity to conceive of any other way of existing. The effect of the process of socialization is to make a particular social structure and a particular human model seem to be natural, and to hide the fact that it is not natural and could be changed.[9]

The apartheid government understood very well the function of schooling as a method of creating and dominating a compliant population. In the 1960s and 1970s education in South Africa was incredibly conservative, and heavily imbued with the racist logic of apartheid, which intentionally built a schooling system that made blacks feel inferior and whites superior. It is hard to imagine an education more explicitly and intentionally cruel in its design. As Dr Verwoerd had explained when introducing the Bantu Education system, its goal in educating black South Africans was to prepare them deliberately for a subservient status within the white economy.

Although white liberals decried Bantu Education, Turner was critical of the standard liberal critiques, which 'fail to analyse and challenge any values implicit in our educational system, with the exception of racism ... we never question or even notice the framework itself ... And so we do not ask the two vital questions: What role does this structure itself play in the education process, and could there be some other kind of education process?'[10] Turner insisted that the damaging effects of the existing school system 'cannot be remedied by spending more money on education or by changing the syllabus. It is a result not of the content of the education system but of its structure.'[11]

For Turner, the university was merely another step in this long process of socialisation; it was not an inherently liberatory institution. The function of the university, as it then existed, was to corral and confine thinking, not set it loose. As the French student protesters had made it clear in 1968, 'The student is [playing] a provisional role, a rehearsal for his ultimate role as a conservative element in the functioning of the commodity system. Being a student is a form of initiation.'[12] It is particularly at the university level that students learn the kinds of subtle rationalisations necessary to survive and 'make a living' within an unjust system. They might be taught a degree of critical thinking, but this took place within strict boundaries, and certainly the university as a whole frowns heavily on the elicitation of transcendental moral questions.

For Turner, being a teacher was not only about trying to create interesting courses. Rather, he saw education as central to both imagining and creating a liberated society. He realised that in order to live as full participants in a society that allows for maximum freedom, people must first undo their earlier negative socialisation and simultaneously must practise being free. Turner explicitly linked the struggle for a radically democratic society – democratic in the sense of people participating directly in the decisions that affect their lives – to a shift in the ideology and structure behind schooling. He tried to envision how education could be restructured in order to serve the needs of a participatory democratic society:

> How, then, can we design an educational system ... that will rely largely on the child's curiosity and desire to learn, and that will encourage in the child that kind of thinking which makes continuous self-education possible? There are at least two educational prerequisites: The child must go to 'school' voluntarily, and the 'teacher' must no longer be seen as 'the one who knows', but rather as a helpful companion in a common search for truth. The school must be seen as a place which has resources that can be used when needed.[13]

Rick Turner was immensely curious about alternative ways of thinking about and structuring education. He was an avid reader of radical educational theory, and in his writing on education and in his pedagogy one can see a wide range of influences. In particular, his thinking drew heavily on the work of Ivan Illich and Paolo Freire.[14] Freire, a radical theorist from Brazil who is most famous for his methodologies for teaching poor and illiterate people, saw the essential role of the educator as one of uplifting oppressed people, rather than condescending towards them or 'fixing' their ignorance. Ivan Illich, an heretical Catholic who was raised in Vienna but who spent the bulk of his life in Latin America, was deeply critical of institutional approaches to solving social problems, and in particular saw the school system as deeply counterproductive. Illich stressed that compulsory public education produces a society that is obsessed with certifications and status, and yet is unable to think critically.

Turner also took a deep interest in Summerhill school in England, founded by A.S. Neill, the first and most well-known of the schools in the 'democratic' school movement. Democratic schools place all decision-making about the structure and curriculum in the hands of the students. Either through consensus or some form of parliamentary government, the children and adults together – and as equals – discuss the class schedule, agree to basic rules, as well as resolve any conflicts that might arise among the student body. Aside from these agreements, there are no compulsory features of the schooling. Classes are voluntary, and no grades are given.

Turner's engagement with radical ideas about education is remarkable, given the conservative and repressive climate in which he worked. Perhaps even more remarkably, he set in motion a number of initiatives to try to bring these radical ideas to life in South Africa.

PRACTICAL EXPERIMENTS

Turner involved himself in a number of educational projects outside his formal work as a lecturer. It is clear from his choices that he refused to make any firm separation between his formal occupation and any learning opportunities that might arise outside the classroom. Turner was perpetually in search of liberated spaces for learning, and threw himself repeatedly into the work of creating these spaces.

One of these was the Platform, a series of lectures and discussions held every few weeks off campus and close to a transport hub, so that people of all races could get there easily. Turner lectured at Platform on a number of occasions and helped steer the discussions towards imagining innovative alternatives to the existing system.

The Special Branch saw fit to infiltrate the meetings and report on what was being discussed. While it is clear that they were disturbed and felt threatened by the conversations at Platform, and particularly by Turner's contribution to them, it just so happens that their informant had, of necessity, to learn a good deal about radical pedagogy.

GEHEIM/SECRET

On 7.9.1971 in the evening he and Omar Badsha were responsible for the showing of the film 'Summerhill' that was shown at the University, Durban. The film concerned the progressive school by name, Summerhill, that exists in England. No conventional teaching methods are applied here. No discipline and authority exists and the children are free to do whatever they want. After the showing a meeting was held with subject as chair and the film was discussed and everybody agreed that such schools should be started in the RSA. The showing of the film coincided with a lecture of 'Rethinking Education' by Ivan Illich, who is a dedicated fighter for change of the political, economic and educational systems for the world. Illich is active in Latin America and has made good progress in Mexico. Illich claims that the rich are becoming richer and the poor ever poorer, the gap between the two must be made smaller. The child must receive more practical education outside the school and must receive education only in the direction in which he is interested and time must not be wasted on subjects in which he has no interest. This system closely approximates the learning approach of the Summerhill syllabus.

GEHEIM/SECRET

On 15.9.1971 he attends a platform meeting that was held at the University of Durban. The lecture of Ivan Illich was then discussed further. The speakers spoke in favour of the lecture. Rick Turner then proposed that an attempt must be made by all teachers in a cunning manner to propagate the idea at schools and to report on progress. Furthermore he said they must attempt to

convince also a head of a school to attend
the meeting and thereby gain his perspective
on the formation of the Summerhill school
in the RSA. Here he shows clearly that he
argues for a social system that clashes with
the old tested methods.

Growing out of the discussions at Platform, Turner and a small group of friends set up the Education Reform Association (ERA). The idea behind ERA was to create a space for students, teachers and parents to engage with one another and think through new ideas about schooling in South Africa. The hope was that ERA might trigger profound practical changes in the local system. For this reason, ERA was particularly interested in influencing the thinking of black teachers, who were expected under Bantu Education to teach a curriculum of subservience to the apartheid state. However, it was difficult to reach these teachers, and the project never really took off as an initiative.

ERA did succeed in publishing a number of issues of a journal of educational ideas and held a monthly forum for discussion for roughly a year.15 Both the workshop topics and the journal articles focused on the reconceptualisation of teaching techniques, attitudes towards student discipline and authority, and the overall goals of education. The project was conceptually quite ambitious and struggled to find a clear path. In the end it was shut down as a result of Turner's banning order in 1973.

During this same period, Turner also helped to set up a number of summer and winter school sessions at Phoenix, outside Durban. The Phoenix settlement had been founded by M.K. Gandhi in 1904, with the intention of providing a space for communal living and support for campaigns against social injustice. The hundred acres of land were divided into small plots, and a number of cooperative enterprises were established, including a printing press, a crèche, a dairy and market gardens. The community surrounding the settlement comprised impoverished Indians and Africans and Phoenix farm was intended to be of service to them. The settlement was firmly rooted in the principles of non-racialism and non-violence and supported many different opponents of apartheid, including the Natal Indian Congress.

After the Mahatma's departure, the project was taken over by other family members, most prominently Gandhi's son Manilal, who spent his life struggling for social justice in the Durban area. At the time that Turner was involved, the project was managed by Sushila Gandhi, Manilal's widow, and Mewa and Ela Ramgobin. Turner developed a close relationship with the Ramgobins and served as a member of the Phoenix settlement board.

While he was teaching at the university, Turner brought groups of young people of different backgrounds and races to Phoenix, both to attend political education courses, and to engage in the hands-on work of community building. His involvement with the Phoenix settlement was a natural extension of his overall desire to fuse together theoretical discussion with practical experiments in living differently.

GEHEIM/SECRET

Turner and Lawrence Schlemmer, lecturer at the University of Natal, Durban, were the main organisers of a 'Summer School' at Phoenix Settlement, north coast, Natal, from 9–16.1.71. It is a multiracial meeting where no colour divide was applied. His activities during the 'workshop' were described as follows: 'Without doubt his sole aim at the camp was to cause confusion in the minds of people present. He quoted from many communist leaders and philosophers. He stressed that society must be broken down, especially the middle class. I gained the impression that the Bantu were used so he could promote his communist ideals. He preached communism throughout the course and in fact tried to put it into physical effect by making us work in communal groups and by calling us the masses.' ...

GEHEIM/SECRET

On 15.1.1971 he gives a lecture on 'Education and Development' during the 'Summer School' to which is referred in the preceding paragraph. He says, amongst other things: 'People should not only work for themselves, but for the whole community and all share the profits from their combined labour. The only essential being that they must trust one another.'

SIX

A Very Busy Time

'Let us, for once, stop asking what the whites can be persuaded to do, what concessions, other things being equal, they may make, and instead explore the absolute limits of possibility by sketching an ideally just society.'[1]

– RICK TURNER

'WHERE EVERYBODY SHARES WITH EVERYBODY'

RICK TURNER'S MOVE TO DURBAN was his first significant attempt to establish a permanent home for himself after leaving the farm at Stellenbosch. He arrived alone, without his wife and children, but with a tenured position at the University of Natal and a determination to start a new life.

On his arrival, he first shared a house with a number of students but this arrangement didn't last long. Turner soon bought his own house, in the Durban suburb of Bellair, a short distance from the University of Natal and on the border of the large Indian suburb of Chatsworth. The house, at 32 Dalton Avenue, would be Turner's home until his death. The property is set at the very end of an oddly configured, meandering street. Dalton Avenue curves along the hilly landscape, then splits in two just before no. 32, which means that half a dozen or so houses are nestled atop the hill overlooking Turner's home. Turner's property was narrow, with a long, tree-lined driveway leading up to an old colonial-style white house with a wide columned porch and bay windows on both sides of the front door. The backyard stretched for a good way behind the house, with ample room for trees and a garden. In addition, behind the main house was a one-bedroom outbuilding and an outdoor shower.

Turner originally hoped that Barbara, Jann and Kim would move up to Durban and rejoin him, but his separation became permanent and the family remained in Cape Town. Soon after he bought the Dalton Avenue property, Foszia Fisher moved in with him. The house quickly became a very social environment, with several house-mates living with Rick and Foszia at any one time. They included student activists, liberal university lecturers, journalists and guests from overseas. The house was well suited as a communal space, as there was ample room for people to enjoy their privacy, but at the same time there were also multiple spaces available for gathering together.

While the Special Branch used Turner's living arrangements as evidence in their case against him, and characterised them as a 'hippy commune' of dangerous revolutionaries, Turner's house-mates remember their time at Dalton Avenue fondly, and speak well of the easy atmosphere of sharing within the household.

It became hippie

Gerry Maré

In 1970, I was renting a house with a friend. The house later became a hippie commune, notorious in Durban. But the house that we were in only had Peter Larlham and myself. Rick asked if he could come and live with us. One day (he hadn't been there for very long) there was a drug raid on the house next door. Rick heard the commotion because his room was in the front, and he came through to Peter and myself and he told us the police were next door. In the next moment there was a knock at the door, and somebody came in and saw that this house was different in some ways from what was happening next door. Rick introduced himself as a lecturer and so there was no use talking to us students. So the police left, they didn't search the place. I felt awkward at that moment, as Rick had been very unsettled by the whole thing; he knew that this was very bad for his future. He was strict on that; there were never any drugs in the house. Because, he said, 'I don't want to get busted for something like that; there is political stuff going on.' After that incident, Rick moved out of our house.

At Dalton Avenue, we shared a hell of a lot. I mean, each one of us had their own particular area, but there was a lot of sharing. We all wanted a degree of autonomy as whatever unit, as a single person or as a couple, but at the same time we wanted to interact quite freely. Mostly we interacted in the kitchen, which was right in the back, so it was well located for the people in the house to mix with those living out back. We'd cook together in the evenings, and we'd also just sit around drinking wine while we talked. Then, also, people would come by deliberately for seminars or the postgraduate politics course.

GEHEIM/SECRET

He also has a lively interest in the hippy culture of which the followers, the long haired [refugees] live in so-called colonies or 'communes'. In Durban he lived for several months in such a 'commune' and visited and addressed existing 'communes' in Johannesburg. It is exactly on this area where no authority is accepted and recognised, where no God, church or commandment is believed in, where so-called free love is believed in, where everybody shares with everybody (a familiar communist principle), that Richard Turner as self-proclaimed Marxist has effective influence without hindrance and without appearing in the foreground. Let us keep in mind the content of the document 'Rules of Revolution' that was drafted in 1919 by a small group of revolutionaries in Russia and from which a few 'golden rules' are quoted below, then Richard Turner's contribution in this 'commune' creates deep concern:

1. firstly, corrupt the youth
2. wean them away from religion
3. interest them in sex
4. destroy their moral character
5. preach democracy everywhere, but seize power ruthlessly, and as fast as possible
6. destroy faith in leaders of people, by holding them up to ridicule and disgrace

GEHEIM/SECRET

On 16.11.1970 a mixed social gathering was held at his house at 32 Dalton Avenue, Durban. There were 45 guests, of whom 19 were Bantus and Indians.

A busy time, very busy
Foszia Fisher

Being with Rick was quite easy, it was really having a partnership. Between us there is this seven-year difference but it never felt huge.

For example, I can only remember one real

argument that we had in the seven years. We were both intractable. It was about the meaning of the Holocaust. Rick's position was that it was the worst thing human beings could have done to each other, this systematic elimination of people. I said, 'We see the Holocaust as something that we must not repeat, but then we forget, we don't look at what happens on a daily basis, where there isn't overt annihilation.' I said that I thought the consequence of colonisation, with every generation being brought into a place of systematic denial, and having to fight for who they are, is worse. Really, we weren't very far from agreeing.

Fundamentally, we were in agreement about all of the important things. We agreed not to hire servants, I was very clear about that. I believed that you should learn to clean after yourself; take responsibility for the organisation of your space. So we cooked, we cleaned. We lived simply. We didn't spend money on buying artwork or anything. But we didn't have much money, because Rick was paying maintenance to Barbara for the kids, and I wasn't earning any money. But we managed.

The house on Dalton Avenue soon became quite full. First, Lawrie Schlemmer moved in, because he said he would share it until Barbara could decide to come. And then Lawrie's girlfriend came to stay. And then Pete Hudson [a political philosopher now at Wits] and his girlfriend. Then, one of the people Rick had stayed with in that condemned house came, with his wife. After Lawrie had left Bill Roberts came. Then after Bill and his wife got a house together, Gerry Maré drove his caravan to the house and parked it at the back. He never stayed in the house but in his caravan. So there were quite a few people.

We had a small nexus of a community. Everyone made a contribution to expenses, and we shared food. There was no rent system; no one profited, we just shared expenses. We had a garden, on three-quarters of an acre, a narrow long stretch in the back, with space enough for bananas, oranges, mangoes and naartjies, which we planted, and even a papaya tree. We had lots of barbecues in the back, and also informal discussions, workshops on various political topics, and even for a time Rick's honours course would meet at the house. Also, since Rick was an adviser to Nusas, students who were involved in various projects would come by the house and discuss things with him, get his advice on various matters.

I was doing my honours programme through Unisa at the time, and Rick was lecturing at Natal. But we also started the Educational Reform Association, and Rick was writing *The Eye of the Needle*. It was a busy time, very busy. Every part of my being was engaged, mentally, emotionally, physically – it was just brilliant.

DIRECTLY OR INDIRECTLY ENGAGED

Turner immediately threw himself into the task of seeking out sympathetic people and establishing connections with as many of them as possible. He made himself available regularly for giving lectures at meetings of political groups, writing essays and articles, and participating in protests of various kinds. The Special Branch took note of Turner's busy schedule and followed his involvement with the following groups: the South African Institute of Race Relations, the Durban International Debating Society, the Theatre Entertainment Council of Natal, the Students' Representative Council at the University of Natal, the University Christian Movement, Nusas, the Young Progressives, Saso, the Platform and the summer school camps at Phoenix settlement.

In addition, Turner developed working relationships with the Natal Indian Congress, with dissident religious groups and people (the Christian Institute in particular, as well as liberal Jews and Muslims, such as Fatima and Ismail Meer) and eventually also with Harriet Bolton and other members of the trade union movement in the Durban area.

He even established a connection with Chief Mangosuthu Buthelezi, the head of the KwaZulu government, of whose bona fides as a credible leader many were already sceptical. But Turner refused, on principle, to rule out any person or body that might be willing to work towards positive social change. Turner took an interest in so many different civil society organisations because he was determined to find any and all potential openings for change in South Africa. At this level, his involvement was pragmatic; he was hopeful enough to be prepared to accept and work with even the smallest of cracks in the system, to try and find a way to crawl through.

Innocent about human possibilities
Lawrence Schlemmer

Rick was in the politics department, and I was in a different place completely. I was a sociologist who had come out of a background of social work. I was intensely aware of the contradictory fabric of race relations and events in those days. It was not easy to simplify or put things in a neat parallel structure, and I was absolutely insistent on that. I knew, based on my own history, that things were confusing and contradictory and in fact ironic, even in the worst period of apartheid. That's not to deny the moral horror of the apartheid era, not at all. Nevertheless, underneath it there were human beings all over the place, of all colours, in authority, outside authority, in and out of jail, in and out of persecution, tortured and torturers, the whole lot. So I was not going to become anyone's political heavy.

Some people now, who pay homage to Rick Turner, what they fondly imagine is a hard and steely commitment to the revolutionary struggle. Those kinds of people wouldn't have been seen dead with me. But Rick was an innocent. In a remarkable way Rick was honest, literally honest with himself and innocent about human possibilities. He hadn't foreclosed on any options. Rick had an underlying simplicity of commitment, which was almost frightening. It was carefully disguised, not deliberately, but it was effectively disguised by a very cool approach – very cool, very laid back.

So, he and I got along just fine. We ended up sharing a house. We lived together until a couple of months before he was murdered.

While Turner was willing to work with a broad range of people and organisations, this by no means meant that he was unclear about or 'soft' in his own world-view. In fact, his presence within these groups was often a provocative one, precisely because he had so much hope. In the cautious and reasonable political climate at the time, he consistently provoked his allies and acquaintances in the broad opposition to apartheid to keep dreaming, to keep imagining an ideal society, rather than resigning themselves to immediate goals, incremental reforms, limited horizons.

For example, in one of his many speeches to members of Nusas, Turner openly encouraged the students, in the words of an informer, to 'work hard to remove the government from power'. As the climate of repression began to intensify, Turner continued to appear fearless in opposing the status quo. Even when the state took its first open stand against him and refused to issue him with a passport in 1971, he accepted the news as an occasion to speak out against the government. Turner issued a press release to the *Daily News* that read: 'I have carefully considered the criteria for passport refusals laid down recently by the Minister of the Interior. On no reasonable interpretation do they apply to me. However, one cannot expect reasonable interpretations from a Nationalist cabinet minister. I think the present government is undemocratic, barbarous and exploitative. The passport refusal is merely a minor confirming illustration. I shall continue to say what I think.'

Turner's approach was that it was better to be honest about your disdain for the situation than to be silent. Also, he believed that the only way to slow the tide of apartheid's repeated attempts to crush any opposition was to be even more active and vocal. When Professor Basil

Moore, who had founded and run the University Christian Movement, a radical Christian student body, was banned in 1972, Turner joined in a protest against his banning and encouraged students to create a climate where it was no longer possible for the government to ban anyone. According to the Special Branch report on his speech, he said:

> The university is not a purely academic institution and the belief that the state is entitled to a say in its affairs is false. The government does not pay my salary. It is paid by the people of South Africa, who have nothing to do with the government. To distrust the government is a fundamental principle of democracy. The government is a group of frightened, ignorant people. If all students become involved in controversial matters instead of only a handful, nobody would or could be banned. Only by questioning can you begin to accept responsibility for the actions perpetrated by the government in your name.

Turner's early years in Durban were the high point of his life. His work as a university lecturer was animated and inspired a number of positive relationships with both students and colleagues. His marriage to Foszia blossomed into a collaborative and dynamic partnership, which was deeply satisfying to him on many levels. Their shared home in Dalton Avenue soon became a lively and open environment where they lived in a cooperative atmosphere with a number of close friends. The house also served as a gathering place for social events, classes and political discussions of all sorts. At the same time, the spirit of openness that governed his domestic life was also a driving force behind his public presence. He responded to invitations to support initiatives for social change positively and with enthusiasm.

Turner also dedicated a considerable amount of energy to theoretical work. He was a shrewd student of social and political problems, and could produce carefully researched, critical analysis about what was wrong with the present system. Nonetheless, he insisted that materialist analysis was, on its own, insufficient: 'To understand a society, to understand what it is, where it is going, where it could go, we cannot just describe it. We need also to theorize about it ... Theory is not difficult. What is often difficult is to shift oneself into a theoretical attitude, that is to realize what things in one's experience cannot be taken for granted.'[2] Turner saw that there was a lack of ideas and of imagination within the opposition to apartheid, that too many aspects of South African society were taken for granted. Quite simply, without these basic assumptions being shaken profoundly, there was no possibility that fundamental change would happen.

In response, Turner wrote in 1972 what was to be his one and only published book, *The Eye of the Needle: Towards Participatory Democracy in South Africa*. Written within this intensely optimistic period of Turner's life, the tone and spirit of the book are confidently and provocatively utopian. It is written in the same mood of openness to new ideas and ways of living that permeated his life at the time.

THE LIMITS OF POSSIBILITY

One scholar has said quite bluntly about the work: 'In academic terms, *The Eye of the Needle* is not a particularly good book; it was written in perhaps 36 hours, and under such circumstances it is not surprising that it is ambiguous and even at times contradictory.'[3] All the same, it represents the most compact and coherent explication of his contribution to theory. It was written at a relatively low point in the history of South African left thinking, and was greeted immediately with many accolades from its intended audience.

Writing to a newspaper in defence of his own book, Turner said that 'whatever its other faults [it is] cheap, short [86 pages in the original edition], non-academic and free from philosophical name dropping'.[4] Indeed, *The Eye of the Needle* is written in unusually clear and simple prose, despite the fact that it grapples with profound social and philosophical concepts. This approach 'breathed a different spirit' into the political discourse in South Africa. As Tony Morphet explains, 'Most South African writing, both in fiction and polemic, assumes a powerful objective dominance in the social structure – men may protest and bewail their fate but little or nothing can be done to effect any change.' By contrast, Turner's politics were rooted in the conviction that 'Men have made the society in a way that can be completely comprehended, and in the same way men can change the society'.[5]

The particular form in which he wrote *The Eye of the Needle* emerged from the tension consequent on the fact that his ideas of political and economic change went beyond the prevailing discourse in which he found himself operating. The commission for the book, and its original audience, came from a Christian study group known as the Study Project on Christianity in Apartheid Society or Spro-cas. Spro-cas was created to bring together experts (many of them not Christian) in various fields (such as law, education, politics, economics and religion) to produce carefully researched reports on the social and political problems created by apartheid and to propose alternatives. As a member of the economics commission of Spro-cas, Turner was asked to draft a separate book to 'encourage thinking and discussion about ... radical alternatives', which the commission saw the need to consider, but could not include in its report. One member of the commission felt it necessary to include a footnote within the report which stated that 'she does not consider that it is an important task ... to draw up models for unlikely Utopias'.[6] Nonetheless, *The Eye of the Needle* was indeed completed, and published by Spro-cas.

With its title referring to Jesus' famous saying 'It is easier for a camel to pass through the eye of the needle than for a rich man to enter the Kingdom of God', the book was a provocative challenge to well-off and well-meaning whites to realise that their way of life was thoroughly unsustainable and could not possibly be protected in the long run. Turner's diagnosis was harsh:

> Until white South Africans come to understand that the present society and their present position is a result not of their own virtues but of their vices; until they come to see world history over the last five hundred years not as the 'triumph of white civilization', but simply as the bloody and ambiguous birth of a new technology, and until they come to see these things not in the past but in hope for the future, they will not be able to communicate with black people, nor, ultimately, with one another.[7]

The reader is led through a patient process of simultaneously exposing the moral character of the present system and being presented with an alternative vision. Through it all, there is a tremendous spirit of hopefulness in the writing; even the boldest of claims is made with a quiet, simple confidence.

One consistent theme of the book is the process of socialisation, the ways in which our behaviours and values are shaped by our society. Human beings are moulded by the structures of which they are part. We grow into the kinds of people that are allowed to thrive within whatever system in which we find ourselves living. As children, we become members of families, schools, neighbourhoods, cities and nations, all of which combine to sculpt our sense of ourselves and of the world that we have inherited.

Central to *The Eye of the Needle* is a refusal to accept any of society's values as somehow natural or given. One by one, Turner exposes and dismantles the logical structure behind various assumptions that govern society and that arc therefore taken for granted. He explains how, within the present system, the dominant ethics taught in schools and in society at large seek

> to rationalize [injustice], to smooth the edges. I shall call this an internal morality: Pay your debts, give to the poor, don't tell lies, don't steal (i.e., don't deprive people of property that is theirs in terms of the given legal-property system in ways that the system does not permit). In a slave society, feed your slaves properly; don't sell their children until they are eight years old. In war, kill people with bullets, but not with poison gas. These internal moralities make life slightly easier for people within the system, and as such should not be sneered at. But they do not challenge the human model implicit in the system. An ethic which does this I shall refer to as a transcendent morality. It goes beyond the given and asks the fundamental question: 'What is human life for, what is the meaning of human life?'[8]

This process of socialisation, of developing an 'internal morality' that is deeply limited in substance and scope, also lays the foundation for all the different forms of oppression in this world. We come to understand the unequal relationships between black and white, rich and poor, man and woman, as fixed, as if injustice is a basic fact of human existence. As Turner puts it: 'The present nearly always seems to be at least fairly permanent.'[9]

If we accept Sartre's premise that we have the capacity to change our own lives, through reflecting on our values and choosing new ones, we shall realise that the systems in which we live are also able to be changed at any time. That is, we can adopt what Turner calls a 'transcendent morality' and call into question what we have previously taken for granted.

In encouraging his readers to imagine an entirely different set of social relationships, Turner focused attention on what he called 'the human model' underlying society. Capitalism, for example, is a human model in which people are raised to aspire towards acquiring as many material possessions as possible; competitive behaviour is encouraged; and the fact that many people are deprived of basic needs is accepted without question. Turner describes the essential features of the capitalist system in detail, outlining not only what makes the system work, but also the ways in which living in a capitalist society fundamentally degrades everyone within it:

> If I concentrate on things, rather than people, I become a slave. I become dependent on things. I behave in the way in which the things need me to behave. In each relationship with the other I am not free to be open to the other as a person. I have to manipulate the other in such a way as to obtain things. And to manipulate the other I have to manipulate myself. This is my essential degradation, for in manipulating myself I finally lose my freedom.[10]

It is important to remember that while the values of capitalism are at some level imposed on us through the structures in which we participate, at the same time we choose to go along with the capitalist human model. We could also make another choice. Various other social structures could be constructed that reject all the basic assumptions of capitalism, and create an entirely different model for people to aspire towards.

> The fact that something exists is no guarantee that it will continue to exist or that it should exist. A glance at some of the institutions that other societies have taken unquestioningly for granted: cannibalism, slavery, polygamy, communal property ownership, non-competitiveness, nudity, vegetarianism, male supremacy, matriarchy, promiscuity, Puritanism, the rule of divine emperors or the rule of hereditary aristocracies, and even,

on occasion, democracy; should make us a little more hesitant in taking absolutely for granted such institutions as private ownership of the means of production, social inequality, monogamy, the school system, 'national growth', war, and racial oligarchy in South Africa ...

In order to reflect on our values, then, we have to see which aspects of our society are the necessary result of the imperatives of human nature and of organization, and which aspects of it are changeable ... Until we realize what other values, and what other social forms, are possible, we cannot judge the morality or otherwise of the existing society ... We need therefore to explore, and, if necessary, to attack, all the implicit assumptions about how to behave toward other people that underlie our daily actions in all spheres.[11]

Because any form of open expression of socialist or communist values was expressly forbidden under apartheid, and because he was writing first of all for a Christian audience within Spro-cas, Turner countered the capitalist human model with what he called the 'Christian human model'. This model of society he described 'as one of freedom and openness', a society that values 'people over things'. That is, he encouraged his Christian readers to think of their faith in terms of the 'transcendental moral values' that at least *could* be the core of a Christian society. All the same, his emphasis was not on redeeming Christianity or recasting it as an ethical religion. More importantly, Turner attempted to present a socialist human model that would not be weighed down and degraded by the mechanistic and brutal edges of communism as then practised in the Soviet Union or the Eastern bloc.

AN IDEALLY POSSIBLE SOCIETY

What is the use of utopian thought? Does it just distract us from the essential work of facing the problems in front of us? Is it a mental exercise to help us clarify what our options are?

For Turner, utopian thinking was a necessity, an essential step in the process of undoing an unjust and undesirable social system. In his summary outline of the process of developing a political programme, his starting point was utopia, and from there he worked backwards towards tangible strategies:

(a) Give some account of the 'Good Society', of a society which satisfies human needs and embodies only legitimate power relationships rather than relationships based on force;

(b) Give some account of the nature of the obstacles in the way of the realization of such a society; and

(c) Suggest political strategies based on the above.[12]

This approach to politics runs directly counter to that of the majority of schools of thought. For those who attempt to bring about social change, most attention is usually put on developing strategies to respond to immediate problems. Myriad organisations, programmes and campaigns are created with the aim of bringing about some small concessions, taking small steps, within an overall oppressive system.

Turner was opposed to any attempt either to limit political goals to immediate measures of amelioration or to believe that the end goal can be constantly postponed to a later date. While he was openly critical of liberal reforms, he was also deeply suspicious of the methods and ideology of communists. In defence of a third position, Turner put his energy into developing a proposal for a desirable utopia.

Turner imagined an 'ideally just society' as one in which hierarchy is eliminated as much as possible; a radically decentralised polity and economy, which would rely on widespread structures of cooperative decision-making and management. He named such a system 'participatory democracy', and spent the bulk of *The Eye of the Needle* in laying out its broad outlines and the pitfalls he hoped to avoid in bringing it to life. Though the book does not contain a very thorough articulation, from the skeleton form the whole body can be implied. The essential goal was to create a social system that allows people to have maximum control over the decisions that affect their lives and to be fulfilled by their daily activities.

Perhaps most importantly, Turner immediately and eloquently dissolved the separation that usually marks thinking about economics and politics, by stressing from the start that any kind of 'democracy' will only be possible as a result of economic equality. That is, everyone must have equal control of their economic lives in order to have full and participatory social and political lives. This reasoning runs exactly counter to the politics that have become dominant in South Africa since 1994, which claim that the extension of voting rights to the black population is a necessary step in the development of economic equality. Turner refutes this by reiterating that political power has little substance without power over the economy:

> Because the owners of the factory have power over the factory and over its product, they can control the people who are dependent on these things – the workers. As a worker, I have no power over what I produce, where I produce, how I produce, or why I produce … An economic system is a system of power relationships. And power within the economy gives, as we shall see, power in other spheres of society as well. The first essential for democracy is that the workers should have power at their place of work, that is, that the enterprise should be controlled by those who are working in it.[13]

The central site of power would be essentially the smallest: the workplace. Turner's vision for a desirable economic and political system was rooted in the concept of workers' councils. Simply put, workers' councils are democratically governed organisations of workers within each workplace that have ultimate responsibility for managing the daily affairs at the place of work. Councils replace – or at least greatly reduce – the dependence on management hierarchies by distributing decision-making power among all the workers. For Turner, everyone engaged in a task, whether manual or intellectual labour, was a worker and could participate in a workers' council.

From this simple starting point, the idea is that the democratic control practised within the councils would be expanded into cooperation between various workplaces, up to the level of the industry, neighbourhood, city and nation. In other words, Turner envisioned councils being developed at every level at which people participate socially.

Unlike most forms of socialism, participatory democracy seeks to decentralise power and decision-making as much as possible. As opposed to a central committee or presidency having maximum power,

Turner saw that 'we can have a number of different autonomous decision making agencies. This prevents concentration of power and increases the possibility of meaningful participation ... Workers' control of industry and agriculture would occur within the context of a political system based on universal franchise and maximum decentralization, with real powers being given to local and to provincial authorities.'[14] Workers would act as representatives on municipal boards, and municipalities would be directly involved in planning health, education and urban development on a broader scale.[15] Such decentralisation of power would shift the balance of decision-making away from the production and protection of luxury consumer goods and towards meeting human needs.[16]

'AND THEN ACT TO GET IT'

It is important to stress that Turner did not conceive of his description of participatory democracy as a formal programme of any kind. He was certain that human beings are not at base – or at least not *only* – selfish. He trusted that human beings are, or can be, motivated by higher goals than material gain, and reiterated that the aim was to empower people to decide for themselves, rather than to tell them what was necessary. 'The object of this scheme is not to tell people what they want, or what they ought to want. It is to give individuals the maximum possible amount of control over what happens to themselves and hence the maximum possible amount of freedom to decide what they want, and then to act to get it.'[17]

In outlining an ideal possible society, Turner has a basic trust that people will be able to bring to life a participatory democratic society through their own initiative and ingenuity. Further, if they don't yet know how to live within a different human model, they can teach themselves to take part in a participatory democratic system through the structures of the system itself. In his vision of the transition from a capitalist system, he is confident that the act of taking shared control of the workplace will itself teach people how to run all other aspects of their lives. For Turner, laziness, stupidity and indifference among workers are all traits forced on them by an economic structure that dominates their lives and exploits their labour:

In capitalist society the workers are not interested in the enterprise itself; why should they be, since it does not belong to them? They have neither opportunity nor stimulus to see it as a whole and to understand how what each individual does is related to the rest. The situation is one in which they are told what to do, given little opportunity for the exercise of their initiative or intelligence, and so do not develop initiative or intelligence. The enterprise is not only a work place; it is also a socialization process. Once the workers have been through this process, it is scarcely surprising that they do not appear to have the competence to run an enterprise. What the capitalist system has made the workers into is then produced as evidence for the impossibility of any other social system.[18]

Turner insists that if workers learn indifference and incompetence through being subjected to an undesirable system, these negative habits can be unlearned by changing the conditions of work. People can learn new values simply by living them. Turner was adamant that 'Workers' control is not only a means whereby I can control a specific area of my life. It is an educational process in which I can learn better to control all areas of my life and can develop both psychological and interpersonal skills in a situation of cooperation with my fellows in a common task.'[19] Much as the classroom must be radically restructured (indeed, reimagined) in order to provide people with the necessary space to develop as full participants in their society, so too the workplace can become a type of classroom for developing non-capitalist values and practices. 'It is only if the workers participate in the control of the central part of their lives – their work – that they can develop the personal qualities of autonomy, initiative, and self-confidence necessary for [participatory democracy].'[20]

Turner had a strong conviction that any organisation aspiring towards social change must not only develop a radical vision, but must also make a conscious effort to put that vision into practice as much as possible:

On the organizational level we must ensure that all organizations we work in pre-figure the future ...

I distinguish between hierarchical organisations, in which roles are reinforced, and what I have described as participatory organisations, in which the development of autonomy on the part of the individual is

encouraged by the nature of the institutional structures. We are trying
to decrease hierarchy and dependence and increase autonomy, as much as
possible ... We are trying to ensure that those hierarchies that exist do not
place barriers between people and do not require patterns of authority
and deference.

Organizations must be participatory rather than authoritarian. They
must be areas in which people experience human solidarity and learn to
work with one another in harmony and in love. The process of political
change through the development of organizational solidarity must itself
be a participatory experience if people are to become conscious of the
possibilities of freedom.[21]

This desire to 'pre-figure the future' was already present in Turner's time
at Welcarmas, and it became prominent in his life choices once he moved
to Dalton Avenue in Durban. Outside his home life, Turner attempted
repeatedly to find organisational settings that would be sympathetic to
his utopian approach to social change.

At the very least, *The Eye of the Needle* had a profound impact on
its principal audience, Spro-cas. Before its publication, Spro-cas had
been a staunchly liberal organisation, with no interest in the prospect
of socialism. Yet by 1973 Peter Randall, Spro-cas' director, could write:
'Above all, we recognise the need to be clearer about the society we want:
we see that it is essentially socialist in nature, and this gives us a greater
stake in working for change, i.e. it is in our own interests to do so.'[22]
Spro-cas also began to develop a much more radical approach to race,
and initiated a 'White Consciousness' group in an effort to support the
Black Consciousness Movement. In addition, a new constitution was
drafted for Spro-cas that would decentralise its organisation and create
more democratic structures. Unfortunately, the willingness of Spro-cas
to embrace Turner's proposals was relatively rare in South Africa at the
time.

Many South African leftists regarded *The Eye of the Needle* as
either unintelligible or insufficiently programmatic. In spite of Turner's
tremendous openness and his willingness to work with a wide array of
organisations, the power of pragmatism tended to overshadow him. *The
Eye of the Needle* – and the approach to social change that it represents

– is perhaps all the more powerful, precisely because pragmatism has in so many cases – and certainly in South Africa – crushed idealism in the process of transforming society.

SEVEN

A Concrete Alternative

'A class analysis starts from the recognition of the existence within a society of structurally imposed inequalities, and the problem then becomes one of explaining how those inequalities are maintained and how they are perceived by those who either do or do not benefit from them ... Sometimes theorists write as though class consciousness were something which you either have or do not have, but this is very misleading.'[1]

– RICK TURNER

A WAY TO ENGAGE

IN A LETTER TO HIS WIFE (which was later read as evidence in court) Turner complained of his involvement with Nusas: 'The only problem is that I now find myself compelled into a leadership role on campus. My advice and consent has to be got for everything, etc. Both embarrassing and undesirable that they should need a leader.'[2] For many students, he played a crucial role in helping develop an understanding of capitalist society and a commitment to involve themselves in struggling towards a more just society.

Part of his powerful influence on his students lay in the way he encouraged them to engage more deeply in the world around them. Turner felt strongly that as part of the population with rights and privileges, they should engage with their community directly and attempt to help prepare others for the prospect of social change. He took seriously the provocation of Black Consciousness and felt that it was crucial for socially conscious young whites to find ways to connect to white adults – who necessarily had a stronger stake in the system – and try to shift the overall mentality of white people. Of course, this was not a one-sided process. The student activists were not simply delivering a message; they were also changed by the process of trying to persuade others.

Engagement was something foreign

Gerry Maré

Rick's notion of social change was that he wanted people to find ways to be engaged. I remember, there was an educational protest of some kind, and a march was proposed, but Rick said, 'No, we are not going to march or anything. What we are going to do is to set up an alternative space for teaching.' And what Rick basically did was that he got students to take charge of refining their ideas about this issue. He said, 'You are going to draw up a pamphlet, and you are going to hand those out to people personally door-to-door. And you are going to say, "Here, I want you to read this because I want you to sign this petition."' That kind of engagement was something foreign to most of us in the student movement.

I received the short end of the stick, because I'm Afrikaans speaking, so I had to go out to a largely Afrikaans working-class area and try it out, talking to people at the high school. That was a real test. I was whisked into the toilet by the senior boys and by some of the teachers. They basically threatened to fuck me up. 'We don't give a damn what you are here for, we are not interested in hearing you out … communist.' In fact, the police arrived and told them to let me go.

After graduating, I went overseas briefly because I decided that if I could find a place where I could become socially involved without being a South African in exile, I would do it. I had never been overseas. The one place where I had more contacts was the Netherlands, because I'd studied Afrikaans and Nederlands literature. Also, there was a whole lot happening in Amsterdam; the Provos were trying to create exciting reforms, and so on. Anyway, I thought I would try that, but it was totally alien to me, so I came back three months later.

I came back, and I said to Rick – frustrated beyond belief – 'How do I join MK?' I had done military service, so I thought I could be a soldier. But Rick just looked at me and he said, 'If you want to talk about this thing, just go away. Speak to someone else; I'm not interested.' So I thought: But how else? Rick said, 'Well, go and stand for the municipality, you've got the right to do that, you are a white person, you've got the vote. Say what you believe in and try to convince people.' That was a challenge. I couldn't do it. But that's what he wanted people to do: to convince people, to find a platform from which you can do it.

THE ONLY SPHERE

While Turner certainly encouraged his students to find any available opportunity for intervening in their society, he was particularly focused on finding ways of challenging the tremendous economic inequalities. His emphasis on class struggle was based on an analysis of the growing importance of black industrial workers to the South African economy. He saw that while in the 1950s (when apartheid was beginning to be entrenched) the proportion of blacks working in industry was relatively low compared with agriculture and mining, capitalist 'development' in the 1960s had made the country more reliant on black industrial workers – and therefore they had more power than ever before. Turner was convinced that the economy was the only sphere in which the power of Africans was growing, a power that could potentially be made even greater through trade unions and other forms of organised working-class action.[3]

Inspired by a class analysis of society, but without a clear programme, student activists reached out to workers in the hopes that their initiatives would lead to increasing workers' organisation. In 1971 a group of students at the University of Natal formed the Wages Commission to investigate the wages paid to black workers in relation to the 'living wage'[4] and then took steps to help workers advocate the kind of wages that would allow them a basic dignity. Many of the key participants in the Wages Commission were students of Turner and were heavily influenced by him.[5]

Looking back, many people in the trade union movement – particularly communists of various stripes – feel strongly that the shift towards working-class politics was essentially a refusal to cooperate with the Black Consciousness Movement. Martin Legassick, a member of the Marxist Workers' Tendency, which was later expelled from the ANC – insists: 'Radical white students regarded with contempt and as a waste of time the idea of trying to engage with racist whites in door-to-door campaigns or in other forms of activity – they turned to the black working class as an alternative.'[6] Perhaps this is an accurate interpretation of the motivation of some of the Wages Commission members. Furthermore, Turner *was* consciously looking for new openings, to help white students out of their immobile position into which Black Consciousness had cast them. Nonetheless, it seems clear that Turner did not see involvement in working-class organisation as strictly antagonistic to cooperation with Black Consciousness activists or as an invalidation of the basic positions of Black Consciousness.

Turner's encouragement of white students to involve themselves with labour went side by side with his encouragement of them to embrace Black Consciousness as a type of radicalism and engage in exactly the kinds of activities that Legassick claims they found contemptible, such as canvassing in white communities. The belief that Black Consciousness and trade unionism could be mutually compatible may have been a weakness of Turner's understanding of the political situation of the time. But it may also have been an expression of the tenacity of his utopian perspective that he sought all possible openings, rather than holding any one position in contempt.

The Wages Commission began by interviewing support staff at the University of Natal, gathering detailed information about the wages they earned and their life circumstances in general. Armed with this information and data about a decent 'living wage', the group called a meeting of workers on campus, which was well attended, and began their campaign. From this humble but encouraging start, the Wages Commission became involved in larger questions facing black workers off the campus.

As African workers were legally defined as outside the category of 'employees' under apartheid law, the only legal mechanism for making reforms in black wages was through the Wage Board. Despite the grave limitations of this forum, the Wages Commission used Wage Board hearings as a way of mobilising workers. They helped workers to formulate demands and then brought these demands to the Wage Board hearings.

The techniques that the Wages Commission used were relatively simple and modest in their reach. But in the volatile atmosphere of exploitation at the time, they had a big impact. The commission was effective because of the relative privilege of the student activists, which gave them greater capacity than their black counterparts to engage with workers without adverse repercussions. Although the commission had no formal role in the Durban strikes of 1973, its influence was certainly felt there. Students certainly did not play a leading role in the strikes. Still, some of the initial strikes happened in factories in which the Wages Commission had been involved, and often the wage demands made by strikers were similar to the recommendations that the commission published for a 'living wage'. And after the strikes, a number of the Wages Commission members became heavily involved in the emerging trade union movement.

It just developed

Halton Cheadle

I've often said that if the ANC had been recruiting, I would have joined; but they weren't there. For two or three years I had been part of the group thinking that students should play the role of preparing whites to change. But when it came to the end of that, I started thinking based on a class analysis of the society (and, again, this is affected by Rick) and no longer accepted the idea that only blacks can lead organisations.

So, I broke away from Black Consciousness and the idea of playing a supportive role to blacks, in about 1973; in fact earlier, in 1972. I became a Marxist. Based on Marxism, I started believing in the necessity to connect with the working class. I certainly considered myself as a Leninist in 1972. But what kind of a Leninist are you that won't join the only official Leninist party? I mean, it's just nonsense. When I think back now, it's nonsensical. Being a Leninist, to us, meant that we believed strongly that we had to organise the working class, that it's just nonsense to leave them unorganised. Workers are absolutely critical for the national democratic revolution. I think that would be an ideological difference between Rick and me; he was not interested in being an organiser. But, again, at the time, there were no institutions. Where were the institutions? We were in the process of building the unions up from scratch.

The massive oppression of the 1960s had effectively obliterated the trade unions, partly because many of the trade unions had become nothing more than recruiting grounds for Umkhonto weSizwe. Basically, there were no unions, or at least very few black unions around, and so I started asking, Why aren't black students organising black workers? They weren't. And so, a group of us decided that our role was to organise black workers. Our emphasis was on ensuring that these unions we were creating would be run by workers themselves. We moved away from the issue of black or white. The issue was simply that the workers should run the union.

However, our entrance into union organising began within the student movement. Charles Nupen, Karel Tip, David Hemson, myself and a few others started a thing called the Wages Commission, in 1971. I don't remember Rick being part of the initial discussions about establishing the Wages Commission in Nusas. But it would have been discussed with him; he was central to so many discussions. The Wages Commission model was taken up in Johannesburg and Cape Town, as an established structure through Nusas, and this led to a revival of trade union activity.

The Wages Commission began as a project by looking solely at the university – looking internally at wage issues for workers on campus. There was nothing to it; we called a meeting and people came. I don't know what would have happened if no one came. From that initial step, we started to get involved in what was called the Wage Board. The Wage Boards would have public hearings on wages for a particular industry. So, for example, we went into the docks and said that there was this Wage Board hearing and the Wage Board set minimum wages through the wage determination and we then had a meeting, with hundreds of dock workers. I remember just that we couldn't fit in the hall. We elected a steering committee, and then we formulated demands, which we later took to the Wage Board meeting.

Normally these Wage Board hearings were just with employers, no one ever came to them. There was a so-called workers' side, where they would have indunas, a tribal headman. Look, I mean it was all organised in typical colonial style. What they did was to reproduce the tribal structures as part of the authoritarian structure inside the factory. So, the supervisor was your induna. It was disgusting. So these guys were the so-called spokesmen for the black dock workers. And when they got up and spoke, they didn't do anything to advocate for the worker. Then we came in front of the committee, with hundreds of workers with us, and put forward a petition that was signed by thousands of dock workers. So this was a powerful mobilising tool.

We latched on to the concept of a living wage. Now, the living wage was about double what people were in fact getting. So, this became our strategy right through into the mid-1980s. We gave the workers information about what a living wage was, and that of course fed into their demands. Of course they were unrealisable demands. But those were the demands we put before the Wage Boards. We were trying to be rational, in the face of a brutal system of exploitation. So, this concept of a living wage was a mobilising tool; it became a rallying cry.

We also started a general benefit fund. The idea was that we would recruit people into the fund and provide very simple funeral benefits. Then, we broke it into sectors: we had clothing, we had textiles, we had metal, we had docks, which we later turned into unions. Workers originally joined the benefit fund and through that we would get factory committees, and then we would have representative factory committees, then a branch committee, and then we moved to being a union. And so we did that throughout 1972–73. These early unions later became some of the core Cosatu unions.

But we didn't know when we started that we were going to create such large unions. It just developed. It took a while before we even began formulating the idea that we should try to form unions. From there, we decided that the way to do it strategically, in order to avoid the state immediately repressing us before we got anywhere, was through the benefit fund. But we worked through trade union offices, early on. There was a woman called Harriet Bolton, who was the general secretary of the Garment Workers' Industrial Union. She gave us office space and the use of the hall. People started coming on Saturday morning with complaints and to sign up. It was quite soon that we developed the strategy where we would say to the person who came in from the factory, 'Listen, get further people from the factory, let's start putting a committee together.' And so we had these shop stewards' committees, effectively. And then we would coalesce them and create branches and do training. After the Durban strikes in 1973, more and more strikes started happening. Then, steadily but surely, we started targeting factories, multinationals, and so on.

There wasn't a clear strategic plan when we started, but it evolved quite quickly. But the fact was that we absolutely hit the nail on the head. No one was organising; we started organising. By the end of 1973, we had established four or five unions, comprising about a hundred thousand workers, organised in one year.

So, there was a shift away from the strategic vision that Rick had outlined, but it wasn't a fierce break. I would say it was more just that different focuses developed. From about 1973 on, Rick was by and large accepting that there was a role for whites to play among workers. But we all mellowed at some stage or another.

Putting an end to the angst

Dan O'Meara

Rick offered us this idea that it is only by working with black workers that whites can effect change. That was a hugely radical idea. It meant that we could get out of the whole ambit of the Spro-cas policy. Spro-cas was a group of older people, connected to the Liberal Party, people who didn't want to get into trouble or incite the police. We weren't interested in that. I didn't even bother to read any of the Spro-cas reports; they just seemed totally irrelevant, totally unaware of the post-1968, post-Saso realities.

Rick's analysis started to give the white left a sense that there was something that we could do, something that we could do that Saso couldn't. We could do it because the law protected us in our whiteness, so we could start organising black workers, without getting into shit with the state. Whereas, if Saso tried to do that, they'd all go to prison immediately. Also, Black Consciousness was essentially a middle-class movement, whose writings and conversations were completely inaccessible to uneducated, working-class blacks. Then, the irony was that the whites – who were university-educated, privileged – who got involved in trade union organising were actually able to relate better to black workers.

The first attempt to engage with the working class was the Wages Commission, which grew out of Nusas at the University of Natal. For white middle-class students the Wages Commission really made them look at the reality of apartheid. We all knew that black people were poor, but to really look at what they're earning, and the circumstances in which they're earning it – it was an enormous eye-opener. (Don't forget, 1972 was the absolute high point of white prosperity in South Africa.) Rick's consciousness-raising ethos was hugely successful.

Without the Wages Commission, that generation who ended up on the Marxist left would not have done so. It was a way into working-class politics. The influence on the students that were involved cannot be overstated. First of all, it put students in contact with black workers – something that never otherwise would have happened to them, outside of meeting the gardener or the servant in the family home. People used to go into the townships and interview; so you not only got the details of their lives, you saw how they lived in ways that you would never have done before. It was hugely dramatic; it was shattering for many people. Then they'd come home and see the way that their parents were living and the kinds of things their parents were promoting and they'd just get enraged.

Most young whites, without access to a project like the Wages Commission, would have stayed in that angst-ridden moment of asking constantly, 'What is our role?' It just put an end to that angst. It was very clear. Here's your role: you live in this unbelievably awful society, where there is the worst poverty in the world, the worst income disparities on earth, and you can see it with your own eyes, so you must be part of the solution.

More significantly, the Wages Commission began to enable the organisation of black workers. From the perspective of black workers the Wages Commission provided a bunch of people who were now prepared to start organising in the factories. Biko's group could have done this, but they didn't have a class analysis, and Black Consciousness was focused more on community projects, not in the factories.

So, here comes this group of privileged people who are not going to be smashed by the police immediately, because the police don't quite know what to do. So for about two years – it was a brief little moment – the people who came out of the Wages Commission could start organising and they were left alone by the police.

The Wages Commission created a climate and an organisational structure that supported a re-emerging union movement. For example, Cheadle and the others in the Wages Commission didn't set out to instigate strikes, but they did focus on the Frame group of factories, singling them out as uniquely exploitative; and that's where the strikes occurred initially. The Durban strikes in 1973 changed the circumstances, and made it clear that any kind of new resistance was going to be based in the working class. Without that group of organisers from the Wages Commission, I doubt whether an organisation would have survived *after* the strikes.

MAKING SENSE OF WILDCATS

In January 1973 a wildcat strike at Coronation Brick and Tile factory just outside Durban set off a wave of strikes throughout the Durban area, involving more than 150 companies and 100,000 workers.[7] 'There was no formal beginning. Sometimes the decision to strike was taken in informal meetings outside the gates. In other instances, workers simply stopped work in one part of the factory, and others joined in … They rarely elected a negotiating committee and often did not even make any formal demands. When addressed by management they would take up en masse a particular demand. The mood at these meetings with management seems often to have been euphoric, with much good-humoured insult being flung at managers.'[8]

The strikes spread rapidly from factory to factory, and even the municipal workers joined in: '16,000 employees of the Durban Corporation closed down the city's essential services: rubbish quickly piled up, a backlog of corpses built up as graves went un-dug, and perishable food decayed in the city's markets.'[9] As one strike ended, another would begin, or workers would be inspired by the sight of striking workers marching and would join in.

The strikes were spontaneous, without coordination from any political party or trade union, and the demands were frequently for wage increases of 100 per cent or more. 'Most workers named a figure approximately double their current wage. Those on R10 suggested R20; those on R20 suggested R40. The evidence suggests, therefore, that there is no wage level, within the range which is "possible" given the present dispensation, which is likely to satisfy the aspirations of workers ... The initial demand is significant. It does seem to express, in veiled terms, a rejection of the whole system.'[10]

The Durban strikes were remarkable not only for their tremendous size and their spontaneity, but also because they were, all things considered, astonishingly successful. In the harsh climate of repression at the time, one would have expected such strikes to be met with mass dismissals or police brutality, but neither occurred and most workers gained at least a small wage increase. As Turner argued: 'The fact that the strikes were not organized by some central body also accounts for the relative measure of success which they achieved. It was quite impossible for the state to take action against more than 150 autonomous groups of strikers. Short of putting nearly 100,000 workers in jail, there was nothing that they could do.'[11]

Working in collaboration with a handful of other researchers and trade unionists, Turner wrote the only detailed account of the episode, entitled *The Durban Strikes 1973: Human Beings with Souls*.[12] Much of the book is simply a careful account of the events that transpired. Using extensive interviews with workers – both Africans and Indians[13] – the book attempts to understand why the workers struck, how they organised and made decisions, and whether there was any substance to the repeated claim made by government officials that the strikes were the result of 'agitators'.[14] Turner was particularly intrigued by the fact that the strikes were responded to with goodwill. Employers frequently granted many of the workers' demands (or at least made some concessions in the form of wage improvements), very few workers were fired, and the police showed considerable restraint. Interviews were carried out with a couple of dozen employers to try to understand this reaction. Furthermore, a number of white citizens wrote sympathetic letters to local newspapers during the strikes, calling for improved working conditions for Africans. Interviews were also done with a random sampling of whites[15] to try to understand whether this reaction was widespread or merely that of a few outspoken people.

The conclusion of *The Durban Strikes* was that the strikes pointed towards the urgent need, and feasibility, of legally recognising African trade unions.[16] While this argument was rationally based and clearly articulated, it is nonetheless somewhat jarring to read, as the thrust is so strikingly different from Turner's other writing.[17] Whereas, in *The Eye of the Needle* the thrust is one of inspiring the reader to imagine social change of a utopian kind, here Turner joined others in advancing reasonable demands that would suit employers, the government and white society.

Put succinctly, in *The Durban Strikes* Turner reconciled himself to the fact that white people wanted 'stability' more than 'justice,' and he offered them trade unions as a means towards stability – not justice. He wrote: 'It is also necessary to make it clear that the degree of change which whites seem willing to envisage is not towards a just society, but rather towards a less unjust and more stable society, with the emphasis on stability, rather than justice ... Since there is at present little likelihood of a change occurring on the level of formal political rights, it is necessary to analyse the part which could be played by trade unions in institutionalizing conflict.'[18] In other words, he argued at length for trade union organisation to be seen as a means of reducing the disorder and unpredictability of wildcat strikes. The argument put forward was that unions do not increase worker unrest, they decrease it. Union leaders 'render considerable assistance' when it comes to 'advising against and restraining their members'.[19] Why did Turner and his collaborators make this argument?

Rather than appealing to and supporting a sense of power and self-assertion within the working class, *The Durban Strikes* instead directed attention towards the ruling class – who are constantly afraid of the potential power of black workers. The authors spoke directly to that fear, and told the rulers that they could be less afraid if only they would channel the rage produced by an unjust economic system into clear and simple legal channels – namely, trade unions. 'Trade unions ... are the precondition for stable industrial peace in South Africa ... a disgruntled and alienated work force, disinterested in their jobs and only able to express their grievances through wildcat strikes and in bloodier forms of protest, such as the tragedy at Carletonville,[20] which occurred as we were completing this manuscript, is not in anybody's interest. The only alternative is trade unions.'[21]

Pragmatic reasoning aside, the more fundamental question remains: Why did Turner come to the conclusion that wildcat strikes are dangerous, unstable or undesirable?

The wildcat nature of the Durban strikes was a crucial component of their relative success. It wouldn't have been too far-fetched to suggest that spontaneous and decentralised methods of working class struggle should be encouraged and broadened. But *The Durban Strikes* analysed spontaneous acts of rebellion as expressions of powerlessness, as opposed to organised forms – such as unions.[22] The book thus implied that such strikes should be 'prevented via orderly trade unionism' and 'orderly negotiations'.[23]

This account points to a weak link between Turner's theoretical writing on workers' self-management and his strategic thinking in the present tense. Having studied the Durban strikes so thoroughly, he still remained blind to their real strength, opting instead to call for 'rationalising' worker–management relations. It is not the role of radical opponents of an economic system to tell the rulers of that system how they can more rationally or peacefully exploit and oppress the population. Nonetheless, in making the case for the legal recognition of African unions, Turner did just that.

A CLASS ANALYSIS STARTS

From reading *The Durban Strikes* alone, one might get the impression that a liberal reform of labour policy was all that Turner desired. Turner's thoughts on trade union organising must be placed within the overall context of his ideas. In an article produced in 1974 and written under

Foszia Fisher's name, after the publication of *The Durban Strikes*, Turner's analysis of the strikes took on a whole new understanding.

This piece, entitled 'Class Consciousness Among Colonised Workers in South Africa', focused principally on what strikes 'mean' in terms of the consciousness of the workers involved.[24] Given that the Durban strikes came at a time of relative labour calm, how can we determine the extent to which worker frustration was deep-seated and unresolved? That is to say, while it is obvious that wages for African workers were appallingly low, and that workers were ready to take risks to improve their wages, what else about their oppression were they aware of? Were their grievances temporary or systematic?

Instead of a simple 'yes' or 'no' answer, Turner saw the development of class consciousness as the process by which personal anger becomes translated into an awareness of an unjust social system. Can it be said that the 100,000 workers who went on strike in 1973 were defying *a system* of inequality? To this Turner answered, 'There may well be a highly dissatisfied consciousness present, repressed by the apparent total absence of channels of action, and unable to verbalize itself. This is illustrated particularly in the case of wildcat strikes, where some incident suddenly permits this consciousness to crystallise, often in very radical forms.'[25]

So, having been denied any normal channels of discontent, the workers in Durban nonetheless found a way to 'verbalise' quite clearly. It is possible to be aware that you are being exploited, and even that the exploitation is systematic, without taking action – if no course of action seems possible. However, 'the very success of the strikes indicates how rapidly a sense of power can be acquired when some event reveals the possibility of effective action.'[26]

Having spoken at length in *The Durban Strikes* about the need to give legal recognition to trade unions, Turner again touched on this theme in his 'Class Consciousness' article, but with a very different emphasis. For example, he wrote again about the risk of 'destabilising' society if unions are not allowed, but was more sympathetic to instability: 'To the extent that employers refuse recognition of strongly organized trade unions, they may encourage the development of more revolutionary class consciousness ... Unless employers can provide a better form of integration, a changing political climate ... could lead to a quite rapid development of class consciousness beyond economist demands.'[27] Here Turner was not pleading for industrial peace. Instead, he was simply pointing out that workers' values change quickly as a result of their increased sense of power, and given the predictable way in which the regime would react, workers might well push past 'economist demands' – namely, industrial peace. Furthermore, as in *The Eye of the Needle*, Turner warned against limiting the demands to one of constantly negotiating with management, and pushed for broader control of the workplace and more meaningful forms of labour. He then pointed out that, potentially at least, all workplace struggles in South Africa could be struggles around control.[28]

Perhaps most remarkably, given the space dedicated in *The Durban Strikes* to praise of unions, Turner spoke in his 1974 article quite sympathetically towards working class scepticism about unionisation. He explained how resistance to forming unions comes, also, from 'those who have seen many forms of trade union and political organisation be effectively repressed. These workers may feel that the unions are not viable. They may feel that given the present balance of forces it is easier for workers to make gains by using methods of informal control in the factories, and through leaderless wildcat strikes. *They may also be right here.*'[29]

Overall, Turner's tone in 1974 was hopeful. He was inspired by the bold wage demands of the Durban strikes, 'but the fact that this could only be expressed by making "impossible" money demands also tells us something about the level of class consciousness of these workers'.[30] In addition, though he saw racialism as a 'crude type of theory' and not likely to be the dominant factor in the coming struggle, he was not confident about workers moving in a clearly anti-capitalist direction or developing a vision of 'an alternative form of society'.[31] But, certainly, Turner was not trying to say that workers are static, ignorant or content. On the contrary, he was clearly impressed by the speed of the class consciousness developing among black workers, and predicted that it would accelerate rapidly.

In conclusion, while Turner did seem to feel strongly that fighting for trade union legalisation was a necessary strategic step, his persistent interest was the broadening of class consciousness and the expansion of the possibilities of social change towards radical transformation.

TURNING EVERYTHING INTO UNIONS

'You might think, "the working class want change, they want power, they want this" ... but asking what people want, you don't always get what you expect them to say. So the first meeting down at Bolton Hall when there was a group of people and the idea of some kind of organisation came up and the workers who were there were asked, "What would you want this organisation to give you?" they said, "Funeral benefits." They were all asking for that because it's such an enormous burden on any family if some member dies.'[32]

– GERRY MARÉ

Black militancy and working class organisation developed rapidly after the Durban strikes of 1973. In response, a number of those who had begun with the Wages Commission grew steadily more involved in the workers' struggle. These young radicals were extremely dedicated and energetic. Their passion paid off, relatively quickly – and explosively. Having once become involved as catalysts, they quickly saw themselves as traditional organisers, taking up leadership roles among workers.

For example, the General Workers' Benefit Fund, which pooled members' money so that burial expenses would be covered, was a small initiative among black workers to cooperate and live better lives. While, in hindsight, people might view the fund as a clear precursor of the black trade union movement, it did not start out with such a clear line of progression in mind. A group of workers simply decided that putting a little bit of money aside to cover burial costs would be a good idea. In response to this initiative, the young student leaders decided that the fund would make a good foundation for trade unions. They encouraged the workers to turn their benefit fund groups into more formal organisations: to issue membership cards and collect dues, to gather to discuss grievances and elect representatives.

As a result of their successes, Halton Cheadle, David Hemson[33] and others shifted towards Marxism-Leninism; towards a programmatic politics that justified their own role as leaders. It was 'a shift that happened very quickly in fact, partly because we were so successful'.[34] Seeing themselves as the leading lights of a coming revolution, they abandoned

Turner's approach towards social change. Instead of trying to engage people's values carefully in the direction of a shift in consciousness, the young trade union leaders learned to steer events in their favour, to acquire and utilise power.

In the new political life after 1973, the old left would steadily re-emerge, and Turner's more anti-authoritarian and utopian radicalism would be seen as less viable.

The irony or tragedy

Dan O'Meara

This is the irony or the tragedy of Rick: just at the moment when this first generation of his students move into organising, they abandon Rick's way of thinking, and they move to Marxism. So there's not, as it were, a real second generation that follows. For example, Halton Cheadle was in many ways Rick's best creation, and also went way beyond Rick. His skills were as an organiser and an agitator, more than as a coherent intellectual. Already in 1972, Cheadle was dissatisfied with Rick's form of analysis. Rick made his honours students read Sartre's *Being and Nothingness*. The students were hugely dissatisfied with it. I remember Cheadle coming to my office and saying that he'd just told Rick that reading Sartre is like going to a shooting gallery and shooting with a gun whose barrel is bent; you could never hit anything with it. Rick was very hurt by that, of course. That was the beginning of a sign that the people who had been fostered by him intellectually were moving beyond him. Well, not beyond him, because they were never his equal, but they were moving in different directions. Everybody remained loyal to him, they all kept in communication with Rick, even through the banning years; but they shifted course.

The positions that he was advocating, say between 1970 and 1974, were just passed by. He was a catalyst, but his ideas ended up not informing the analysis of South Africa. It happened because he lost his platform. Rick was a public person. He was a formidable communicator, an astonishing teacher. Suddenly he didn't have access to his audience anymore. Furthermore, the central points of Turner's philosophy – the interplay between individual responsibility and the broader culture – were radically changed by the emergence of Black Consciousness and by the Durban strikes.

The kind of gutter Marxism (mechanistic Marxism) which emerged in South Africa provided a very easy answer to the new circumstances in the country after 1973. I became a Marxist at just that time, and it was psychologically an immense relief to me. It enabled me to answer all the questions that Rick's positions couldn't really answer for me. Marxism simply said, 'Yup, this is the way it's going to happen, these are the people you're going to have to work with, and this is the solution. And, here is a role for you.' Rick's analysis didn't provide a recipe: Marxism did. Rick's answers were far too complicated.

PART THREE

The Banning Years

Paddy and Jane Turner before Richard was born. (Courtesy of Jann Turner)

The cottage at Welcarmas farm.
(Courtesy of Jann Turner)

Richard Turner and John Clare in the uniform of St George's Grammar School, Cape Town, 1959. (Courtesy of Barbara Follett)

Richard Turner, 10 years old. (Courtesy of Jann Turner)

Richard as a young adult, reading. (Courtesy of Jann Turner)

PROF. INSKIP

University of Cape Town student sit-in, 1968. (UCT Manuscripts and Archives)

THE CAPE ARGUS, THURSDAY, 'AUGUST 15, 1968

ON STUDENTS'

SITTING IN

DEMONSTRATING STUDENTS *overflowed on to stairways and info corridors in the Bremner Building of the University of*

UCT students take over Bremner Building.
(UCT Manuscripts and Archives)

PROTEST MARCH: Hundreds of University of Cape Town students at the start of the protest march yesterday. After a mass meeting on the campus, the students marched in a long column to the university's administration buildings — half a mile away. They sang protest songs and carried banners and posters.

The student protest descends the steps from Jameson Hall. (UCT Manuscripts and Archives)

Student protesters organise a makeshift snack bar within Bremner Building. (UCT Manuscripts and Archives)

APPEALS TO REASON

PROF. D. INSKIP *reasons with Maties through the police loudhailer.* Col. G. E. McIntyre, *Divisional Inspector of Police for the Western Cape, stands beside him.*

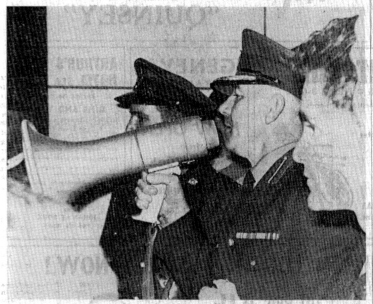

COL. G. E. McINTYRE, *Divisional Inspector of Police for the Western Cape, orders the crowd of students to disperse and go home, at U.C.T. last night.*

UCT authorities and the police attempt to defuse the situation.
(UCT Manuscripts and Archives)

*Barbara Hubbard and Richard Turner as undergraduates,
Cape Town. (Courtesy of Barbara Follett)*

*Rick Turner in the early 1970s. (Courtesy of
Jann Turner)*

Rick Turner, photographed by Foszia Fisher. (Courtesy of Jann Turner)

Jann and Kim Turner as young children. (Courtesy of Michael Hubbard)

Foszia, Rick and Jann on Brighton Beach, Durban, 1970s. (Courtesy of Jann Turner)

(From left) Barbara Hubbard, Kim Turner, Foszia Fisher and Jann Turner at Richard's funeral. (Courtesy of Jann Turner)

Funeral procession. (Courtesy of Jann Turner)

Mourners at Rick Turner's funeral. (Courtesy of Jann Turner)

Rick Turner in the early 1970s. (Courtesy of Jann Turner)

Dr Turner's daughters, Jann, 13, and Kim, 9, read the words of Martin Luther King . . . "A man dies when he refuses to stand up for what is true."

Jann and Kim Turner addressing mourners at their father's funeral.
(Courtesy of Jann Turner)

Rick Turner probe dropped

THE Harms Commission has decided not to continue with its investigations into the murder of Natal academic Dr Rick Turner because of a lack of facts "and other clues."

Mr Justice Harms says, however, that there are two suspects — former Bureau for State Security (BOSS) spy Martin Dolinchek and an unidentified man described "as a so-called rightist political activist."

Dr Turner was murdered at his home in Durban on January 8 1978 after having been restricted in terms of the Suppression of Communism Act.

Investigate

"His mother requested that the commission investigate his death (as) she believes the State to be responsible for her son's death," says the Harms report.

"She furnished no facts to substantiate this, but she did append a report by a private detective ... he reported that 'at this stage I have no evidence indicating that a member of any of the governmental agencies could possibly be suspected'."

Mr Justice Harms says Dolinchek "was involved in the Seychelles invasion and was, there, sentenced to imprisonment.

"He is not available to give evidence and in an interview with the deceased's mother, he did not furnish her with any useful information.

"A second suspect is known as a so-called rightist political activist who was in 1979 convicted of offences relating to his political persuasions."

Allegations linking the man to the Turner murder "led nowhere".

● The commission found there was nothing sinister about two SA Defence Force lieutenants trespassing on the Verwoerdburg property of human rights lawyer Brian Currin.

The report said the men had been investigating the illegal use of an SADF vehicle which had been stopped near Mr Currin's property. ◻

The state's investigation into its own culpability for Rick Turner's death was lukewarm, at best. (Newspaper clipping courtesy of Michael Hubbard)

*Rick Turner, during the banning years, with Jann and Kim. (Courtesy of
Michael Hubbard)*

Foszia Fisher, looking through the window at 32 Dalton Avenue, where Rick Turner was shot. (Courtesy of Michael Hubbard)

EIGHT

Not Limited At All

'Don't you realize what a ban is? It isn't a preventive measure, it's a way of punishing people the State cannot punish under normal law. Many of the banning restrictions are designed simply to inconvenience or exasperate. At first it doesn't seem too inconvenient to have to report to a police station once a week – but after a year it seems an intolerable inconvenience. Talking to one person at a time is designed to inconvenience you by making you repeat everything you said to the last person to the next person as well. It is to keep you looking over your shoulder, even in your own home. It is to maintain that kind of tension. Besides, all these provisions are designed to make one commit technical crimes. They couldn't make you a criminal before, so they set up artificial provisions, and if you are caught contravening these you are technically a criminal.'[1]

– STEVE BIKO

AS A FORM OF REPRESSING DISSIDENTS, the apartheid state used 'banning orders' to neutralise people. During the four decades of apartheid rule, more than 1,500 people were banned. Perhaps even more effective than arrests and assassinations – which often have the effect of making martyrs out of rebels – banning sought to isolate and silence people. Banned people were removed from public life (for up to five years), forbidden to participate in any form of political activity, forbidden even to simply socialise.

Furthermore, banned people were subjected to constant surveillance by the security police and by informants, their phones were often tapped, and they were regularly harassed by the police in random and abusive ways.

By all accounts, banning worked, at least to a certain extent: the banned person did become more isolated and less visible in the public domain. Banned people were, by necessity, constantly aware of the restrictions placed on them; every moment, day after day, month after month, year after year, was curtailed by a thousand little rules and restrictions. Banning orders were designed to be virtually impossible to follow, in order to trap people into committing what Steve Biko called 'technical crimes', so that they could be punished further. The constant awareness of being watched and belittled by policemen and bureaucrats, combined with the loneliness of isolation from dear friends, surely wore down the spirits of everyone subjected to a banning order.

Nonetheless, many banned people were resilient, dynamic individuals and none of them submitted willingly or fully to their restrictions. In most cases, the fact of being 'banned' merely increased their determination to resist. People found any and every loophole in their banning orders and devised ingenious methods to maintain at least a modicum of friendship, intimacy, family life and political struggle intact, in spite of everything. Decades later, the whole phenomenon of banning orders appears as just another confirmation of the idiocy and barbarism of government, and of apartheid in particular.

* * *

Rick Turner was banned on 26 February 1973. As a banned person, he was not allowed to be with more than one person at any time (other than family members). He was prohibited from setting foot on any university campus or in any factory, from speaking with any students or workers, or from entering any neighbourhoods or areas designated for African, Indian or coloured people. He was forbidden to publish his writing, and everyone else was forbidden to quote anything he said or wrote.

The banning order came at the height of Turner's activities as an educator, writer and activist. As a result of the banning, he was forced to adapt himself to deeply compromised circumstances and develop entirely new methods of social engagement. While he certainly suffered under the strain of his restrictions, he was nonetheless remarkably prolific throughout his banning years. Sadly, the banning years were the last years of his life, as he was murdered just a month before the order was set to expire. As he never had the chance to re-enter public life, many of his activities during the last five years of his life have remained hidden for decades, unknown to most people.

INVITED TO GIVE EVIDENCE

> Commission: In fact, you are politically a very active man, is that correct?
> Turner: I would say active, for an academic on an English campus, very active.
> Commission: Could you explain that please?
> Turner: Well, most of the academics are not very active or are completely inactive. So relatively speaking I am very active.[2]

Turner was banned along with 15 other people: seven members of Nusas, as well as eight members of Saso. These bannings were the direct outcome of the Schlebusch commission of inquiry, which had been set up by the government in 1972 to investigate a handful of oppositional organisations, so as to determine whether they should be viewed as a threat to the state. Four different bodies were targeted: Nusas, the Christian Institute, the University Christian Movement and the South African Institute of Racial Relations (SAIRR).

The members of these groups were called to testify before the commission without having any charges pressed against them and without any clear explanation of the purpose of the commission or the potential risks to those who participated. Formally, people were 'invited' to give evidence. However, despite the fact that the government called it a commission rather than a formal court, those who refused to give evidence had charges pressed against them in court, and the so-called findings of the commission were used as justification for harsh legal measures against both individuals and organisations that had given evidence.

The leadership of the Christian Institute and the SAIRR both refused to testify, out of fear that the commission was merely a set-up to provide the state with sufficient evidence to ban people. In the event, these suspicions proved to be accurate. The punishment for refusing to testify was a small monetary fine; far less of an imposition than a five-year banning order.[3]

Rick Turner was called to testify before the Schlebusch Commission on account of his role as an adviser to Nusas. Turner's reaction was to write a letter, outlining the ways in which he felt that the commission fundamentally misunderstood the role of Nusas (and universities in general) within a democratic society (which apartheid claimed to be). Stated politely and in the same patient, explanatory tone that was characteristic of Turner, the letter was nonetheless meant to convey his profound objection to the entire proceedings.

MEMORANDUM TO

COMMISSION OF INQUIRY INTO CERTAIN ORGANISATIONS.

I have been invited, apparently in my capacity as a member of the NUSAS Advisory Panel, to give evidence before your Commission. I would like to stress that I place this memorandum before you in my private capacity as a South African Citizen, rather than in my capacity as a member of the Advisory Panel.

As it is not clear to me why the Commission was set up in the first place, nor of what offences NUSAS and the other organisations concerned stand accused, I cannot, in this memorandum, either support or refute those charges. However, NUSAS has, in recent months, been the subject of a number of vaguely worded ministerial attacks. It has been accused of such offences as "internal terrorism" and "corrupting the youth". It seems to me to be important for the work of your Commission that these charges should be analysed.

The above, and similar, charges, may be referring to one of two things. Either -
a) it is being alleged that, in addition to its normal public activities, NUSAS is carrying out clandestine activities which involve "subversion" etc. or

b) it is being alleged that the normal public activities of NUSAS
are of such a nature as to subvert and corrupt.

However, it seems reasonable to assume that if these charges refer
to the first case, to clandestine subversive activities, then, as
this is a police matter, NUSAS, or those members of NUSAS allegedly
involved in these activities, would have been brought before the
courts, rather than before a Parliamentary Commission of Inquiry.
Thus I conclude that the accusations refer to the second case, to
the alleged results of NUSAS's public activities.

If this is the case, then it must be said immediately that these
accusations involve a misunderstanding of the nature of the
university, a misunderstanding of the nature of democracy, and a
misunderstanding of the central values of Western civilisation.
So before considering NUSAS any further, I feel that it is important
to get some clarity on these issues.

The university does not exist at the
government's pleasure.   A free university is as necessary to a
democracy as is an elected government.   The only responsibility
which the government has in respect of the university is to protect
its freedom.

The attempt to communicate through protest can only threaten a
government when that government is incapable of producing valid
counter-arguments.   Far from being undemocratic, it is of the
essence of democracy that protests of this kind should occur.   They
are essential for the spread of political debate, help to keep the
public informed of opposing view points, and, in the best cases, can
bring new and important truths to the attention of the public.

I have been willing to associate myself with NUSAS over the past
three years because it seems to me that within NUSAS students were
indeed trying to understand their society from a universalistic
position, rather than trying to act as a pressure group for the
interests of a particular segment of society;   and because it seems
to me that they are doing this in an open-minded, peaceful and
democratic way, and as such are carrying out their duty to the
public who finance the university.

Despite his serious misgivings, Turner eventually decided to comply with the commission's 'invitation' that he testify. His decision to participate in the commission was not rooted in fear, but was rather an expression of his general political orientation, which was transparent, open and honest. Furthermore, Turner was aware that the proceedings would be thoroughly documented, and he appreciated the opportunity to state his position on a number of political questions and to be clear about the activities he was engaged in.

> Schlebusch: It seems to me that you apparently say many things that you don't intend to ... with a meaning that you don't intend to convey?
> Turner: I think everybody does that nearly all the time.

For the commissioners, their primary concern was to establish that Turner had a powerful (and, in their eyes, detrimental) influence on white students. They attempted to prove that his involvement with Nusas had led to the organisation taking more radical political stands and bolstering its general willingness to oppose apartheid. Turner repeatedly admitted that he was asked for advice by students, and even that his advice was acted upon. However, he did not agree that his involvement with the students meant that he was directing them; rather, he saw himself as a facilitator. For example, Turner's description of his participation in Nusas leadership training is typical of his understanding of his role in relation to students: 'What I did was, I simply asked the students to talk about their problems and led the discussion from there.'[4]

But the inquiry was by no means limited to student activism. Turner was asked to speak about a wide range of activities. Based on its own infiltration and surveillance, the state had gathered a considerable dossier of reports of meetings, protests, seminars, lectures and cultural events in which Turner had been involved, as well as a great deal of his published writing. In each instance, the commissioners asked Turner to confirm that he had been a participant and had said the things he was quoted as saying. In the main, Turner agreed without hesitation that he had been present at the events mentioned, and repeatedly asserted that he still concurred with his previous statements. While he willingly took responsibility for his own actions, he steadfastly and repeatedly refused to give information about anyone else who might have been involved. It was clear from the entire proceedings that the state had already gathered all of the evidence it required (to its own satisfaction) to ban Turner, and was merely testing his willingness to supply any further 'intelligence' which it might be able to use against him or others.

The Schlebusch Commission was quite concerned by Turner's involvement with various organisations. He was asked to speak about his level of participation with nearly 20 of them, some political, some religious and some merely cultural.[5] Much of this questioning was indicative of the small-minded and paranoid attitude of the South African security forces, and little else. Turner was actually a member of only a few of the organisations that he was asked to speak about: Spro-cas, the SAIRR, the Education Reform Association, the Citizens Action Group, the Committee for Clemency and the International Film Society. That a film society should be cause for alarm to a government commission investigating potential threats to state security gives some indication of the state's mentality. Clearly, Turner's interest in cultural activities, his awareness of ideas from outside South Africa, was – in and of itself – threatening.

In most cases, Turner had only attended the organisations in question on one or two occasions, usually to give a talk, and sometimes as a participant in a meeting of some form. Many of the groups had goals and values that were dramatically different from his own. For Turner, engaging with a wide range of different organisations was merely an expression of his overall appreciation of and belief in dialogue. For the state, this level of engagement with an array of groups seemed to represent a particularly untrustworthy sort of personality. The South African security apparatus appeared on the whole constitutionally incapable of comprehending that Turner was not an 'operative' for some organisation or other (especially not a clandestine, hierarchical Party) but rather an autonomous and intelligent person.

Urgently aware that the law strictly forbade the advocacy of communism in any form, Turner's main defence for his comments on Marxism, socialism and communism was that he was a professor of political science, and therefore his duty as an academic required him to study seriously all variety of political thought. For example, when asked to comment on a particularly damning indictment of apartheid-style capitalism that he had written – 'Capitalism refracted through the apartheid structure is far more inhuman, far more irrational in terms of the needs of the people than is the welfare state capitalism of Western Europe with all its failings. Direct and indirect thought manipulation is far more thorough here where even the most anodyne news items are impregnated with racialism' – Turner nonchalantly replied, 'I think it is a fair academic comment on the situation in South Africa, which I will certainly stand by.'[6]

In spite of any attempts he made to deny them, Turner's anti-capitalist sympathies were undeniable, and clearly apparent to the commission.

> *Excerpt from a talk given to the UCM, which begins 'I am not a Christian'.*
> 1. *God talk is either completely meaningless or else consists in referring to some phenomenon or fact as God and implying that you are thereby saying something more about the fact without saying what it is that you are saying about it. Meaningless talk is irrelevant.*
> 2. *What is relevant is the problem of this world, of man. This problem can only be solved by exploring this world in the light of reason, not by referring to the Gospels, since the Gospels only express an ethic, a good ethic, but one that is powerless unless it rests on an accurate analysis of the situation.*
> 3. *An analysis of the political situation shows that men are responsible for the violence of their societies and that the only way out of this, the only way to love one's neighbour, is through the attempt to build a socialist society.*
> 4. *Religion has often served, and often still serves, as an opiate and as an obstruction to this endeavour. What should be relevant to an organized church should be the attempt to turn their religion from being a tranquillizer to being a revolutionary stimulant.*

While Turner's commitment to socialism was certainly genuine and quite openly stated, in fact the state needed next to no evidence in order to justify its decision to ban him. As Donald Woods wrote, 'Theoretically, a banned person is entitled to ask the minister the reasons for his ban, but what happens is this: every banning order begins with words to the effect that whereas the minister is satisfied that you are engaging in activities which endanger public safety, he hereby ... and when you apply to him for his reasons, his reply is that the reason for the ban is that he is satisfied that you are engaging in activities which endanger public safety.'[7]

I HEREBY PROHIBIT YOU

TO: RICHARD ALBERT DAVID TURNER
(I.N. 014/532651)
32 DALTON ROAD
BELLAIR
DURBAN

NOTICE IN TERMS OF SECTION 9(1) OF THE SUPPRESSION OF
COMMUNISM ACT, 1950 (ACT 44 OF 1950)

WHEREAS I, PETRUS CORNELIUS PELSER, Minister of Justice, am satisfied that you engage in activities which are furthering or are calculated to further the achievement of any of the objects of communism, I hereby, in terms of section 9(1) of the Suppression of Communism Act, 1950 prohibit you for a period commencing on the date on which this notice is delivered or tendered to you and expiring on 31 March 1978 from attending within the Republic of South Africa or the territory of South-West Africa:

a) Any social gathering, that is to say, any gathering at which the persons present also have social intercourse with one another;

b) Any political gathering, that is to say, any gathering at which any form of State or any principle or policy of the Government of a State is propagated, defended, attacked, criticized or discussed;

c) Any gathering of pupils or students assembled for the purpose of being instructed, trained or addressed by you.

NOTICE IN TERMS OF SECTION 10(1)(a) OF THE SUPPRESSION OF COMMUNISM ACT, 1950 (ACT 44 OF 1950)

Further, I hereby prohibit you for a period commencing on the date on which this notice is delivered or tendered to you and expiring on 31 March 1978, from:

(1) absenting yourself from the magisterial district of Durban

(2) being within

    (a) any university, college, school, etc.

    (b) any body, organization, group or association of persons mainly consisting of students or scholars, and particularly the National Union of South African Students

    (c) the premises of any factory

    (d) any harbour

    (e) any area set apart by any law for the occupation of Coloured or Asiatic people

    (f) any Bantu area

(3) communicating in any manner whatsoever with any person whose name appears on the list of prohibited people under the Suppression of Communism Act or the Riotous Assemblies Act

(4) performing any of the following acts:

    (a) preparing, compiling, printing, publishing, or disseminating in any manner any publication which

        (i) discusses, refers to, criticizes or attacks any policy or principle of the government

        (ii) contains any matter related to any unlawful organization

        (iii) contains any matter which is likely to engender feelings of hostility between the while and non-white inhabitants of South Africa

(b) giving any educational instruction in any manner
or form to any persons other than a person of whom
you are a parent

Given under my hand at Cape Town on this 26th day of
February, 1973.

MINISTER OF JUSTICE

Under apartheid law, banning orders were not considered to take effect
until they had been hand-delivered to the person in question. A Durban
police officer handed Turner his banning order, after tracking him down
to a party at a friend's house. This gathering would be the last social event
that Turner would freely attend for the rest of his life.

When Turner received his banning order, he immediately applied for a
series of exemptions. For banned people, winning any kind of exemption
allowed for a crucial amount of breathing room for the years to come.
Even to have the right to attend one social gathering a month would be
a profound shift in the general feeling of isolation. Furthermore, most
police officers would not read the banning order or exemptions carefully,
and so would be less likely to interfere with someone who had any kind
of exemption, for fear of making a mistake.

While most people applied for a small exemption, such as the right to
play chess at a chess club or to continue to play sports, Turner essentially
applied for an exemption from all his restrictions. On the prohibition
against interacting with students, he applied for an exemption to 'perform
[his] normal teaching duties'. On the prohibition against publishing, he
applied for the right to publish scholarly articles and books. He also
applied for an exemption in order to be able to enter coloured and Indian
areas of Durban.[8]

Predictably, his application for exemptions was denied.

GP-S-(F-L)

Section 'A.1'

SUID-AFRIKAANSE POLISIE SOUTH AFRICAN POLICE

SAP 148(f)

DEPARTMENT VAN JUSTISIE

11 -6-1973

PRETORIA

DEPARTMENT OF JUSTICE

P/sak - P/Bag X302 Tel. adr. - add. "KOMPOL"

Verw./Ref.:	S.1/8242.
Navrae/Enq.:	Lt.-col. P.H. Fabricius.
TEL.:	29281 x 311.

VEILIGHEIDSTAK
SECURITY BRANCH

HOOFKANTOOR
HEAD OFFICE

PRETORIA

8.6.1973.

The Secretary for Justice,
P R E T O R I A.

RESTRICTIONS : Richard TURNER.
10/3/2/1 - 56 (VB) dated 7.5.1973.

1.   The applicant has a marked ability to influence
others and was ardently followed by students and student
leaders while he was a lecturer at the University of Natal,
Durban. He is described by connoisseurs in the field of
political and social science as a Marxian revolusionist.

2.   In an era of racial- and labour conflicts, conditions
are ideal for applicant with his influence and knowledge
of social science and philosophy to promote the idea of a
social and economic change in the R.S.A. TURNER has the
gift to write and to convey his views to his readers.

3.   In view of the above it is considered highly
undesirable that TURNER be allowed on the premises of -
or to lecture at any educational institution, including
the University of Durban-Westville or to publish works in
any form.

4.   Regarding applicant's request that the prohibition
in respect of areas set apart for the occupation of Coloured-
and Asiatic persons be relaxed, it must be stressed that
applicant played a prominent part in the activities of the
Natal Indian Congress and the Coloured Labour Party prior to
being restricted. TURNER has for some time been living
with a Coloured-Indian half-caste woman Fozia Fischer, who
has been furthering his subversive activities and has acted
as his mouthpiece, since his restriction. It is felt that
against this background, the concession applied for, should
not be granted.

Brigadier.
f/COMMISIONER : SOUTH AFRICAN POLICE.
H.C.V. GILLIERS

NOT LIMITED AT ALL

GEHEIM/SECRET

Regional office [of the security police] Durban was approached to deliver commentary on subject's activities. On 1 April 1974 it is reported as follows: He lives with Foszia Fischer who is directly involved with the black labour force and his influence can be felt in the labour unrest. Foszia Fischer has the ideal opportunity to act as middle man for Subject and his associates. Furthermore he moves around freely and reconnaissance services brought to light that he is in regular contact with many persons across Durban – public restaurants and private houses. The existing restrictions have not limited his movement at all and visitors still regularly visit his house.

Like most other banned people, Rick Turner's reaction to the banning order was to attempt, to the fullest extent possible, to ignore the restrictions, or at least not to let any of them actually limit his life. The wording used in the order was painstakingly precise and so constructed as to leave no possible room for loopholes. But the irony was that the restrictions were so severe that they became absurd in practice. In trying to control virtually every detail of Turner's life, the state put itself in a position where it could not possibly succeed.

For example, the prohibition against 'giving any educational instruction in any manner or form to any person other than a person of whom you are a parent' is ridiculously difficult to enforce. How could any police force ever reasonably hope to stop someone from educating other people 'in any manner or form'? They could successfully remove him from his classroom at the university, and even prevent him from setting foot on campus, but they could never stop him from being an educator.

Allowing Turner to educate his children meant, of course, that both Jann and Kim learned at a very young age that they had been born into a deeply unjust society and that their father suffered dearly for daring to oppose it. Despite being restricted to the Durban area and able to see his daughters only briefly each year (they lived with their mother, in Cape Town), Turner continued to have a steady presence in their lives through regular correspondence. His letters were often in the form of small collage books, and were designed to be educational. He explained in language comprehensible to a nine-year-old girl everything from how to build a new bookshelf, to what exactly a banning order meant, to what kind of a city Johannesburg was, and why the young people in Soweto started their uprising in June 1976. Describing the wave of wildcat strikes in Durban at the start of 1973, Rick wrote to Jann: 'Lots of men said that their bosses were not paying them enough money. So they said they would not do any more work until they got paid more. All the factories stopped, and so the bosses had to pay more, to get the workers to work again. I want to write about it, so I have to try and find out what was happening.'[9]

Even at the level of the university, Turner's influence could not be completely curtailed. During the banning years, Rick sustained positive relationships with a number of his peers from the university. He met regularly with Fatima and Ismail Meer (despite all three being banned), with Raphael de Kadt and Tony Morphet. According to informants working for the security police, Turner's influence as a lecturer made a lasting impact on the overall curriculum of the political science department, even after his banning. Further, the university Senate voted unanimously in June 1973 to continue paying his regular salary, regardless of the banning order in effect. The decision was meant to convey to the state an absolute unwillingness to demonise Turner for his convictions.

Through all manner of ambiguities and loopholes, Turner continued to find ways to be active politically and intellectually, and maintain his connections with student activists and others with whom he had a strong affinity. While he was not entirely under house arrest, his movements were severely restricted and were watched carefully by the police. As a result, the house at 32 Dalton Avenue became the centre of Turner's life during the banning years. To the extent possible, Rick and Foszia kept their home as a space that was welcoming to a wide array of people, full of vibrant conversations and a feeling of community.

Our community

Foszia Fisher

Having a full house was also good because it meant that if we were raided they would be hard pressed to prove anything. Well, they couldn't say who could or could not live in the house. All they could stipulate was that Rick couldn't be with more than one person at a time. They couldn't tell him how to live. The house could always be full of people. When the police knocked on the door or when they descended, Rick just had not to be in that space where everybody was. And the rooms were all connected, so one could easily disappear. But if we were on our own, we would have been at high risk. So, it was a conscious decision to live in a community.

But our community began to lessen over the five-year banning period. People gradually moved out during the banning years. Also, with the banning order we didn't go out as much as we had before. People would come and visit from Johannesburg and Cape Town, but only on occasion, so we spent a great deal in each other's company, talking. I guess in those eight years we lived together, in a funny way we had more time together than most people have. After Rick died, I think the people I saw was even less.

What was interesting with the banning was that Rick was forced to be more in the background. It made him prolific with his writing, and he stayed active as he was able, but he could not take a leadership position and other people were obliged to put themselves out there. I think that's always good. As a leader, Rick wouldn't have pushed anybody; he would be challenging, but he wouldn't assume an authoritarian role. Still, one of the debates we used to have was about how automatic it was that people made space for him to assume leadership, and I said to him, 'You must be careful – people are relying too much on you, that's always bad. They just assume that you will provide the answers. People get lazy and there is always a backlash to that.'

EDUCATION IN ANY MANNER OR FORM

While the banning forced Rick Turner into the background, this didn't at all mean that he ceased being a leader within the circles of those fighting for social justice. In fact, during the first year of his banning, Turner's influence on activist initiatives was felt quite strongly, both through his advice and support to others, and through his writing.

As Turner's main influence among students came as a result of extended and frequent lectures and conversations, being cut off from the campus and from his normal teaching duties was certainly a powerful blow. Nonetheless, he did stay in close contact with a number of young student activists and continued to play a mentoring role through one-on-one meetings at his home.

GEHEIM/SECRET

On 5.5.1973 a delicate source reports that Barbara Stonestreet from Cape Town (previously wife of subject) said to Foszia Fischer that she (Barbara) will contact NUSAS restrictees in Cape Town and will convey any news that she may gather to subject.

In addition, Turner continued to have a presence at public gatherings, by writing speeches that his friends were able to deliver. While this surely seemed an ingenious technique at the time and did succeed at getting his message out, it did not in any way manage to elude the watchful eye of the Special Branch.

GEHEIM/SECRET

During a meeting held on 20 March 1973 at the University Natal, Durban, that dealt with 'Race and Society', Professor Lawrence Schlemmer spoke on 'Does race difference necessarily lead to political conflict: an examination of some theories'. Subject could not attend this meeting because of his restriction but drafted his piece for Schlemmer. Here he says the following: 'The people who took the leadership in the labour strikes were seen by the authorities as agitators and because of this were suppressed. Educated blacks feel together with white liberals frustrated and they are taking action to change their lot.'

The most important issue of 1973 for Turner was the steady growth in organising labour in the aftermath of the wildcat strikes at the start of the year. He found multiple outlets to engage with labour struggles, and in this way built solid working relationships with a group of close friends.

In the months after the banning order, Rick Turner simultaneously initiated three projects: the *South African Labour Bulletin* (a periodical), the Institute for Industrial Education (a correspondence course for workers) and a labour research group. Though Turner wrote the majority of the content of the first edition of the *Bulletin*, over time the constraints placed on him by his banning made it impossible to do much more than contribute the occasional article under a pen-name. Nonetheless, the *Bulletin* continued publication and after his death even gained prominence, with a reputation for being the most steadfast and thorough South African periodical to cover news related to working-class concerns (while remaining always independent of trade unions).

The third project, to establish a group focused on researching labour issues, never really got off the ground. It was the second initiative, the Institute for Industrial Education (IIE), that quickly became the project in which Turner became most deeply involved.

As an idea, the IIE came out of the group of people who worked together with Turner on the research and writing of the book *The Durban Strikes*. Foszia Fisher served as director for most of the life of the organisation. Other close friends involved were Halton Cheadle, Omar Badsha, Lawrence Schlemmer and Eddie Webster. In addition, the IIE had clear sympathies with the emerging black trade union movement, and actively sought collaboration with trade union leaders such as Harriet Bolton, John Copelyn and Alec Erwin.

The IIE was never intended to be a training programme, but rather a broader educational programme, with the same values and goals that informed Turner's own classroom at the university. Turner's writing provided the bulk of the curriculum and content. This had two main components. The first was to study the structure of capitalism and the role of workers within that structure. The second dealt with working-class organisation. There was a constant interplay within the curriculum between these two components.

The broad outline of the lessons was as follows:

1. *People only work for other people when they have no alternative*: that is, when they have no direct access to the means of production, and so cannot work for themselves. This means that those who control the means of production have power over those who do not.[10]

2. *There is much INEQUALITY* in the distribution of income. This inequality is connected with: (a) property ownership, (b) education and training. We can therefore divide society up into three CLASSES: OWNING CLASS, MIDDLE CLASS, AND WORKING CLASS. Although there is some movement between classes, most people stay in the class in which they were born.[11]

3. *The interests of the working class are in conflict with those of the other classes* in two ways ... It is in the interests of the working class for there to be greater equality. It is in the interest of both the middle and the owning class to keep society unequal. There is also conflict over

discipline and control ... Workers would like to have more control over their lives and their jobs. They would like to make decisions instead of just obeying orders ... On the other hand, managers try to keep control over anything if they can.[12]

And then ...

4. Therefore, as workers, you must organize in your own interests.
5. There is a history, in South Africa and globally, of workers organizing in their own interests.
6. There are some basic organizational skills necessary to build a workers' organization.
7. There are some problems you might come across in the process, which could be better avoided if you are aware of them.

Creatively open-ended

Lawrence Schlemmer

The Institute for Industrial Education was creatively open-ended. Nothing was pre-planned. That was the last thing Rick would have done. That's where his creativity, his serendipity, his ability to look for things that would surprise you, came into play.

What Rick was saying, through the IIE, was, 'Listen, these workers are oppressed people. We've got to take their consciousness seriously and see where they're at. We need to give them the intellectual tools and the awareness to occupy whatever power base they're going to create, meaningfully.'

He asked us not to decide *for them*, but to let them see for themselves what they must do to change their situation. Our task was to give them the tools to grow. This was very untidy for an ideologue on both sides of the political spectrum, and Rick was not a tidy person. He did not operate within anybody's boundaries. Except he had a commitment which was as resolute as anyone.

155

The idea with the IIE

Foszia Fisher

The idea with the Institute for Industrial Education was to enable people to be free participants and functioning members of society at every level – not just in the factory, not just as workers, but as people. For workers to be able to make decisions about their own lives, they needed to have enough information to express what it is that they want. The goal was to have people thinking for themselves, rather than simply getting the solution from someone else.

Since the working hours were very long and very hard, it was a lot to expect people to spend at meetings. So, we thought we would have weekend long gatherings, like quarterly or monthly, for workers to come together and discuss things, to reflect on their studies. The level of literacy was quite low; I mean, some people could read, or at least they could read in Zulu (so the workbooks were printed in both languages), but a lot of people could not read at all. So, the gatherings would give an opportunity to have workers support one another, to go through the ideas together.

But, at the time, if anyone would have discussion groups, the security police would see it as people engaging in revolutionary or underground activities, so that would make them even more mindful. So, while we definitely wanted to create spaces where people could come in and talk and discuss, we also realised that the more we did, the more we would jeopardise the project and the individuals involved. We only had maybe two of the weekend seminars between 1974 and '75, before everything happened.

Mostly we just focused on giving the workbooks to as many people as possible and hoping that somehow within the way that they lived they would manage to have conversations with fellow workers without making it become obvious. There was something about trusting in people's natural ways of connecting with each other.

We put a lot of trust in people, and it mostly worked really well. The workbooks had questions in them, and workers would send the answers back. Then, we would comment on their responses and talk to them, either by writing back to them or sending messages via the union organiser. There would be some kind of interaction.

There were a number of reasons for adopting the correspondence format for the Institute. First, there were practical considerations. Turner was banned from engaging in any kind of educational setting whatsoever, and was furthermore banned from writing anything at all. A correspondence course allowed him to produce educational materials anonymously, and without ever stepping foot inside a university.[13] Furthermore, state restrictions on educational institutes were more lax than those placed on political organisations or trade unions. Therefore, with a modicum of legal credibility, the IIE hoped to survive longer than other initiatives, as well as raise funds abroad. In addition, as an approved organisation, the IIE could expect to attract more workers to take part in the study than if the project were viewed with suspicion by the authorities.

As the ultimate usefulness of the curriculum depended on workers applying their knowledge to their own circumstances, it was crucial that they share their studies with each other. The foundational document of the IIE stated this goal as follows: 'We hope to encourage each student who enrols in the course to recruit a few more workers in the firm so that they will be able to work as a group, helping each other with problematical concepts, discussing problems during their lunch breaks and travel time and working together on practical projects ... The questions will be designed so as to make it necessary for the student to use the concepts acquired in the course to think about his or her own work situation.'[14]

'Trusting in people's natural ways of connecting' was a central part of the vision behind the IIE. In its own words, the IIE conceived of its educational programme as 'not oriented towards examinations and achievement of social status, but rather towards exploration and the development of skills in action, and social cooperation'.[15]

ODDLY POWERLESS

GEHEIM/SECRET

On 29.8.1973 the Security Police effected a raid on Subject where the following people were present: Foszia Fischer, Halton Cheadle, David Hemson and Eddie Webster. Subject was not trapped with the group and he explained that the last three visitors were for Foszia Fischer. The people mentioned are all concerned with the 'Institute for Industrial Education'.

All the ways that Turner found to remain involved in politics after he was banned went against the restrictions outlined in his banning order. Any form of participation in publishing was expressly forbidden. Any process of reproducing or distributing Turner's writing was illegal. Any gathering of a group of people (larger than two) having any kind of 'social intercourse' was forbidden, in particular any gathering that 'discussed, referred to, attacked, or advocated' any policy or principle at all. Also, the intention behind the prohibition on Turner entering any factory or workplace was clearly to keep Turner out of labour struggles. The Special Branch surely had knowledge of his involvement with labour (quite likely, even fairly intimate and detailed information) but was oddly powerless to stop any of it or even to prove that he was doing it.

While Turner's first year as a banned person passed relatively well, and while he found a number of ways to stay connected to dear friends and to social movements, it was not a situation that could really last. The state was quite determined to minimise his impact on the growing 'unrest' in the country. In the years to come, the authorities would continue to put pressure on him, to harass him and his family, and seek ways to further isolate him from his friends and community.

NINE

The Days Grow Lonelier over Time

'Partly, I suppose, it is a function of the frustration of being here at a very interesting time, but not being able to take any political part. Basically, however, I feel that for the moment I can best contribute by doing some good philosophizing, and I have reached the point at which I intellectually need the stimulus of a good philosophic community.'[1]

– RICK TURNER

TO BE A BANNED PERSON was to be made to suffer a slow but steady erosion of all significance, a letting go of any and all possible impact on others. The stipulations outlined in the original banning order were merely the beginning of a determined campaign of erasure. If the labyrinth of limitations didn't immediately succeed in shutting the person down, there were always other ways of trying to force people to disappear.

In Rick Turner's case, the banning was a terrible nuisance, but he was able to manoeuvre round it fairly well. He also had a lot of help from Foszia and others who cared about him. Unfortunately, time was on the side of the state, and time itself was one of the most corrosive elements of the banning experience. Five years is a long time. A lot can happen in five years, but banning is meant to ensure that virtually nothing does.

The 'subject' is meant to endure the slow decay of normal levels of productivity into a deeper and deeper state of silence and isolation. Then, if five years of relative obscurity wasn't long enough to erase the person's will-power, the government could always decide to reinstate the banning order for an additional five years. Banning was a waiting game, and only the state had anything to gain from time passing. The architects of apartheid always knew that their regime might have an expiration date. They saw threats to their existence in all directions (and often with good reason). Banning prominent dissidents was a way of buying time, of expanding the shelf life of a doomed project.

After the first year of Turner's banning order, the Special Branch realised that something would need to be done to further limit his activities and his impact on others. They understood clearly the methods that Turner was using to circumvent his restrictions, but this was not enough to allow them to arrest him or stop him entirely. A number of different strategies were debated by the authorities, including putting Turner under full house arrest and banning Foszia Fisher. However, in the end, the most effective method to reduce his impact on social movements was to place increasing pressure on his peers and collaborators, to cut him off from any sympathetic audience, from any real outlet for his intellectual work. Worst of all, where the state was unable to succeed in isolating Turner, the movement itself cut him off, as we shall see. As a result of these combined pressures, Turner's last years were increasingly lonely, although he struggled always to maintain his intellectual capacities, to keep thinking and writing.

* * *

STRONGER RESTRICTIONS

GF S·(F-L)

SAP 148 (f)

SUID-AFRIKAANSE POLISIE  SOUTH AFRICAN POLICE

P/sak - P/Bag X302   Tel. scr. adc. 'KOMPOL'

Verw/Ref	S.1/2242
Nav ac/Enq	Maj. P.J. Rossouw
Tel	29221 x 310

GEHEIM

VEILIGHEIDSTAK
SECURITY BRANCH

HOOFKANTOOR
HEAD OFFICE

PRETORIA

2.10.1974

Die Sekretaris van Justisie
P R E T O R I A

STRENGER INPERKING : Richard A.C. TURNER

1.   Sedert TURNER op 27.2.1973 onder groep 'C' ingeperk is, gaan hy syns onbelemmerd met sy ondermynende bedrywighede agter die skerms voort. Hy is n geleerde; besonder intelligent en is die breinkrag agter die aktiwiteite van sekere radikale studente en persone soos Foszia FISHER, die VERULERS e.a. wat onder die skyn van humanitêre dienste onder nie-blanke werknemers eintlik arbeidsonrus aanstook.

2.   Dit word voorgestel dat Richard TURNER se inperkingskennisgewing gewysig word dat hy onder Groep 'B' tot sy tuiste te Daltonweg 32, Bellair en die landdrosdistrik van Durban ingeperk word en dat hy sy tuiste nie mag verlaat behalwe op die volgende tye:

    (i)   Tussen 7 vm. en 6 nm. gedurende weeksdae, d.w.s. Maandae tot Vrydae; en

    (ii) Tussen 10 vm. en 12 n.d. op Sondae.

Verder word aanbeveel dat hy geen besoekers aan gemelde tuiste mag ontvang nie, behalwe.

    (a) n mediese praktisyn vir bona fide mediese behandeling;

    (b) die volgende persone wat op gemelde perseel inwoon;

        (i)   Derek WANG

        (ii) Veronica WANG

        (iii) Wendy TAYLOR

    (c) sy twee kinders Jan en Kim TAYLOR en sy moeder mevrou W.J. TURNER.

2/....

- 2 - GEHEIM

3.	'n Aanvullende memorandum ten opsigte van Richard
TURNER word hierby aangeheg asook die gebruiklike Justi-
sie-vraelys.

4.	Foszia FISHER met wie hy saangeleef het en wie
ongetwyfeld sy mondstuk was na sy inperking, het op
27.9.1974 vanaf Jan Smutslughawe met 'n enkel reiskaartjie
na Londen vertrek. Dit word vermoed dat sy nie weer sal
terugkeer nie.

5.	'n Aanbeveling ten opsigte van haar inperking word
dus agterweë gehou.

Brigadier
h/KOMMISSARIS - SUID-AFRIKAANSE POLISIE
M.C.W. GELDENHUYS
/Isur

Stronger restrictions: Richard A.D. Turner

1. Since Turner was restricted under group 'C' on 27.2.1973 he has continued almost unhindered with his subversive activities behind the scenes. He is an intellectual; exceptionally intelligent and is the brains behind the activities of certain radical students and persons like Foszia Fisher, the Websters, etc. and others who actually foment labour unrest under the pretence of humanitarian services among non-white workers.

2. It is proposed that Richard Turner's restriction order be revised so that he is restricted under group 'B' to his home at 32 Dalton Rd, Bellair, and the magisterial district of Durban and that he not be allowed to leave his home except at the following times: (i) between 7 a.m. and 6 p.m. during weekdays, i.e. Mondays to Fridays; and (ii) between 10 a.m. and 12 midday on Sundays. Furthermore, it is recommended that he receive no visitors at the aforementioned home except: (a) a medical practitioner for bona fide medical treatment; (b) the following persons who live on the premises mentioned: (i) Derek Wang (ii) Veronica Wang (iii) Wendy Taylor; (c) his two children Ian and Kim Taylor [sic] and his mother Mrs W.J. Turner.

3. A supplementary memorandum in connection with Richard Turner is attached herewith as well as the usual Justice questionnaire.

4. Foszia Fisher, with whom he lived and who was undoubtedly his mouthpiece after his restriction, left for London from Jan Smuts Airport on 27.9.1974 on a one-way ticket. It is suspected that she will not return again.

5. A recommendation in connection with her restriction is therefore being held back.

Rick Turner's relationship with Foszia Fisher was special for a number of reasons. The most remarkable thing was that it was allowed to continue at all. As an openly cross-racial relationship, living together as they did in the same household, their daily love violated the most basic principles of apartheid. It would have been far easier to prove that Turner was guilty of racial mixing than that he was a communist. Other white men were harassed much more for having relations with black women that were far less permanent and profound.

Had the state wanted to cause him a great deal of suffering, hassle and public humiliation, it would have been a relatively straightforward process to press charges against him for his marriage. There would of course have been the rather delicate and embarrassing matter of having to prove somehow that Rick and Foszia were in fact lovers – quite literally, the police would have needed to catch them in the act – as well as myriad other sordid details. To pursue such a trial would have laid the state open to ridicule and protest from various angles, and would have required an explanation for the decision to prioritise such a petty issue as a matter of state security. But then again, the pettiness of racialism was central to apartheid policy. Prosecuting Turner would have been quite a reasonable choice, in so far as apartheid was reasonable.

Perhaps the Special Branch believed it unwise to focus on the marriage because they felt that they could eventually come down on Turner for something even more damning: some imagined conspiracy with guerrillas, some liaison with Moscow or some wild hippie rebellion spreading across university campuses. Whatever the state's reasons for keeping quiet about Rick's love for Foszia, the threat posed by the marriage was clearly more than skin-deep.

The ways which Rick and Foszia found to continue working together on intellectual and activist projects, even after the imposition of the banning order, were clearly of grave concern. The Special Branch knew that in their private life at home, politics played a prominent role, and that many guests who came to the house were actively involved in organising against apartheid. They knew that Rick and Foszia had created the IIE as a collaborative effort, with Rick doing the writing and Foszia acting as the director. They understood clearly that Foszia was able to disseminate Turner's ideas in the wider world and to bring news back home to him.

Furthermore, Foszia was, in her own right, quite active and influential.

That Foszia was never arrested for her political work or placed under a banning order remains a bit of a mystery. In a secret memorandum of 1974, the Special Branch claimed that they saw no reason to ban her because she was leaving for England on a one-way ticket. But then, of course, the state had had to approve of this journey, and allow her to fly on her South African passport (even though she was going to England to attend a Marxist conference, to present a paper that Turner had written). Perhaps the police genuinely believed, or hoped, that Foszia would stay in Europe permanently, thereby leaving Rick at home alone, without anyone to help connect him to the outside world. Nonetheless, the idea of banning Foszia was dropped, and she was allowed to return to South Africa after her short trip to Europe. Then, of course, as the Special Branch must have known she would, Foszia returned to her political work and remained a steadfast ally of Turner's.

The issue of banning Foszia was raised again in 1976: the police even came to the house in Dalton Avenue to discuss the matter with her. Ironically, the fact that she was living with Rick, in a white neighbourhood, provided a logical barrier that proved difficult for the state to get around. In a letter to a friend, Rick explained the strange set of contradictory forces that tripped the Special Branch up in their attempts to take action against Foszia:

As you know, Foszia has been working in the trade union movement here in Durban. She was recently visited by SB people wanting information about her and hinting at a possible banning order. Among other things they wanted to know her address, but refused to accept this address, on the grounds that the Minister could not break the law by banning her to a white group area.

She and I went to see the local commander, Colonel Steenkamp, and discussed it with him. He said that they did not wish to interfere in our personal lives, but reiterated the argument about the address, and said that if Foszia did not provide an alternative address, then they would, if necessary, provide one for her.

Finally, my mother, who is staying with us, agreed to employ Foszia as a secretary companion, so that she would then be entitled to stay on the premises as a bona-fide employee. We naturally refused to provide any alternative address. They were a bit dubious about this, but we have not heard anything since this occurred at the end of January.[2]

Even though the state never acted directly against Foszia for her marriage to Rick or for her political work, it did take action against a number of Turner's other allies. At exactly the moment when the Special Branch was discussing the option of placing Turner under house arrest, proceedings were under way to ban a number of young activists who had played a critical role in developing the trade union movement for black workers.

Within the first year after the 1973 Durban strikes, some 100,000 workers joined the newly formed trade unions, and smaller, less dramatic strikes continued throughout the year. Much of the organisation among black workers was driven by a group of energetic young white radicals, who together formed the Trade Union Advisory and Coordinating Council (TUACC). Initially, the IIE had a collaborative relationship with TUACC, and members of the union structure also cooperated in running the institute. Thus, when David Hemson, Paula Ensor, Halton Cheadle and others were all banned at the start of 1974, this put a serious dent in TUACC's efforts, and at the same time also limited Turner's capacity to influence the emerging trade union movement.

Banning people who were sympathetic to Turner and who collaborated with him on different projects not only reduced Turner's impact on the movement, but also increased his isolation. Over the years of his banning, successive waves of repression would continue to narrow his social life down to a smaller and smaller circle around his own home.

In September 1974 a few dozen Black Consciousness activists were arrested for demonstrating in support of the newly independent (and socialist) Mozambique, and then were subjected to a long legal process.[3] Turner was eventually called to testify before the court about his sympathetic stances in relation to the defendants, and to answer to the accusation that his book *The Eye of the Needle* had played a role in radicalising the black activists. Nine of the accused were convicted, in 1976. In the same year, another set of banning orders was handed down to labour organisers, once again weakening the resources of the budding union movement.

In addition, a number of close friends suffered other forms of harassment by the state, such as being held under the 90-day detention law, having charges pressed against them, and having police pressure placed on their employers. Also, all through Turner's adult life many of his socially conscious peers made the decision to leave South Africa altogether, rather than live under the stifling atmosphere of apartheid. John Clare, his childhood friend, had left already in 1963; Andrew Colman, his friend from Rhodes, left in 1969, Michael Hubbard, his brother-in-law, left in 1971. A number of the young leaders within Nusas (some of whom were banned along with Turner) also fled the country. Some were able to leave voluntarily and legally, some were forced out, and many others found ways to escape illegally. This movement of anti-apartheid activists into exile accelerated in the 1970s.

All these factors combined to reduce Rick Turner's capacity to play any kind of role in openly opposing the apartheid state. Having effectively whittled down his sphere of influence quite severely, the Special Branch decided in 1975 not to go any further with the stronger restrictions on Turner that they had once thought would be necessary.

Meanwhile, within the ranks of the opposition, divisions began to arise between Rick Turner (and his allies) and leaders within the trade union movement, many of whom had once been close friends. In the end, the IIE, which had begun as a hopeful collaboration between union organisers and academics, would collapse into oblivion, with all the power and money going to the unions – and bad feelings in both directions.

* * *

G.P.-S.41079—1969-70—20,000

J 300

KAAPSTAD   LÊER No. 10/3/2/1-3107
                FILE

DEPARTEMENT VAN JUSTISIE/DEPARTMENT OF JUSTICE

+377

DIE SEKRETARIS / MINISTER
THE SECRETARY

G E H E I M
============

INPERKING : RICHARD ALBERT DAVID TURNER

1.   Die Minister het by geleenthede navraag gedoen oor
die wenslikheid daarvan om Turner strenger in te perk.
Hierdie voorlegging word na aanleiding daarvan gemaak.

3.   Voordat die gedagte van 'n breë ondersoek aan die
Minister voorgelê kon word, het Kompol aangedui dat hy
'n nuwe aanbeveling in verband met Turner se strenger
inperking sou maak. Gedurende Oktober 1974 het Kompol
toe aanbeveel dat Turner onder groep (b) ingeperk word.
Kompol het aangedui dat Foszia Fisher gedurende September
1974 na Londen vertrek het en dat daar vermoed is dat
sy nie na die Republiek sou terugkeer nie. (2.10.74).
Kort hierna het Kompol telefonies aangedui dat Foszia
Fisher wel na die Republiek sou terugkeer en het versoek
dat Turner se strenger inperking agterweë gehou word
tot tyd en wyl daar sekerheid oor Fisher verkry is. (Nota
(b)). Kompol berig nou soos volg:

"Dit wil voorkom of bogenoemde (Turner) in die jongste
tyd nie met dieselfde ywer van voorheen met sy bedrywighede voortgaan nie. Sedert hierdie Departement se
enersgenommerde skrywe van 2.10.74 waarin strenger
inperkingsmaatreëls teen hom aanbeveel is, is min
oor Turner verneem. Dit is moontlik dat die arrestasie
van die 36 SASO en BPC-lede gedurende Oktober 1974

wat tans nog aangehou word n heilsame uitwerking
op linkse elemente oor die algemeen het en is die
klimaat vir die voortsetting van sy doelstellings
nie meer so gunstig soos voorheen nie.

Bostaande in ag geneem is dit miskien wenslik dat
daar nie op die huidige net die oorweging van strenger
maatreëls,teen hom voortgegaan word nie". (17.1.73)

5.   Voorheen was Turner baie bedrywig in die beïnvloeding
van studente se denkrigtings en in hulle aktivering.
Hy het dit gedoen deur talle vergaderings, simposiums,
besprekingsgroepe en ander byeenkomste dwarsoor die land
toe te spreek, deur artikels vir verskeie publikasies
voor te berei en verál deur studente aan die universiteit
waar hy n lektor was, binne en buite sy klasse intens
te bearbei. Die inperkings waaraan hy tans onderhewig
is, het hom effektief sy studente-invloedsfeer ontneem.
Of strenger inperking dieselfde ten opsigte van sy invloed
in arbeidskringe sal vermag, is te betwyfel. Hy is daar
nie openlik bedrywig nie. Hy gee heimlik raad deur middel
van tussengangers, in persoonlike gesprekke en met die
voorbereiding van skriftelike stukke. Selfs n groep (a)-
inperking sal nie verhoed dat hy hiermee voortgaan nie.
In die lig hiervan en met die oog op Kompol se jongste

aanbeveling, doen die Departement aan die hand dat Turner
nie nou strenger ingeperk word nie. As sy invloed in
die arbeidsveld dit regverdig, kan dit moontlik liewer
oorweeg word om aandag te gee aan diegene wat sy raad
in die praktyk toepas. Ons sal hieroor met Kompol skakel.

SEKRETARIS VAN JUSTISIE

A|S(V)

1. The Minister has on occasion made
   inquiries about the desirability of
   stronger restriction on Turner. This
   submission flows from that.

3. Before the idea of a broad
   investigation could be presented to
   the Minister, Compol [the Security
   Branch headquarters] indicated that
   it would make a new recommendation

in connection with Turner's stronger restriction. During October 1974, Compol then recommended that Turner should be restricted under group 'B'. Compol indicated that Foszia Fisher had left for London during September 1974 and that it was suspected that she would not return to the Republic. Shortly thereafter Compol telephonically indicated that Foszia Fisher would actually be returning to the Republic and requested that Turner's stronger restriction be held back until clarity was obtained about Fisher. Compol now reports as follows: 'It will appear that the abovementioned (Turner) does not continue at present with his activities with the same vigour as before. Since this Department's same memo of 2.10.74 in which stronger restrictions on him were recommended, little has been heard about Turner. It is possible that the arrest during October 1974 of the 36 SASO and BPC members, who are still being held, has had a salutary effect on leftist elements in general and the climate for the pursuit of his aims is no longer as favourable as before. Taking the above into account, it may be desirable not to continue at present with the consideration of stronger measures against him.'

5. Previously Turner was very active in influencing the direction of students' thinking and in making them active. He did this through addressing many

meetings, symposiums, discussion groups and other gatherings across the country, by preparing articles for different publications and especially by intensively cultivating students at the university where he was a lecturer, in and outside his classes. The restrictions in place at the moment effectively removed him from the sphere of influencing students. Whether stronger restrictions will achieve the same in terms of his influence in labour circles is doubtful. There he is not openly active. He gives secret advice through go-betweens, in personal conversations and with the preparation of written documents. Even a group 'A' restriction will not prevent him from continuing with this. In this light, and taking into account Compol's latest recommendation, the Department proposes that Turner should not be more strongly restricted now. If his influence in the labour field justifies it, one should rather consider whether attention should be given to those who give practical effect to his advice. We will contact Compol in this connection.

ONE-DIMENSIONAL HEROES

'No, I don't think Rick Turner was marginalised. He was overtaken by the one-dimensionsial heroes. I'm not saying that they were not heroes, but they were all one dimension. And it's this one-dimensionality that tends to produce the Stalins of the world, the

Mugabes, and so on. It can produce these weird excesses that deny the fact that all these struggles depend on human beings with all their untidiness and complexity. Every revolution we know of has ended up killing its own children in some shape or form. It's when you invent your future that you come up with situations where the end point of the revolutionary struggle, however brave, turns out to be something like what happened in South Africa, where now there is the most remarkably rapid process of elite enrichment that the world has ever seen. Billionaires have been created within two weeks! I'm sorry: if political purity produced that kind of estrangement from reality, then it's shit.'[4]

– LAWRENCE SCHLEMMER

In the initial conception of the IIE, the goal was to develop a mutually collaborative relationship between academics, workers and trade unions. As the mostly white trade union federation, TUCSA, was not sympathetic to organising African workers, the IIE's principal contact with unions was made through the Trade Union Advisory and Coordinating Council (TUACC). TUACC had been formed in 1973 to develop an infrastructure for building 'open' trade unions among African workers.[5] However, the IIE's friendly relations with unions proved to be one-sided, and after insisting for two years that the institute ought to be controlled by the unions, TUACC eventually shut it down.

The story of the IIE, and particularly its decline, is a tragic tale of the potential pitfalls and shortcomings of all social movements. On the one hand, the problems that led to its downfall had to do with class privilege and the difficulties involved in privileged people attempting to provide leadership to the oppressed. At another level, the conflicts that ran the IIE into the ground arose from two very different concepts of how to build structures that could effectively oppose an oppressive system. From another angle, the whole story of the IIE seems like an unfortunate waste of energy, as the squandering of the goodwill and resources of intelligent and capable people. It would be best to understand the IIE as a collaborative process gone awry.

Part of the tragedy of the IIE story was that the radical milieu in Durban was, relatively speaking, rather small, and many of the relationships that grew tense politically were first of all – and afterwards – also those between close friends. A number of those who later took prominent positions within the burgeoning black trade union movement knew Turner quite well and were influenced by his ideas to become involved. Ironically, both 'sides' of the argument – mostly happening between white university-educated and middle-class activists – could claim (with some clear justification) that the other side was imposing itself on the workers, inhibiting their intelligence and capacity to self-organise. That the two groups could so closely mimic each other in their critique indicates that they all had relatively similar starting points.

In essence, everyone agreed at an abstract level that the end goal ought to be a radically transformed economic and political system, loosely understood to be 'socialist' in some form. Further, they had all reached these conclusions through careful study at university level, as a result of which they had all made the firm decision that merely grappling intellectually with these issues was not enough; they must find ways to engage directly with the struggles of black workers. Both Turner and the leaders of TUACC put a strong emphasis on the idea of workers controlling the conditions of their labour and building their own organisations.

Of the group of students at the University of Natal that were influenced by Turner, the most notable were Halton Cheadle, David Hemson, Alec Erwin and, to a lesser extent, Gerry Maré. These young radicals found support in older union activists, such as Harriet Bolton, a dissident organiser within TUCSA, Omar Badsha, an Indian communist organiser within the Chemical Workers' Union, and Harold Nxasana, an African trade unionist from a previous generation of unions. In addition, the IIE attracted liberal–left academics, particularly Eddie Webster, Lawrence Schlemmer and Tony Morphet (who was not in the leadership of the IIE, but was sympathetic to it) and of course Foszia Fisher. Meanwhile, a similar group of young white socialists developed in Johannesburg at Wits University. The most prominent of these students to arrive in Durban was John Copelyn, who ended up playing a very powerful role in both the life and death of the IIE.

Arrival in Durban
John Copelyn

I came down to Durban from Johannesburg in March of 1974. At the beginning of February in '74, David Hemson and David Davis, both trade union organisers, were banned. Soon after, Halton Cheadle was banned as well. So, when I went down to Durban it was like immediately after this huge wave had crashed onto the shore and it felt like dispersion and desolation all around. So, by the time I went down I became the general secretary of the union within a week or two. I was like the last man standing.

They gave me a job in the Institute for Industrial Education and I became the editor of the first issue of the *South African Labour Bulletin*, which was all written before I got there. I mean, Rick was fully the engine behind that project. He had written the content completely and had it all typed and everything. All I had to do was print it all out, and have my name on there as the editor. Anyway, that was my starting point with them. In a way I feel ungracious to have come along afterwards with a lot of criticisms because all of them played a fantastic role in getting the movement going.

You engage in the working class
Tony Morphet

In a way TUACC was saying we don't have the time to go into this expanded educational procedure; we need to organise! We need shop stewards to know when to call a strike and when not to, and we need shop stewards who won't be caught and captured and become union officials. They were very good about that. The power of the union was on the shop floor, not in the union offices.

Turner was actually a threat, or became quickly a threat to that approach, because it's the other way around for Turner. What he wanted was access to give people ideas. So in a way he was anti-organisation. He wanted to be able to reach into the union with ideas. That's what he wanted to do. The unions were the place where he could reach workers. He wanted to reach working people and talk to them about themselves, as he always did: talking to you about you, not to tell them what *he* wanted, not to organise or enrol anyone, or get them into any official position.

Still, Turner assumed the unions would welcome him.

No matter how similar their starting points, it soon became evident that the political orientation that provided the guiding principles for the IIE was profoundly different from that of organising trade unions. Turner saw himself as providing the necessary information (and asking important fundamental questions) for workers to be able to develop solutions for themselves. Turner's approach was very different from the 'vanguard' approach that has a clear programme and simply needs the working class to carry it out.

The vanguard
Foszia Fisher

The thing is that we weren't clear enough to know that we were disagreeing on process. The process that the union organisers were interested in was very much a top-down approach. The goal for the Institute for Industrial Education was not a top-down process, but bottom-up.

John Copelyn, for example, made a solid career

as the vanguard of the unions. Then, at some point he withdrew from politics. Now he runs, is it e-tv or something? He invests union money in the stock exchange; he knows how to work with money, and he's made money for the unions. But what changes have the workers or 'the workers' organisation' made to a democratic South Africa? I don't know.

I guess I didn't want to know. When all these people I once worked with became politicians, I kind of stopped wanting to know. As far as I can tell, there is nothing that has happened since the end of apartheid that would make me feel like, 'I worked with these people and I'm so pleased to have known them because they have made a huge difference.' I don't see that.

I don't see on the day-to-day level for workers in South Africa that there have been major changes in the way people are employed. Is there any kind of truly innovative thinking about the way business is run in South Africa, compared to the way business is run everywhere? No. There is no change.

At the root of the union critique of the IIE lay the claim that education was being squandered on the wrong people, and therefore undermining the ability of the unions to educate their members.

The IIE always did attempt – certainly from the start – to make its curriculum available to union members and leaders, and in fact hoped that as the unions grew they would explicitly support the institute both by encouraging their workers to be students of the IIE and by providing financial assistance. An IIE memo to TUACC in 1975 clarifies that the institute was interested in increasing union participation, but from the IIE's side it sounds as if the unions under-utilised the courses available to them. 'We have decided to give priority in admission to the course to union members and are at the moment waiting on the unions to enrol their members to the course ... None of the unions has yet taken up its full quota.'[6]

At the same time, the IIE did make the courses available broadly, and advertised in local newspapers and by other means. According to the trade unionists, this level of openness to anyone becoming a student of the IIE was problematic. Harold Nxasana,[7] who was engaged in translating the IIE course workbooks into Zulu, argued, 'We only got workers who thought the course would get them white-collar jobs.'[8] In this way Nxasana expressed the general feeling of frustration within TUACC that the IIE was encouraging the 'wrong' kind of worker to study with them.

TUACC leaders generally expressed disdain for any kind of education programme that wasn't specifically targeted at building a union cadre. On the one hand, this objection was defended by the argument that union organisers were exhausted, overworked and severely strapped for resources. Certainly the strains on the black trade unions in the mid-1970s were serious. No doubt organisers were intensely committed and worked in very trying circumstances, with few successes. In light of these tremendous barriers, TUACC leaders were reluctant to spend too much of their energy on a process of general education for black workers.

But the TUACC leaders did not object to the IIE merely because they saw it as a 'waste of time'. On a more fundamental level, they raised objections about the whole purpose of the education being offered. The whole idea of education as a 'creatively open-ended' process troubled them.

Who gets educated, and why?
John Copelyn

The practice of it was, as I saw it, that you got basically a more educated, more entrepreneurial kind of black person applying to become a student of the IIE. This kind of person wasn't interested in working class organisation, but was rather trying to get a diploma so that he could maybe become a personnel manager, or something like this. The idea of having our energy dissipated by educating future managers just seemed to me a waste of time.

There was nothing in the content of the curriculum that any of us in the union found offensive. Rick was very subtle in the way that he described the world as a class-conflicted world. Just understanding the world around you in those terms is very enlightening. I wasn't anti any of that, to be frank. I was just against having that as our contribution to the world when we were trying to build a trade union movement.

In a trade union movement lots of people don't read, or don't read very well, or they just don't like reading. A guy that's only educated through Standard four before becoming a weaver – these are the kinds of people that become union activists. Now, either you start with where they are actually as a group and say, 'What are the things that have made you come together? What do you want to do together?' Or you can say, 'I don't want to start there, I want to start with the theory of civilisation and let me try and plug it in very simply so that most of you can understand, let me try and use simple words so you don't get lost in linguistics.' That's the sort of approach that the IIE had. I would say that's a very different orientation.

You know, what is training and what is education? If I free your mind and whatever it is and make you class-conscious … it's education? If I give you skills that allow you to run your organisation well and to control it well … that's not education? I think that's the heart and soul of what I saw the difference to be.

As far as men like Copelyn and Alec Erwin were concerned, worker education needed to be focused solely on the pressing need of building a dedicated core of activists in the factories. Fair enough. However, in Turner's view this was simply not 'education', in the broadest and most transformative sense of that word.

There is a complicated irony to the conflicts around the nature of education that should be offered. Both sides could rightfully claim that the other side was talking down to or speaking for workers, rather than empowering them. Copelyn is correct to point out the limitations of the IIE workbooks, which 'use[d] simple words' yet were written without consulting any workers, and were then presented to them with no chance to discuss the contents with the author. Furthermore, the simple fact that the IIE was an initiative brought to the workers rather than originating organically from themselves limited the extent to which it could be an empowering educational process.

However accurate their critique of the curriculum or the structure of the IIE, to limit the reach of an educational institute because the topics in the curriculum are too broad or too far removed from what is perceived to be the worker's best interests hints at paternalism. Why should Copelyn or anyone else in the top of the union hierarchy decide on the workers' behalf that an IIE education was a 'luxury' or that it was wasted if made available to a worker who did not want to be a shop steward?

The trade unions that developed after the 1973 strikes made much of the claim that they were 'democratic'. Surely this was not all just rhetoric. In terms of financing, election for position, as well as the concept of 'nonracialism'' and the development of black leadership, there were conscious steps taken to deepen democracy within the unions (as compared with previous incarnations of South African unions). This commitment to democracy deserves recognition, but it shouldn't be exaggerated, either.

Of course, Copelyn is wrong that Turner wasn't interested in workers developing 'skills that allow you to run your organisation well and to control it well'. In fact, Turner wrote at length about the need for workers to develop these skills. Even a cursory reading of the workbooks clearly demonstrates that an overwhelming majority of the material was focused on workplace struggles. At least half of every workbook dealt with 'nuts and bolts' issues, such as how to negotiate with management, how to gain union recognition and how to build democratic structures within the union. However, as Alec Erwin describes it, in response to the low levels of literacy among union members, worker education programmes in the unions were increasingly based on the need to 'work from the specific to the general, whereas the correspondence course worked from the general to the specific'.[9]

Furthermore, exactly as Copelyn implies, Turner was not content merely to 'train' people to build a union and negotiate for better working conditions. Instead, he saw it as essential that people were able to develop a broader social consciousness, to imagine and fight for a radically different social system. Trade union democracy is of little value if it is not part of a broader process of transforming a system of exploitation into one of participatory democracy at all levels of society.

Whether well founded or not, the claim that the IIE was directing workers' attention away from the concerns of the factory floor gathered a lot of traction, and helped to increase tensions between TUACC and IIE. A particularly intense dispute blew up around an attempt to add to the list of courses offered by the IIE a 'community education' course which would be run in collaboration with Inkatha. While this was not the most fundamental of the conflicts between TUACC and the IIE, it did raise a number of important issues. The relationship between the IIE and Buthelezi (and the KwaZulu government more broadly) was complicated, and it is not surprising that it led to conflict.

From the start Turner and Fisher tried to establish mutually beneficial ties with Buthelezi, who was nominally the 'chancellor' of the IIE for the bulk of its existence. Though this was a controversial appointment at the time – and although Buthelezi later proved to be a much more reactionary 'ally' than anyone in 1973 foresaw – most people, including those ardently opposed to him, tend to defend the decision in the context of its time. The justifications given are similar to Foszia's, who says, 'Was Buthelezi the kind of person he is now? No, he grew into that person. He wasn't that at first. He was somebody you could talk to, he was shy, he was not sure about many things.'[10]

In short, there was a sense that, in the political desert of the early 1970s, it was a sound tactical choice to establish links with Buthelezi. His sanctioned status with the Pretoria government seemed to insulate the IIE against possible reprisal. Furthermore, Turner and Foszia saw it as a good thing that many workers seemed to trust Buthelezi as 'their leader'. Foszia describes one of the perceived benefits of making Buthelezi the IIE chancellor: 'The first round of certificates that we gave, he handed them out. It was great, the workers loved it, it was in a sense, "My chief gave me this," you know it meant something.'[11]

But the decision to work with Buthelezi ran deeper. Turner's analysis of the possible benefits (for radical social change) of the homeland system generally and of Buthelezi in particular was overly optimistic at best and a tragic error of judgement at worst.[12] He essentially underestimated the potential risk involved in assisting a government-sanctioned tribal leader, and the risk of implication with Zulu nationalism more generally. In his article on 'Class Consciousness', Turner wrote: 'tribal affiliations may be manipulated as a weapon to be used in conflict within worker organizations, but they are not likely to form the basis for alternative types of organization'.[13] The horrific 'civil war' in Natal in the late 1980s and early 1990s, with Inkatha at the centre of it, proved him wrong.

Turner's attention was focused elsewhere when thinking about KwaZulu. One side-consequence of the 1973 Durban strikes was that the KwaZulu government was put into a unique position, and forced to make some official comment about the exploitation of local (Zulu) workers. As many of the workers either had permanent homes within the boundaries of the homeland or were daily commuters from one of the outlying suburbs of Durban that formed part of KwaZulu, the strikes took place partially within the KwaZulu 'jurisdiction'. The first group of workers who went on strike were encouraged to return to work after hearing a speech from the Zulu king. After this, the king did not make any further interventions in the strikes, and a dynamic young man named Barney Dladla, who was the Minister of Labour in the KwaZulu government, stepped forward. He took stands that few ministers of labour ever do. Dladla encouraged workers to withdraw their labour and even to go to jail if need be, with the full backing of the KwaZulu government.[14] Actions such as these ignited Turner's imagination as to the possibilities of using the power vested in the homelands to assist more militant struggles developing in the urban areas. In addition, Dladla firmly presented himself as sympathetic to the involvement of Halton Cheadle and others in the early stages of building black trade unions. Initially, Dladla's pro-union stance came with Buthelezi's backing, and therefore the full backing of the KwaZulu government, but this was short-lived. Within a year or two, Dladla was forced out of office by Buthelezi, and the relationship between the unions and the homeland government quickly deteriorated.

When Dladla and Buthelezi fell out, the IIE was put in an uncomfortable position. Still, it chose not to make any kind of formal break with Buthelezi. At the same time, Lawrence Schlemmer, a liberal sociologist at the university and a good friend of Turner's, began to develop a steady working relationship with Buthelezi. It was Schlemmer's involvement in the 'community education' curriculum[15] that led to the feeling among radical activists that the purpose of the course was more about aiding Inkatha than anything else. Omar Badsha remembers that the whole process ended in one extremely unpleasant meeting.

'You've got your back against the wall'
Omar Badsha

Now, I understand that when you are fighting for space, you try to use every avenue. When you've got your back against the wall, then you see Buthelezi as progressive. But, the IIE community education course was directed at building Inkatha, not the community. No, there is no getting away from that.

Unfortunately it became personalised, to my great regret. Rick must have just felt that we were pig-headed and difficult, which we were – I was. Because it was just dragging on, this tension, this contestation. It had to come to a head and it came to a head there.

I see now in retrospect that the process of shutting down the IIE was much too personalised. The conflict became focused on Foszia, and she was quite stubborn in response. There was a campaign to get rid of her. But I don't think we thought through who would run the education programme after getting rid of Foszia. We were so dependent on Foszia and Rick to generate the actual material for the IIE; now it seems obvious that the organisation would disintegrate once we split from them.

In retrospect, Badsha and others in TUACC were right to distance themselves from homeland politics, and from Buthelezi's politics in particular. In time, Buthelezi did prove to be vehemently anti-union and helped create a political machine that took violent action against trade unionists and harassed them to an appalling degree.[16]

At a certain level, the conflict between the unions and the IIE had nothing to do with the subtleties of what makes for a good education. The union leaders were simply offended that the IIE refused to follow their commands. Seeing themselves as the rightful and obvious leaders to direct the workers' struggle, TUACC made an attempt to turn the IIE into a subcommittee of the union. According to Johann Maree, the reason was quite simple: 'They objected to the independence of the IIE as this enabled it "to take its own decisions and formulate its own direction".'[17]

Control

John Copelyn

The notion that the IIE would have money and the trade union movement would not just drove me off the bloody twist, you know? That they could be serving lunch at all their meetings and the trade union movement would have no carpets on the floor and so on ... all of that sounded stupid to me. I wanted to basically channel the money they had to the trade union movement.

What I despise is an organisation that claims to have a supposed independence from the trade union movement. I despise an organisation that has the freedom to raise money in the name of workers.

I believe in organisation and I believe in education being subordinate to organisation. Whether that's a Stalinist tendency or whatever, I wouldn't know.

I feel that in class struggle there isn't a place for concepts like academic freedom, you know. Basically all your academics are middle-class people; their so-called classlessness is a lot of shit. The question is, Are you prepared to serve the working-class movement? Are you prepared to subordinate yourself to it? If the trade union movement says, 'What we really want is curriculum around a certain topic', do you drop everything and do material around that kind of a topic or do you say, 'No, we academics know better than you'?

I was in one camp and Rick was definitely in another camp. Let's say I was less interested in the education, and I was more interested in the organisation. That's the bottom of it.

I've got to accept responsibility that I put an enormous amount of pressure on them to stop doing the correspondence course aimed outside the trade union movement. As a result, Foszia was left with a very stripped down correspondence school; very little resources were allocated to it. Foszia was the most dedicated person sitting in that office. Then, suddenly she came into meetings, and we had mobilised 51 per cent of the people to start saying that we weren't happy with the IIE ... It was terribly frustrating for her.

Eventually, the 'enormous amount of pressure' and 'terribly frustrating' atmosphere had the effect of pushing Foszia out of her leadership position within the IIE. Foszia officially resigned in October 1975.[18] To all intents and purposes, with the removal of Foszia the IIE ceased to exist. Officially, Alec Erwin became the chairperson of the working committee of the IIE and Copelyn was made a full-time education officer for TUACC. In this way, the project limped along for another half-year or so, but the commitment to carrying on with educational programmes was gone. In response to the police detention of the leadership[19] and other union problems which appeared dire, Copelyn came to the conclusion that 'to be involved with the IIE was a luxury. There was just too much organisational work to be able to sit back and design programmes.'[20]

The destruction of the IIE was described by those responsible as a necessary step in order to move forward with the trade union movement.

In a way, this is just a convenient way to absolve oneself of any moral responsibility for the choices made. What was in fact gained by abandoning the methods of the IIE and 'building a strong labour movement' instead? The successes of the unions are clear enough; they make the kind of social changes that one can calibrate and quantify. In contrast, the successes of a project like the IIE are far harder to estimate. The IIE was potentially a safeguard against any kind of 'dumbing down' of the people in the name of liberation. There is no way to prove that South African workers would have been better off with the kind of education Turner's workbooks provided, instead of the shop-steward training offered by the unions. The difference is qualitative, rather than quantitative; it cannot be counted, but it can be felt.

Perhaps the pragmatists were more efficient than Turner ever could have been, more shrewd at negotiating, more conscious of the dynamics of power – how to slowly build organisations with hundreds of thousands of members and usher in changes that affect millions. Alec Erwin speaks confidently of the successes gained by shifting away from the IIE and focusing on building the unions. 'I think we were right, because we built unions against all odds, and those unions have played an absolutely decisive role in the political liberation struggle.'[21]

Indeed, the people who dedicated themselves to building trade unions in South Africa were certainly heroes, but, in Schlemmer's words, they were 'one-dimensional heroes'.

FROM ROUSSEAU TO SARTRE

As the climate of political repression darkened and more of his peers were either banned or went into exile, the house on Dalton Road became emptier, quieter. House-mates moved out, and gatherings of all kinds became less comfortable and less frequent, because of the restrictions. Rick Turner maintained a small handful of close friends in his final years, as well as his deep connection to Foszia and twice-yearly visits from his children, but all in all it was a much smaller social network than he had once known.

For those who were close to Turner during the banning years, it was impossible to ignore the surveillance and harassment that slowly came to be seen as normal. It is now known without a doubt that Turner's phone calls were all recorded and transcribed by the Bureau of State Security (BOSS) and that a handful of his immediate neighbours had agreements with the Special Branch to pass on information about Turner's activities. Rick and Foszia grew accustomed to being constantly followed, constantly watched by police wherever they went, as well as in their own home. Jann and Kim became used to having their vacations with their father interrupted repeatedly by mandatory visits to 'check in' with the local police. On repeated occasions, Turner's house and property were attacked and sabotaged in different forms by the security forces. Car tyres were slashed, attempts were made to fire-bomb the house, and so on.

In this tense, wearying situation, Turner focused heavily on his intellectual pursuits. He was, in any case, a great lover of reading and writing. He kept abreast of the news, both locally and internationally, and hungrily sought out new ideas from all over the world. He was a determined and disciplined academic, sitting down to work every day, taking a break for tea in the late morning, and then carrying on with his work. Turner's calling and passion was to study philosophy. As the banning years lengthened, and most other outlets for sharing his ideas were closed off, Turner began the most ambitious philosophical project of his lifetime.

> 'Sartre has said that existentialism is the attempt to draw out all the implications of the denial of the existence of God. I would say that it is more accurate and more illuminating to say that it is the attempt to draw out all the implications of the fact that there is no human nature. This implies that men can create and control their own society, since it is men who hold present society in being through their alienated praxis.
>
> 'But it also implies that when I explain to the other that he is responsible for what happens in his society, he can agree and still refuse to do anything about it.'

* * *

'*The first principle is that freedom is essentially difficult. There are no simple solutions, precisely because there is no human nature, and so man has to invent himself. Freedom is not something which can simply be guaranteed by a declaration of human rights.*

'*The second freedom is freedom to think.*

'*In a class society culture, and so education, is unconsciously impregnated with the ideology of the dominant class. This 'serial brainwashing' must be replaced by a conscious indoctrination of those principles and methods of thought which will eventually permit an escape from indoctrination and from the pre-reflective, unconscious building up of a picture of the world.*

'*If this is not done, most people will have understandings of the world which are closely conditioned by what is. Those few individuals capable of escaping from indoctrination by themselves will be the only eyes to benefit from a society which guarantees freedom of thought without providing the tools for thinking with.*'

– RICK TURNER,
'NOTES ON SARTRE'S POLITICAL THEORY'

Returning again to his study of Jean-Paul Sartre, Turner attempted to write a full-length account of Sartre's philosophy, which would also ground Sartre's theory in an analysis of a number of earlier philosophers – Rousseau, Kant, Hegel – whose thinking helped to provide a foundation and counterbalance for Sartre's thought.[22] Turner felt that his earlier doctoral work on Sartre had been largely a-historical, and therefore weak in analysis. His philosophical studies during the banning years aimed to contextualise Sartre's work sufficiently well in order to understand the precise contribution of his ideas.

The extant 500-page manuscript is quite thorough. It was intended to be a full account of the philosophical, ethical and political implications of Sartre's thinking. Nonetheless, Turner's prose is relatively simple and clear, as the goal was to make the philosophy as accessible as possible.

In view of the fact that Turner was forbidden to publish under the banning order, the manuscript (loosely entitled 'Notes on Sartre's Political Theory') could not be published during his lifetime. After Turner died, Andrew Nash, who was at the time a young student of philosophy, offered to edit the manuscript, write an introduction for it, and get it published. Sadly, the project remained stalled for over a decade, as the family could not agree that Nash should proceed with turning the manuscript into a book. By the time everyone was persuaded about the need to bring it out, in the early 1990s, there was no longer a publisher willing to take it on. In the absence of this book, it is difficult to assess the full scope of Turner's philosophical work and the impact it may have had.

What is certain is that Turner intended his writing to be of use to the growing movement against apartheid, at whatever point that may have been possible. He was deeply frustrated by the fact that the banning order kept him out of the growing determination of people in South Africa to rebel against the government. In response to this isolation, Turner calculated that his greatest strength was as a philosopher, and felt that the best contribution he could make, under the circumstances, was to produce philosophical writing. While the writing itself is very much theoretical, and not explicitly linked to South African realities, it was nonetheless intended to be a gift to the radical opponents of the status quo.

Reading the unpublished manuscript now, one sees an attempt to grapple thoroughly and effectively with a wide range of problems related to the radical restructuring of society. This is of course the same impulse contained in *The Eye of the Needle*; both texts are rooted in the longing for an ideal society. However, in 'Notes on Sartre's Political Theory' there is much more analysis of the structures of capitalism (and capitalist ideology) and the barriers in the way of abolishing class society. Having been banned for engaging in left-wing activities ironically deepened Turner's conviction that present society is driven by class struggle, and that this is fundamentally unacceptable.

By delving more deeply into Sartre's philosophy, particularly his *Critique of Dialectical Reason*, Turner could expand his theoretical writing beyond matters of personal choice – which had been central to both his earlier writing on Sartre and to *The Eye of the Needle* – into critical thought about the structure and aspirations of groups of people and of organisations (both oppressive and liberating). In detailing Sartre's political theory, Turner's hope was to provide a theoretical base (for both himself and others) on which to confront the practical problems that inevitably plague social movements.

While Turner's intellectual work was very much rooted in his own personal drive to make use of his powerful mind, it was at the same time a pastime that allowed him to continue to engage with his friends. In addition to the support he got at home, from Foszia and from his friend Lawrie Schlemmer, he also maintained a number of other intellectual friendships. Tony Morphet, for example, hosted Rick at his house every Wednesday afternoon, giving Turner space to write and to talk through his work.

'I am the way in which I make myself into a tool in pursuit of survival, and the way in which I do this is a function of the surrounding world, of what I can produce and of how I can produce it. I am what I make myself to be, but what I make myself to be is determined by what I can produce. I am the product of my own product.'

– RICK TURNER,
'NOTES ON SARTRE'S POLITICAL THEORY'

Discovery of Marx
Tony Morphet

I can remember him talking about Marx, because Marx had just arrived. I mean, I know he has been around since 1848 but in South Africa …

Anyway, I said to him, 'What's in the middle of Marx?'

'Oh,' he said, 'a man is a product of his own product.'

I said, 'What?'

'Human beings generate a product and they are the product of that product.'

I thought about it for weeks to get any kind of grip on it.

I ended up talking to Rick again. 'Go back, tell me about the product of the product.'

We got into history, we got into sociology, we got into socialisation, but all at the very simple, very quiet level, not wanting to recruit you. That was, I think, the mystery of it: he didn't want to recruit anybody to anything. But people were drawn in of their own wish and will through that particular process.

Turner's own discovery of Marx was mostly from Nupen; Turner was originally a liberal. But Turner's particular way into Marxism was focused on the question of how to have a rich, easy consciousness, instead of being cramped down and processed by an oppressive society. The answer is to learn to understand the forms of oppression around you and distance yourself from them; to make a way out through the counter-culture. Rick also read the 1844 manuscripts of Marx, which is the same stuff, actually. It's in those texts that you hear about 'fishing in the morning, tilling the soil in the afternoon, and a critic at night'. Beautiful stuff, all about escaping the cash nexus and finding out the values of a fulfilled life.

So what Rick's socialism is about is a world that is freed from the constraints that seem to be embedded in ordinary social life so that you can live from the interior rather than the exterior. You are about self-fulfilment; you are not about functioning. And it takes Rick a long time to understand that what you have to have for that is some form of social control of production. But production is important. You can't just drop out, unless there are other people producing. So, what do you do about production? You have to create structures that fuse together this sense of individual fulfilment with communal fulfilment. It's about getting back the human dimension into the social organisation, that's what Rick is driving at.

A PHILOSOPHIC COMMUNITY

Clearly, the last few years of the banning started to wear on Rick Turner, politically, psychologically and even physically. However diligent Turner was at his studies, he was still lonely, and he found it slow going to make sense of the difficult material on his own. The isolation became more and more of a burden, and he longed even more to be part of a fulfilling intellectual community.

During his final years alive, Rick and Foszia began drafting a proposal for the kind of political and intellectual community that would be ideal for them, which they called the New International School of Social Research.

```
NEW INTERNATIONAL SCHOOL OF SOCIAL RESEARCH
at BELLAIR


South Africa is a racial oligarchy in which social
definitions in terms of wealth and race delimit the
social reality of the entire population. What is
the relation in such a situation between social
institutions and personal attitudes? Why do racial
attitudes have such salience? Why do the dominant
white groups (and those following them, probably
most of the rest of the population) live almost
exclusively in terms of material values, to the
exclusion of person values?

What is the relation between the socialization
process necessary to train whites for a position
of dominance, the authority structure in education
and work, and the domination of male over female?
To what extent are whites oppressed? Alienated,
or de-personalized by their roles in the overall
institutional structure?
```

How do blacks internalize and live their oppression?

If whites are oppressed, which are the situations in which they can most easily be made aware of their oppression and so motivate themselves to attack the institutions?

If blacks have internalized their oppression, what are the mechanisms whereby this operates, what situations in their daily lives are most likely to make these mechanisms break down?

These and other questions involve three inter-related fields of action/research:

1) Theoretical:

an investigation of the nature of being human; of alienation, of 'real' or 'false' needs, and of the relations between the individual and the social structure. This involves problems in the theory of social science, in philosophical ethics and in religious theory.

2) Empirical:

experimental study of particular situations in South Africa to uncover the particular ways in which social structure and the various categories and the individuals' perception of reality interact and change in this specific context.

3) Practical:

devising and putting into practice projects designed to de-alienate people, by making them aware of their oppression and helping them relate to other people to change the institutional basis of oppression.

A possible example of this would be devising educational programmes for pre-school children (at present free from governmental control), taking into account the financial, social and cultural difficulties connected with the different groups and to use these programmes both for the development of the children and as a basis for building parent-organizations and for bringing home to parents the nature of family authority structures.

Teaching

Our objectives would be two-fold.

1) the specifically South African one of teaching free from racial restrictions. This would be possible through making it a non-fee institution. All 'students' would be volunteer research assistants, taking part in the administration of the institute. This would both get around legal restrictions and involving full participation of all staff and students in decision-making would prevent the growth of faculty/administration-student cleavage and the concomitant development of authority structures.

2) The more general one of developing ways of moving away from the lecture/discipline approach which is characteristic of our universities in the direction of project-oriented group work. Students would participate in the institute, research projects, and would be guided in their primary reading by the 'staff', in terms of the theoretical and practical problems which they encountered in their research.

We would operate at a 'post-graduate' level, but our criteria for admissions of students would depend more on personal commitment and intellectual maturity than in formal qualifications.

We envisage an initial staff of two directors and five full-time research assistants, all paid

relatively low salaries. Administrative tasks
would be carried out by students - this would
include general office work, the preparation of
institute publications, and so on.

This would:
a)   cut expenses
b)   prevent an alienating 'brain work' vs. 'dirty
     work' divide
c)   and as mentioned above, prevent cleavages and the
     growth of institutionalized authority.

In a world where paper qualifications are important we
would try to arrange for leading overseas academics
to act as external examiners for our students' work
so that foreign universities would have some criteria
in terms of which to judge them.

The aims of the New International School for Social Research speak
to Rick Turner's enduring hopefulness, in spite of the long years of
loneliness of the banning. At the moment when he was completely cut
off from all forms of teaching, he nonetheless dreamed of bringing to life
a school that would give him an opportunity not only to be a teacher,
but also to radically redefine fundamental notions of what education is
all about. Years after he had been punished for being an agitator among
his students, Turner still firmly believed that the best atmosphere for
learning is among equals, working collaboratively on shared projects.
In his ideal school, artificial hierarchies among human beings would be
confronted and abolished, both in the curriculum and in the structure of
the schooling itself.

While the proposal itself speaks explicitly about South African
problems, and so was designed for a South African audience, it seems
possible that such a project could have been initiated anywhere, and
could also have been part of a daydream of a better life in exile. Though
he did his best to rise above it, at some level the banning was simply
unbearable, and Turner had no option but to begin dreaming of a way

out. Studying philosophy was Rick Turner's response to the isolation of the banning years. He not only saw it as a way to focus his energy in the short term, but he also hoped that it would allow him to rejoin the kind of intellectual community he so desperately needed.

Turner's study of philosophy during the banning years was concerned with understanding the historical context of Sartre's ideas. Towards this end, Turner studied the work of Rousseau and Kant, as well as the influence of Marxism on Jean-Paul Sartre. Studying Marx led to an investigation of Hegel, one of the key contributors to the Idealist philosophy which developed in Germany in the early 1800s. Turner took a keen interest in the German Idealists, and became determined to understand their ideas, as well as critical responses to them, and how these all related to Sartre.

Once a week, Rick would meet with Raphael and Elizabeth de Kadt, to share a meal together and learn to speak and read German. To eat together under the banning order required that they keep a separate table set with a plate of food on it in another room, so that if the police raided – which they did, on occasion – Turner could quickly withdraw to his own private table, and feign that he was not actually interacting with them. Raphael was a dear friend and colleague, and Elizabeth was fluent in German and so able to help Turner become more comfortable in the language. By learning the German language he hoped to be able to grapple with Hegel and other German philosophers in the original. Turner himself described the experience of reading Hegel as 'a dense thicket of argument inside which I am still lost'.[23]

In 1976, Turner began to make plans for travelling to Heidelberg in Germany to study German Idealism in greater depth, with the benefit of the academic libraries there, as well as undertaking coursework in the language. He established a connection with a sympathetic professor in Heidelberg, Michael Theunissen, who knew Turner's previous philosophical work and agreed to support him in his further research. Furthermore, Turner applied for a Humboldt Fellowship, in order to fund his year abroad. The politics department at the University of Natal supported his decision to study in Germany, and offered him sabbatical for 1977.

Having made these arrangements, Turner then set about trying to persuade the government to agree to let him leave. It was, of course, an enormous request. He had already surrendered his British passport in 1971, and had been denied a South African passport when he applied for it a year later. On top of this, the banning order was not due to expire until March 1978, so Turner was requesting to leave the country a full year before his banning was complete. The apartheid state in general had a great dislike of dissidents leaving the country. Once beyond the South African border they were able to speak out against apartheid much more freely than they could ever do at home. In respect of someone as articulate as Rick Turner, there would have been a well-founded concern that allowing him to spend a year in Europe would give him free rein to ridicule and criticise publicly the state of affairs in South Africa.

Understanding the tremendous difficulties involved in getting clearance to travel to Germany, Turner debated his options carefully, and sought the advice of friends who might be able to assist in the matter. He reached out first of all to Frederik van Zyl Slabbert, who had taken a seat in parliament as a member of the opposition Progressive Party. After saying why he wanted to go to Germany, he tried explaining why the Minister of Justice might agree to let him leave:

> From the Minister's point of view, I think that there is at least one good reason why he should let me go. Being out of the country for one or two years will further weaken any political ties he might think that I have here, and will certainly break any residual links which I might have with student politics. If I go on a South African passport, with the intention of returning to my job here, there is a strong guarantee that I will not engage in any political activity while I am outside the country. However, if I were to leave on an exit permit, or, as seems to be more fashionable, by crossing the border, the state would have no further control over me.
>
> Not, I should say, that I have any intention of doing either of those things, inter alia because my children are here. There is also quite a good guarantee that I would return if I had a passport.
>
> I do not know whether they intend to reban me in 1978. But if they feel they would like me to be out of the way for a little while longer, without their having to go to the bother of banning me, I would be willing to stay away a while longer; perhaps for two or three years, instead of one. If I do get permission, I will be applying for a Humboldt fellowship, which is

renewable for a second year. I have been told informally that I should not
have any trouble getting one, but that they will not make the grant until I
have received clearance from the South African government.[24]

In other words, Rick Turner was willing to agree, on some formal level,
to distance himself from the movement against apartheid in order to
have an opportunity to engage in the kind of academic environment that
would allow him to thrive rather than atrophy. In addition, it seems that
his sincere wish was to be able to return to South Africa after a brief stay
away, in order to maintain his connection to his family. One must read
such letters with a pinch of salt, as it should be assumed that they were
read by the Special Branch, and that Turner would have written them
with this in mind. All the same, assuming that he was mostly honest
about his intentions, he had no desire to go into exile, to leave South
Africa permanently.

Turner petitioned Slabbert to help present his case before the Minister
of Justice. Slabbert refused, as he felt that his intervention wouldn't
help, and that he should instead try to get a personal interview with
the minister himself. Turner then reached out to an old friend from
Stellenbosch, Johann Degenaar, who was prominent in the South African
philosophical community, for help with the matter. He said to Degenaar
that he was 'certainly willing' to meet with the minister, 'but it has
occurred to me that either some of the philosophy association people or
somebody I knew at Stellenbosch might have some chance of helping me
by intervening personally'. Sadly, Degenaar was also unable to help.[25]

In his follow-up letter to Degenaar, Turner said that he felt that
neither Degenaar nor Slabbert had understood him properly. He clarified
his position:

I did not wish to argue to the minister that I am now a 'good boy'
who deserves special treatment. Rather, I am arguing that I am a bona
fide academic, engaged in technical, philosophical research which has
nothing to do with South African politics. Insofar as a ban is meant to
be preventive, rather than punitive, there is no reason why the minister
should not let me go to Heidelberg, where I can intervene in South African
politics even less effectively than I can under my present restrictions here.

This argument seems to me to be logically impeccable – whether it is politically and psychologically impeccable is of course another matter! However, it is the only argument that I have.[26]

There is no doubt that Turner was a bona fide academic, and that his interest in engaging in philosophical research was genuine. However, as he himself alluded, Turner's political stances – in opposition to apartheid, capitalism and Soviet communism – remained steadfast as well. Turner remained to his death a firm advocate of a socialism rooted in autonomy and small-scale democracy. Nonetheless, as it was 'the only argument' he had, Turner drafted a letter to the Minister of Justice, claiming that his time abroad would have no connection to his politics.

I appreciate that you may want some kind of guarantee that my interest in philosophical research is genuine. Of course ultimately I can offer no more than my assurance that it is. But I would like to point out that, as I will be returning to South Africa when I have completed my research, it would clearly be foolhardy of me if I were to wish to engage in political activity while overseas. Moreover, I have applied for a Humboldt Fellowship in order to finance my work in Germany. If I am awarded such a fellowship, I will be morally obliged to the Humboldt Foundation to use the funds for the purpose for which they are granted, as well as being morally bound to my University to use my study leave for the purpose for which it is granted.[27]

However 'impeccable' the logic of the argument may have been, the Minister of Justice didn't buy it in the slightest. In fact, the order to deny Rick Turner the right to travel was as emphatic as the original banning order. In their motivation, the Security Branch noted that 'Turner still displays an almost unequalled antagonism towards the State and, given his ability, is the person to whom those who wish to foment labour unrest in Natal turn for advice. In addition he is a Marxist who will never change his way of thinking. He therefore remains a security risk.'

Having been denied the right to study in Heidelberg, Turner had to face the prospect of another year in South Africa under the banning order, and he began to grapple with possible scenarios that might come after the banning would expire. All through 1977 his desire to leave for Germany remained steady, and he kept up both his research and his search for possible ways to get permission to leave. He continued to reach out to his allies at the university and friends both in South Africa and abroad, hoping that someone might be able to shift the opinion of the government in his favour. Meanwhile, Foszia and Rick discussed their alternatives at length and tried to imagine what might lie ahead.

Of course, Turner hoped for the possibility that his banning order would be lifted, and he would be allowed to return to his normal teaching duties. Perhaps, as the outline for the New International School for Social Research hints, Turner may have even hoped that he would be given room to re-engage in the political work into which he had so ambitiously thrown himself before the banning. To plan on such a possibility would have been tremendously naïve or a grave misunderstanding of the extent to which the state viewed him as a serious threat.

Though it was hard to stomach, there was always the chance that things would only get worse with time. There was the dreadful possibility that the banning order would be reinstated and Turner would have to face another five years in isolation. Or, perhaps the state would have to find even more vicious ways to silence him. It would have been impossible for Turner and Foszia to really comprehend all the nightmare scenarios that lay before them at the end of his banning years.

G.P.-5.

SAP 148 (f)

SUID-AFRIKAANSE POLISIE   SOUTH AFRICAN POLICE

P/sak - P/Bag 302   Tel adr. "KOMPOL"

VEILIGHEIDSTAK,
SECURITY BRANCH.

Verw./Ref.:	S.1/8242 (A.1)
Navrae/Enc.:	Maj.P.J. Rossouw
TEL.:	29281 x 310

HOOFKANTOOR.
HEAD OFFICE.

GEHEIM

PRETORIA.

0001

26.10.1976

A.   Die Sekretaris van Binnelandse Sake
     P R E T O R I A

B.   Die Sekretaris van Justisie
     P R E T O R I A

REISGERIEWE : R.A.D. TURNER
A. 76103/66
B. 10/3/2/1 - 3017 gedateer 11.8.1976

A.1.   U Streekverteenwoordiger, Durban se BE.71/7 van
19.10.1976 verwys.

2.   Bogenoemde is op 27.2.1973 onder artikels 9(1) en
10(1)(a) van Wet 44 van 1950 (Wet op Binnelandse Veiligheid)
vir 'n tydperk van vyf jaar tot 31.3.1978, ingeperk. Kragtens
die kennisgewing onder Artikel 10(1)(a) word hy onder andere
verbied om die Landdrosdistrik van Durban te verlaat.

3.   TURNER openbaar steeds 'n byna ongeëwenaarde vyandigheid
teenoor die Staat en is weens sy bekwaamheid, die persoon tot
wie diegene wat die arbeidsonrus in Natal aanblaas, hulle wend
vir raad.

4.   Daarbenewens is hy 'n Marxis wat sy denkwyse nooit sal
verander nie. Hy bly dus 'n veiligheidsrisiko.

5.   Hy het ook by die Minister van Justisie aansoek gedoen
om vir 'n jaar (1977) na Duitsland te gaan ten einde filosofiese
navorsing te doen. Na verneem word het die Minister die aansoek
geweier.

6.   Hierdie Departement staan die toekenning van reisgeriewe
aan TURNER teen.

2/...

TEN

Scream from the Rooftops

'To maintain political control of South Africa a certain type of government is required, and it is impossible to separate completely what it must do to blacks from what it does to whites. A minority cannot rule a majority by consent. Therefore, it must be prepared to use force to maintain its rule and this in turn requires a cultural climate that sanctions killing. The spies must inevitability act among the whites as well as the blacks, for dissent anywhere may be contagious, and hence fatal.'

– RICK TURNER

'If they want to beat me five times, they can only do so on condition that I allow them to beat me five times. If I react sharply, equally and oppositely, to the first klap, they are not going to systematically count the next four klaps, you see. It's a fight … If you allow me to respond, I'm certainly going to respond. And I'm afraid you might have to kill me in the process even if it's not your intention.'[1]

– STEVE BIKO

RICK TURNER'S ASSASSINATION did not take place in isolation. While his murder was one of the first of such blatant attacks by the apartheid security forces, it was nowhere near the last, and it happened within a climate of tremendous repression. During Turner's lifetime – and even more so in the years after his death – the state demonstrated an ever greater willingness to use excessive force against dissent. No longer resorting to legal measures to detain and banish the opposition, it became easier and cleaner to destroy opponents by assassination, parcel bombs and worse.

Many of Turner's close contemporaries suffered fates similar to his. The most prominent of these catastrophic events was the death of Steve Biko – the charismatic Black Consciousness leader who had been banned at the same time as Turner. He was brutally murdered in police custody in September 1977, just a few months before Turner's death.[2] Within weeks of Biko's murder, on 19 October 1977, the state banned 17 Black Consciousness organisations as well as the Christian Institute[3], and arrested almost 70 key black leaders.

Donald Woods, a white liberal and long-standing editor of the East London *Daily Dispatch*, who had developed a sympathetic relationship with Biko and his comrades, was very outspoken about the horror of Biko's murder in detention and was promptly banned as a result. After enduring months of harassment and death threats, on 1 January 1978 he appeared in Maseru, Lesotho, with his wife and children and made a very public display of boarding a plane and leaving southern Africa for good. He had fled the country by disguising himself as a priest and hitchhiking across an obscure border post in the Drakensberg mountains. His wife and children drove in a separate car and were able to arrive in Maseru undetected.

Donald Woods's escape was a major victory, both for him and for the anti-apartheid movement, and a tremendous embarrassment for the state. Once in exile, he was vocal in his condemnation of apartheid, and published a widely read biography of Biko.

Nightmare as warnings

Foszia Fisher

In November of '77, I had this really funny dream of the two of us ...

In our bedroom there's the bay window and a wall behind our beds and a wall across from the window.

The way we would sleep, Rick was in the front of the bed and I was toward the wall. And *his* dream was that somebody had shot through the window and the bullets had pierced him and then me. My dream, the same night, I was unusually in front and the bullets had gone first through me and then through him. So we woke up with exactly the same dream.

Before that, we had never thought about being shot. It was not something that we worried about or even thought about.

On Boxing Day [26 December], Rick's daughter Kim had a dream and woke up screaming. She had dreamt that the house was on fire ...

I guess the warnings were there ...

I had a sense of it, and yet it wasn't close.

There were so many different ways that we were being alerted to something changing in our lives, but there's no way you know what to do with that information. But it's in you, and it sits like undigested food ...

I just remember being shocked, we were just totally shocked. And there were no words. I remember going to the memorial meetings about Steve Biko; listening to the speeches. It was just more of the same. It didn't make it feel as if it was getting worse, it was just more of the same.

When Donald Woods left the country, we had no idea. We knew he ran the newspaper. His comments were not outrageous. It was only later that we learned to what extent he was involved with Steve Biko, but I had no idea. But that caused a ripple, and we did talk about it and we were surprised. But it didn't concern us.

It's a huge border and people come and go all the time. If you want to make a drama, you can.

You can't live your life thinking, 'When's the bullet going to come?' You just have to go on living and taking it. Not letting it define your reality. And I guess that's what we did.

So in a sense we were careful and yet very vulnerable. We knew that the society we were living in was a violent society. But we didn't prepare for either of us being killed.

From this distance you can see patterns, but when you were there you couldn't.

In Durban, the state violence happening elsewhere in the country arrived in the form of an assassination attempt at the home of Fatima and Ismail Meer. On the night of the attack on the Meers, in 1978, a firebomb was thrown into the garage adjacent to their house and a shot was fired before the culprits quickly sped away. Although there was considerable damage to the building and their gardener was injured, the Meers survived the attack unharmed.

At 32 Dalton Avenue, discussions were under way about Foszia taking a trip to Botswana. Two German friends, husband and wife, wanted to visit Rick and Foszia, but because of their work as critical journalists were denied visas to South Africa; instead they were going to be in Gaborone. Rick and Foszia felt that perhaps their friends could exert some influence to help Rick obtain authorisation to travel to Germany to take up his post-doctoral fellowship. With his banning set to expire in only one month's time, and with the possibility of some external diplomatic pressure from Germany, there was some hope that he would finally be able to go.

A back-up plan

Foszia Fisher

It was also our thinking that if the banning order would be re-imposed, we would leave South Africa. We were interested in finding a legal means to leave South Africa. But if that didn't work, we would have needed a back-up plan. Because this was not good for him. He was doing stuff in South Africa but he needed people

to be engaged with. Our plan was, if the worst came to
worst – we didn't know there was a worst beyond that
– we would leave and go to Germany and work towards
having some sort of conference centre in Europe where
we would run various kinds of discussions on strategy,
on change. It was not just going to be specifically about
South Africa. It was going to be about living wherever
you are. That would have been our plan.

The decision about whether Foszia should travel to Botswana had a couple
of other components. One idea that was considered was whether either
of Turner's daughters, Jann or Kim, who were visiting for the holidays,
should go along on the trip. Foszia was planning to stay in Gaborone with
Mike Hubbard, the girls' uncle, and Jann and Kim would have enjoyed
the chance to visit him. Furthermore, when the girls came up to Durban
it was usual to take a trip somewhere (despite the fact that the banning
order made even day excursions an incredibly cumbersome ordeal).

The idea of bringing one of the children along was considered seriously
and an effort was made to get their passports mailed from Cape Town.
Looking back, Rick's mother Jane felt that the phone calls between Rick
and his first wife Barbara might have played some negative part in leading
to Rick's death.

His private life made a little
more unbearable
Jane Turner

It seems to me that the telephone has played a large
part in the murder of my son. Not just any telephone,
but the telephone in his house, which had been tapped
by the security police during his five years of banning,
making his private life a little more unbearable.

The week before the murder my son telephoned the
mother of his children in Cape Town, asking her to send
him the passports of the children. He asked for the two

passports as it hadn't been decided which child should go. (The passports were not available so neither child could go.)

The listeners, then, knew that he would be alone, apart from the children, that weekend. (Did the word passport conjure up visions of flight? Had he actually thought of skipping the country, of course, he'd never have spoken about passports on the tapped phone and he certainly wouldn't have taken the children with him. But would the listeners reason like this? Did one of them perhaps think 'Another Donald Woods – I'll put a stop to that'?)

My daughter-in-law was very badly treated at the border, but when finally the police there phoned the security police in Durban their whole manner changed and she was suddenly treated with courtesy. Why?[4]

The other question to be dealt with was finding someone to travel with Foszia. Rick was unwilling to allow Foszia to make the journey on her own, as he felt that a companion might be helpful in case of an emergency. For many days leading up to the trip, it was impossible to find anyone willing to make the trip. Then, a young undergraduate student, Margie Victor, volunteered to go. Margie was an odd choice, as she was not among Rick's group of students, nor was she a particularly close friend or comrade. Stranger still, when Foszia was later asked about Margie's decision to travel to Botswana, her only explanation was that 'she wasn't doing anything that weekend. I think the motivation was, she and her boyfriend had just broken up. So it was something positive for her to do. So she sort of came up with the idea.'[5]

The journey had to begin very early in the morning, as the South African government had imposed restrictions on the sale of petrol in the aftermath of the Opec oil crisis. There was a limited window of time to make the drive to the Botswana border, before the petrol stations closed. On the morning of Friday, 6 January 1978, the alarm failed to go off. Nonetheless, Rick woke up in time and helped Foszia to get on her way.

In Pietermaritzburg, Foszia and Margie stopped at the house of Lorna Mirren's mother. Mirren, a liberal, had left South Africa for Botswana because she was in an inter-racial relationship, and so faced difficulties living under apartheid. She had asked Foszia to bring some things to her in Gaborone, which turned out to be a suitcase full of clothing. Unfortunately, Lorna's suitcase added to the long and extremely unpleasant interrogation at the border. Foszia and Margie were questioned for a number of hours. The officers were tense and agitated the whole time. They treated Foszia with great scepticism, refusing to believe her answers, and went over and over the same questions, as if she was being evasive.

Trouble at the border
Foszia Fisher

Oh yeah. I wasn't a stray thing. They knew who I was. They knew my name. They knew I was with Rick. They asked Margie, 'What are you doing with her?', because they knew Margie wasn't part of our circle. Margie, I don't think they gave her a body search, but they did me.

They wanted to know if I had money. He wanted to confiscate the money. He wanted to keep the money, and then I said, 'How on earth am I going to pay for petrol if you don't give me back the money?' So he gave me the money.

There was a question about the money and there was a question about the clothes: what I might be smuggling out of the country, and why I was going out of the country. How long was I going out of the country? It's hard to know from where I am now whether they were insinuating that I was the advance party for Rick's escape. So, the questions were all along those lines:

'Is Rick in Durban?'

'I don't know.'

That line of questioning from the police was constantly repeated; the police thought he was about to escape.

They were questioning me about something and I said, 'You don't have to take my word. Just call your colleagues in Durban and they will tell you.'

They were fine after that. There had been tension, tension, tension. And it was like the air in a balloon had been released.

'Here, have your money. Go on your way,' and then, 'have a good journey.'

And then Margie said, 'I think we should go back.'

I said, 'Why?' and she said, 'I just have this feeling.'

I said to her, 'There's no point. We have to go. Whatever is in process, is in process.'

We never would have got back in time. That's what I said then. We left on Friday and arrived in Botswana Friday night. I spoke to Rick on Saturday, about midday. So yes, we would have made it back in time.

I wish I had turned back. Because then if I had been back, Rick wouldn't have answered the door. The only reason he did was that he was worried about me.

Foszia woke up in Gaborone on the Saturday morning and took a drive around town with Michael Hubbard, exploring and talking. Afterwards, she met up with the friends from Germany, Gesila and Reinhardt. As Michael Hubbard had no telephone in his house, Foszia called home to Durban while she was out that afternoon. Rick was very happy to hear from her, as he had been worried after so many hours of silence. He had earlier in the day called Barbara, hoping that she might have some news from Gaborone. Foszia told Rick about her difficulties at the border, but also reassured him that everything was fine.

For dinner, Foszia went out to the house of Jenny Curtis and Marius Schoon. Jennie had been a member of Nusas and had fled the country after receiving a banning order. Marius was a member of the South African Communist Party as well as the African National Congress. Though both were viewed with hostility by the South African government, Foszia saw no reason not to have dinner with old friends.

It's a big border
Foszia Fisher

Marius thought I was undisciplined. We had discussions about: 'If you believe in liberation you have to be with the party.' He thought people who worked outside of structures for change were not always helpful. So we were having that kind of discussion.

Q. Were you potentially interested in their help in leaving South Africa? Were they interested in helping?

At that point, only Rick and I had discussed leaving. We had not raised that possibility with anybody else. We didn't need help. There were already ways of leaving. It's a big border. No, we didn't need help. But the security police were convinced that we were part of an underground movement. Because most of the people I knew were. So in their heads, I had to be. I think their thought was: 'The more you do, the more careless you get. If you give them enough room they will eventually get caught.'

Q. Do you think it's possible that the police would understand from your meeting with Jenny Curtis and Marius that you had a connection with the ANC, with the underground?

They knew Jenny was part of Nusas and Jenny had been working with the trade unions in Johannesburg. We would have meetings and stuff, so it wasn't as if we didn't know each other. It wasn't anything unusual linking up. The only person I had not met before was Marius.

Q. So you don't think that the trip to Botswana gave them a pretext to view you and Rick in a new light?

There wasn't enough time for this process to occur. I don't think it was me going across the border that made them think, 'Now it's time to go kill Rick.' I don't think so. I think, and I don't know why I think this, that the plan had been put in place. It wasn't spontaneous.

In those years, Gaborone was home to a number of anti-apartheid South Africans living in exile, many of whom had arrived there illegally. No matter how casually Foszia understood this at the time, it seems very unlikely that the authorities took her association with fugitives lightly at all. Her treatment at the border gives some indication of the extent to which the state was suspicious of anyone in Foszia's position – of living a life of open opposition to apartheid – crossing the border to Gaborone. Moreover, the process of fleeing illegally across the 'big border' to the north was not as simple as Foszia asserts, as many people faced grave danger when leaving. Michael Hubbard, who came to Botswana legally, to work for the university, understood the situation in a much graver light.

Vulnerable in Botswana
Mike Hubbard

One needs to understand the history of that particular phenomenon. In early '78, certainly there were ANC people in Gaborone. In mid-'77, six to eight months earlier, Marius and Jeanette jumped the border and they came immediately to our house and lived there for four or five months.

There were a number of ANC people who lived quite recognisably in Gaborone. I wasn't one of them, but I knew of them. No doubt many others did as well. So, there's a build-up, if you like, of an opposition clustered around the ANC, among whom Jeanette and Marius were certainly prominent.

Eventually, South African commandos came across the border in '85 and shot a lot of them in their houses. Thami Mnyele, the artist, was killed. Another one from Durban, who was a student at the University of Botswana, was also killed in '85. By that time Jeanette and her daughter had been killed by a letter bomb sent to their home in Angola by the apartheid security police.

Back in Durban, that same evening, Rick Turner had dinner with his two daughters and a friend named Kathy Thompson, who was living in the cottage in the backyard. He made Jann and Kim some tea, and read them bedtime stories.

He took a bath.

Just past midnight, he answered a knock at the front door.

'Who's there?'

Jann's statement to the police, given four days after the murder[6]…

```
NAME    .  Jann TURNER
NAAM    :

RACE    .  WHITE            SEX   :  FEMALE  AGE      13 years
RAS     :                   GESLAG          OUDERDOM :

ADDRESS .  'Stepping Stone', 14 Osborne Road    TEL.NO.     663844
ADRES   :     MOWBRAY  Cape Town                TEL.NR. :

EMPLOYED AT  .  Scholar                         TEL.NO.
WERKSADRES   :                                  TEL.NR. :

STATES IN   .  ENGLISH
VERKLAAR IN :
```

I declare that the following statement is true to the best of my knowledge and belief and that I make this statement knowing that if it is tendered in evidence I will be liable to prosecution if I wilfully state in it anything which I know to be false or which I do not believe to be true.

The late Dr Turner was my father. My sister Kim and I are visiting him at his home at 32 Dalton Road, Bellair.

On Saturday, 7th January 1978, during the evening and at about 7.30 p.m. my sister, my father and I had supper together. Then my sister and I prepared for bed.

My sister and I went to our beds in the front bedroom. My father sat on the end of the bed and read to us, the bedroom doors were open except for one. The main bedroom light was on.

My father left to make tea. It was then about twenty or quarter to ten. He brought tea for all of us and again sat on my bed. We all read our own books. We stopped reading at about 10.15 p.m.

At about 10.30 I could not sleep. I felt uneasy. I think my sister was asleep. Our bedroom door was open.

I went into the bathroom, where my father was having a bath. I talked to my father about not being able to sleep. He told me to think about the planets.

I said goodnight to him and went back to bed and fell asleep about five minutes later.

I woke up and heard my father near the front door. He said, 'Who is it?' but there was no answer or movement. He again said, 'Who is it?' and again there was no reply.

My father came into our room and stood about two paces away from the window.

He spoke to himself and said in an irritated way something along the lines of 'who the hell is coming around at this time of night?' He took a step forward and pulled the curtain back and looked out of the window onto the front veranda. He looked slightly surprised and opened his mouth. I heard a loud bang and saw a big flash. I thought that it was an explosion. He let out a loud muffled scream. He staggered back and fell into the bedroom doorway. He writhed around on the floor and made a noise. When he fell I jumped out of bed and shouted, 'Daddy, Daddy, what is the matter?' I was shocked and I cannot remember what happened after that.

The next thing I can remember was that I was at the back door shouting, 'Kathy, there's been an explosion!' The back door was not locked. I went back and found my father lying in the doorway of the lounge and the kitchen. His body was in the lounge and his head in the kitchen. He was lying face down. He could not breathe properly and there was blood everywhere. The house was in darkness. I ran and used the phone and dialed 414 - Cape Town emergency number.

Kathy arrived. She was fully dressed and the lights were switched on. I turned my father over onto his back. He did not speak a word. He was still alive. Kathy told me to stay away from the doors and windows. I did not hear any motor car pull away after the explosion or any noise outside.

Kathy phoned the ambulance. There was a pool of blood and I held his head. I wiped my father's face with a cloth. His face was white. My father was dressed in his shorty pyjamas. I looked for the wound but I could not see it because of the blood.

I have no idea what the time was when I heard my father at the front door.

After I tried to find the wound, I gave my father mouth to mouth resuscitation.

The police and an ambulance then arrived.

When my father entered our room the light in the veranda was off. There was moonlight. The curtain he pulled away is at the window closest to the front.

I have seen my father look through the same window in the past when not sure who was at the front door.

The statement was read over to me before I signed it.

I know and understand the contents of this declaration. I have no objection to taking the prescribed oath.

I consider the prescribed oath to be binding on my conscience.

Jannturner

JANN TURNER.

BELLAIR
12.1.1978 —

L. Bree

STEPFATHER.

Ek sertifiseer dat die verklaarder erken dat hy/sy ten volle op hoogte is met die inhoud van hierdie verklaring en dit tegryp. Hierdie verklaring was beedig/ bevestig voor my, en verklaarder se handtekening/duimafdruk/merk is hierby geplaas in my teenwoordigheid daarop aangebring

I certify that the deponent has acknowledged that he/she knows and understands the contents of this affidavit which was sworn/affirmed before me and the deponent's signature/thumb print/mark was placed thereon in my presence.

Justice of the Peace.
Kommissaris van Ede/Commissioner of Oaths.

Datum
Date 13/1/78

Plek
Place Bellair

AREND JOHANNES EYSELE.
S. A. POLICE P.O. BELLAIR.

Statement taken by me.

A.A. EYSELE D,

The phone call
Mike Hubbard

Suddenly we got this phone call.

It must have come through at around 1 a.m. Ilona Kleinschmidt was on the phone with Foszia. All I heard was, 'What? What? Is he badly hurt? Is he badly hurt?'

And she just slipped down to the floor and curled herself up in the foetal position … and Foszia was saying, "There's no point. There's no point."

We got back to the house and there was just crying and crying. There was no question of going back to sleep. We were just devastated, both Foszia and me. Gesila we had not woken up. And I'm really glad we didn't wake her up because at least there was one person who got a night's sleep. It's really difficult to overemphasise the depth of despair and destruction I could see in Foszia, and that I had been feeling myself. I had two sisters but I never had a brother, and Richard was very much like an elder brother to me.

It was quite devastating.

Scream from the rooftops
Fatima Meer

When Rick died, Islam would call for a quick burial, but his mother, Jane, insisted that the funeral must be attended by as many people as possible. Further, Jane picked the headstone:

'Rick Turner: Assassinated January, 8th 1978. He fought for Justice for All' as she wanted us to scream from the rooftops that he was assassinated; you couldn't say 'killed' or 'murdered'.

Nonetheless, as far as we were concerned he was a Muslim, so he was buried in a Muslim cemetery [Brook Street, downtown Durban] according to Muslim rites.

Every aspect of Rick Turner's death and burial was political, as most of his life had been. The situation was ripe with all the absurd and painful contradictions of navigating a system that constantly negates people's humanity. On the one hand, the state was obliged, finally, to treat Foszia as 'Mrs Turner', the wife of Richard Turner. But this moment of acceptance came at the most appalling time. Foszia was made to pay the highest possible price in exchange for this small, ironic gesture of validation. To be forced to stare down at the body of one's lover, torn to pieces by a bullet – very likely fired from a policeman's gun – and then confirm to an official, 'Yes, that's him,' is a horrifying fate.

That's not him

Foszia Fisher

They had done this autopsy on him and they stitched his body in the most 'we don't care' way. So it was very hard to connect what I saw with Rick.

It was like, 'That's not him. It resembles him. But this is not him. I remember the hair, I remember the chest, but that can't be him. Someone took a cast and put it there, but it's not him.' Nothing prepared me for it. But 'Yes,' I said, 'Yes, it's him.' Then, after a while, the eyebrows, the nose, the closed eyes, the scar I know, I kissed that many times. The ears, the neck. You go through the whole thing and it is, but it isn't, so I signed the paper thinking, 'Wow, I must tell Rick about this. I signed the acknowledgement.'

After the autopsy, there came the question of the burial, the funeral and all of the complicated political questions enmeshed in these arrangements. Rick Turner is buried in a Muslim cemetery in the centre of Durban. His is one of only a few white bodies buried there. The day his body was placed in its final resting place was the first time he had legally entered an area of South Africa reserved for non-whites since his banning began on 26 February 1973. Islam does not acknowledge the colour bar in any way, and Turner's body was accorded the same treatment as anyone else's.

A kind of peace

Foszia Fisher

We sat with his body and the men bathed him, embalmed his body, oiled it, did whatever they do to prepare the body for burial. And then they came and laid him on the floor in pure white cotton. There was no casket but they placed him in the metal frame, so

217

when they took him to the cemetery it would just be the body in the white cotton so the body decays quickly. There's no kind of preservation.

They had put coal on his eyes, so his eyes were closed and there was a kind of peace on him.

It was like he had been dressed up for something.

But again, the same stillness.

Someone took a cast and put it there, but it's not him.

The funeral, of course, was an inter-racial affair: Rick's extended community of friends and family, colleagues and political allies spanned a broad cross-section of the population. The authorities tolerated the gathering for the most part, though of course they had to deal with the thorny issue of deciding whether to allow the number of Rick's friends who were under banning orders to attend. Some were allowed, others were denied. In addition, the security police sent informants to the funeral, to keep tabs on all those whose surveillance files were being constantly updated.

Roughly a thousand people attended the funeral. More than a dozen mourners spoke, giving impassioned accounts of the Rick Turner they had loved, and of the significance of his life and his assassination. The range of people who gave eulogies in his memory reflected the broad reach of his friendships and political connections. Turner had wanted to build meaningful relationships across all the barriers in apartheid South Africa, and the funeral provided an opportunity for representatives from many different communities to step forward and show their respects.

Among those who spoke were a number of university colleagues, including the Principal of Natal University, and Turner's friend Lawrence Schlemmer. Political activists, such as Charles Nupen, a student leader in Nusas, M.J. Naidoo, from the Natal Indian Congress, and Thizi Khumalo, a trade union orgasniser, also shared memories. In addition, religious leaders of various faiths spoke, including a rabbi, a Muslim imam, a Hindu priest and a radical Catholic archbishop.

Richard Turner was laid in his final resting place the way that he had lived: with the love and appreciation of a great many people from all walks of life. For them all, he was memorialised as a man who had 'sought justice for all' and died too young, as a result.

Given the political climate at the time, and the callous indifference and even hatred on the part of the authorities towards Turner and his surviving family, it is not surprising that his mother Jane insisted on 'screaming from the rooftops' that her son had been assassinated. Even young Kim began to grasp hold of the horrible suspicion that the murderer of her father worked for the government:

> In my nine-year-old mind I knew that South Africa was governed by people who murdered school children for refusing to learn a language that was alien to them, and I remember my sister and mother attending Steve Biko's memorial service, and accepting that it was the police who had killed him whilst he was in their custody. Putting all these things together, I could see the political motives behind my father's killing. He had died for daring to disagree with the government, and for me the man who had pulled the trigger became irrelevant, and I felt I knew who his killers were.[7]

STONEWALLED

Having hounded Turner for years, following him wherever he went, tapping his telephone, hiring neighbours to spy on him, the authorities suddenly had to act as if they were trying to apprehend the murderer of a white man in a society organised for the exclusive benefit of white people. They failed miserably, and intentionally. Step by step, right through every stage of the process, for decades to come, the police were simply unable even to act *as if* they were interested in handling Turner's case with the care it deserved.

It took the Durban police half an hour to arrive at the house after young Jann was able to get through to them by phone. When they did turn up, they were gruff, and lacked all compassion for Turner or his loved ones. Jann recalled the event before the TRC.

It's the police, open up!

Jann Turner

When the police arrived he was already dead. He died probably 20 minutes after he was hit. I had tried during those 20 minutes to talk to him, to ask him who he had seen at the window, what had happened, but he never regained consciousness. I know now when he died, although at the time, because his eyes fluttered and his mouth quivered, I thought he was trying to talk to me ...

The way the police arrived at the house was strange. They didn't use sirens, so the first we heard of their presence was a loud banging on the door. When we asked who was there, we got no reply. We were terrified at this point, fearing that the killer had returned to hurt us. We shouted again, 'Who is it?' And I remember getting up and Kathy and I running and Kathy screaming at me to get away from the doors and windows. Three or four times we called out, and they didn't identify themselves.

Finally they said, 'It's the police, open up!'

When I tried to call my mother, an officer in plain clothes grabbed the phone from me, and I was sent in to my father's bedroom, with Kim and Kathy, where we were watched over by a very young and very shaken police officer who kept on saying that my father would be alright.

But he was already dead.

While the police were at the property, they did almost nothing that would normally be required in a murder investigation. Photographs were taken of the murder scene, and Turner's body was taken away; but little else was done. Even the bullet case was not discovered by the police at the scene. This was found on the following day, by the girls' mother, Barbara. She described what happened to her daughter in a later interview conducted in 1993 by Jann Turner.

I got orders from on top

Barbara Follett

At about 20 minutes to 3 a.m., you called me and said, 'Daddy's dead.'

And I do remember shrieking: 'Dead!'

And I remember you saying to me, 'Don't scream, everybody's screaming.'

And I can remember saying, 'Alright, I won't scream, just tell me what's happened, and where's Daddy.'

And you said to me, 'I'm standing over him and he's been shot.'

I immediately began making preparations to come to Durban straight away. The next morning when I walked off the plane, you and Kim were standing there with Lawrie [Schlemmer]. You were both covered in blood and your hair was covered in blood, and it had dried because the sun was hot. Since then, whenever I think of South Africa, I think of the smell of drying blood in the sun. Not only because of you and Kim, but because of all the people that I saw die. I think South Africa is drying blood in the sun.

When I arrived at the house, I walked into the bedroom, and I saw your father's handprint in blood on Kim's sheet, and then I turned round and I looked at the wall and I could see a bullet hole above Kim's bed and I thought, 'That bullet must have ricocheted across the room,' and I walked over to the bed and found the bullet cartridge there.

I picked it up and I walked outside and showed it to the police officer and I said to him, 'Look, here's the bullet, it's a 9mm.'

He took it from me and he said, 'Well, we found the bullet. But we're never gonna find the weapon because BOSS doesn't want us to finish this case.'

'Why? What do you mean?' I asked.

He was quite a nice guy, and I'd met him before, because he supervised your father's banning. He replied, 'I got orders from on top to lay off on this case; [Minister of Justice, Jimmy] Kruger's involved. I can't do anything.'[8]

Any potentially thorough police investigation into Rick Turner's murder would have had to deal in some depth with the role of the state's security apparatus. As a result of his banning, Turner had been closely watched by both the Special Branch and the Bureau of State Security (BOSS). While the two organisations had somewhat different methods and goals (and were not entirely aware of each other's activities), they nonetheless were both primarily focused on surveillance. If, as the Durban police claimed for decades, the murder of Rick Turner was a strictly criminal affair – with no political motive – the security forces would have had a great deal of information that could have led to apprehending any common criminal.

However, as Martin Dolinschek, the BOSS agent assigned to Rick Turner's case, reminded Jann Turner when she interviewed him years later, 'One thing is, if you want to do something, you can withdraw the surveillance, assign them somewhere else.'[9] Agent Gopal, a security police officer who was assigned to carry out surveillance on Turner, was later reported as testifying: 'One week before the assassination, the surveillance was suddenly terminated by orders from his superiors, without any explanation of why this was done.' Whether or not the police agents were given any explanation from their superiors, the implication is quite clear. The surveillance was withdrawn so that no one would be able to witness the events leading up to and following Turner's death.

The security police clearly didn't want to provide any answers about the murder and, fortunately for them, the police had no intention of asking. Had the Durban police been determined to solve the case, they would have had to demand access to all relevant surveillance files. Further, the police would have had to force the security police to explain their decision to suddenly cancel the surveillance that had been in operation 24 hours a day for five years.

The consensus, after numerous investigations into Turner's murder have been conducted, is that Barbara's recollection is probably accurate. It seems clear that someone (if not immediately, then relatively quickly) in a high-ranking position within the apartheid state gave the Durban police orders to 'lay off' the case, to go along quietly with covering up any potential involvement of the security forces in the killing. Even in the absence of explicit orders, the police were clearly unwilling to confront their fellow officers, and were quite content to leave Turner's case unsolved. And so, increasingly over time, the police department resorted to out-and-out lying.

It is now entirely impossible to believe that the murder of Rick Turner was an act of common criminality. Turner was not a common citizen, and far too many details of the case lead to the strong impression that he was murdered for political reasons. Aware of this fact – but still attempting to steer attention away from the state as the most likely suspect – the police began spreading a rumour that perhaps the ANC was responsible for Turner's death.

As it happened, a man by the name of Stephen Mtshali, who had been a member of the ANC (but had turned against them and cooperated with the police), was shot in his home on the same night as Rick Turner (though he did not die).[10] Even though the evidence seemed to point elsewhere, the story began to circulate that the two shootings might be connected. According to Jann Turner's investigation, the police were able to broadcast this ludicrous theory through a sympathetic contact within the news media:

> During the week after my father was killed, Leon Mellet, a crime reporter working for a Durban newspaper (and now a Brigadier in the police force), penned several stories suggesting that my father was killed by the ANC, against whom he had supposedly turned. These articles appear to be a deliberate attempt to smear my father and the ANC, and to throw yet another spanner in the spokes of the police investigation. Leon Mellet

went from crime reporting to have quite a successful career in the police, so apparently he was working for them all along.[11]

The news articles published in the days after Turner's death, while occasionally including an unusual level of sympathy for Rick Turner and compassion for his grieving family, were often full of slander and bizarre theories about the probable cause of his death.

NIGHTMARES THAT LINGER

In the aftermath of Turner's death, the weight of his absence began to press down on all who were close to him. The desperate effort to make sense of something that cannot be truly explained, to come to terms with something that is quite simply unacceptable, started right away and has not stopped since.

To lose a father, a husband, a brother or a dear friend to an assassin's bullet is not the kind of nightmare that can be forgotten easily. The horror of Richard Turner's death lingers palpably among all those who knew and loved him, despite the passing of many years. Although they have continued with their lives – and, for many, this also meant carrying on with the struggle for freedom – the memory of Turner *stays*. His brilliance is remembered fondly, but always, tugging at the shirt-tails of that recollection, is the awareness of the brutal way in which his life was taken.

People carry their trauma in different ways; but the grieving hit everyone.

Tony Morphet recalls what it was like when he arrived in Durban shortly after the death: 'the most terrible trauma everywhere – people in hysterical states. I mean, it cut across people in the most extraordinary manner.'[12]

Foszia remembers the difficulty of returning to Durban after her trip to Botswana and feeling as if the murder were not real enough for her, because she had been so far away when it happened.

So unreal

Foszia Fisher

It's still unreal. I don't know what it would be to make it real for me.

I was at the house and my mother was there, my sisters were there, all my female relatives were there. And they were doing the things, cooking and so forth, and I remember going into the garden and the smell as they put him in the ground. The smell of him was just there with me. It was so weird.

I wanted to have a sense of making it real because it was so unreal, all the different aspects. So unreal. And then I sat in the room where he had been shot. And I looked to see where the bullet had gone and where it had come out. And I argued with him and I said, 'How could you have let it happen? What was the matter with you? Why didn't you move your arm? The bullet would have gone through your arm and not entered your lung or entered your chest. That was the cause of death. That was why you choked on your blood. If you moved your arm the bullet would have gone through, and it might have hit Jann or Kim. So whichever which way, this was possibly the best outcome. I don't know.' But I just remember sitting in the room fighting with him.

There was always in that room a great sense of noise, a great sense of confusion.

Tony Morphet can relate to this feeling of Turner's death being painfully unreal. 'It was apparently completely unpredictable and there was this terrible sense that there might be more and more and more, that it might just go from one person to another. I saw Lawrence Schlemmer the day after the assassination and he said to me, "We don't know how many more of us … [*Sobbing*]" So, the other feeling was a most extraordinary sense of having been broken.'[13]

For the young girls, on the other hand, there was almost a sense in which it was all too real. The abrupt, explosive end to their father's life happened in the girls' own bedroom, and his blood poured out everywhere, such that they couldn't possibly escape the reality of it. For Jann and Kim, their father's death was so uncomfortably close to them, their lives so intimately intertwined with his passing, that the tragedy of it all threatened to drown them.

Nearly twenty years later, Kim said of the absence of Rick in her life, 'What can I say about not having a father? It's been quite difficult. For example, it hurt me a lot, three years ago, when my daughter asked me, "Mommies don't have daddies, do they?" because she couldn't understand why I didn't have a daddy. So I had to explain to her why I don't have a daddy and where he is. How do you explain to a young girl that you have no father because some man walked up to his house and killed him? I haven't explained that totally to her yet, and I don't think I will for a long time. When that time comes, I would very much like to be able to tell her who killed him.'[14]

Jann Turner held close to her father's suffocating body in his last moments on earth. She even attempted to resuscitate him, to use any possible way to perform the miracle of keeping him alive after being shot in the chest at close range. Foszia remembers asking Jann afterwards, 'Did you have a sense that if you knew how to call him, he could come back?' And she said, 'Yes, but I didn't know which way.' This urgent sense that she must do something, *anything*, to help her dying father, would stay with Jann well into her adult life, as she threw herself into tracking down the killer.

Rick's mother Jane, interviewed days after his death, told the newspapers that 'my blood has turned to acid'. Her bitter rage at the tragedy of having lost her beloved son didn't seem ever to subside, and she persistently spent the final years of her life attempting to find his killer and get his story out into the public arena.

The inevitable flurry of questions – *how* did it happen? *why* did it happen? *who* was responsible? – assailed people in different ways.

Foszia has had to fight a bitter struggle against the ghost of her husband's killer, and her own feelings of powerlessness or, by some painful twist of logic, of being partially at fault for Rick's death. 'For a long time I thought if only I hadn't been so pigheaded he would be alive. And then there was something in me that just stopped. I thought ... it wasn't me who pulled the trigger. It wasn't me who made it happen. And then I realised I had to stop. I have to start thinking, "This happened. Somebody did this. And I have to recreate this, I have to make a meaning, I have to do something. I have to stop living in definition to that moment." And yet, somehow I'm implicated in it.'

Tony Morphet, to an extent spared from some of the most intimate torments of grieving, as a result of being more removed from the death, also made a conscious choice to try and cauterise the wound of his loss. 'That's what I did. I cauterised it. The rupture was very unexpected and I suppose damaging. More damaging than one even thought at the time. So, it's not so much closure, but more a sense that some things can't be done, some things can't be known, some things can't be understood properly, some things can't be valued properly. They must be left alone.'[15]

No matter how necessary such a stance was for Tony or others who valued Turner deeply, it wasn't a stance that everyone was able to take.

For Foszia the nightmare of losing Rick continued decades after his death, in various forms. For Jane, the outrage at the system of apartheid for gunning down her son would never relent, sending her across the continent of Africa trying to bring the assassin to justice. Later, in the dawning years of the transition to democracy in South Africa, Jann Turner would return to the country, as an adult, to follow in her grandmother's footsteps. Jann spent two full years, using all her intelligence, diligence and courage to try to uncover the truth behind the death of her father.

Unfortunately, in a country that has suffered through decades of tyranny, where violence was common and where the victims were often murdered by their own government, the search for answers can be a nightmare in and of itself.

Conclusion

'The essential problem is this: How can we design a set of institutions
that will give all individuals power over their own lives without
permitting them to exercise power over other people? How can
we design political institutions that will give people the maximum
freedom to choose what to do with their own lives?'[1]

— RICK TURNER

* * *

WHAT'S IN A LIFE? How can we trace a coherent thread of aspiration and
maintain our dignity in spite of the fact that compromise feels like an
inevitability?

What's in a society? How do we retain our determination to radically
transform all of our social interactions and structures, in the light of the
seeming permanence of the current moment?

Stories. Hints. Scraps. Little bits of evidence that point in possible
directions.

* * *

Every country has its own hell.
It is clear that every country has its own hell, its own savageries and
traumas.

South Africa may have a uniquely horrifying history to contend
with, but it is not the only place where people struggle to break free from

the weight of their history. All of us find ourselves increasingly living within a globalised hell; a system of exploitation and brutality which claims to be both inevitable and permanent. The tangible significance of 'independence' throughout the de-colonised world has been steadily attacked at virtually all levels and socialism has collapsed, leaving many people feeling disillusioned and set adrift amidst what appear to be few fundamental alternatives.

In South Africa, the hell of apartheid has given way to a new desert of possibilities.
Not unlike the situation in many other countries, the hopes and aspirations of South African radicals were not fulfilled by the system change which came about formally in 1994.

The concept of 'winning' – wars of liberation, revolutions, etc. – is a dangerous one. A clear victory is often a defeat in disguise. But when we say that we've already won, our minds shut off. We are infatuated with slogans and programmes and clear and tangible progress. Even if we are able to speak out strongly against the failures of so-called revolutionaries to implement their stated goals once they take power, 'the movement' remains frozen in our memories at its climax: vibrant, inspiring, and utterly disconnected from the compromises and capitulations that followed.

The current governing alliance in South Africa is deeply stagnated, hemmed in by its own frightening mix of socialist rhetoric, Stalinist organisational principles and capitalist policies.

The basic features of the disappointing and painful compromises that are built into the new South Africa are so well known that they have essentially become a cliché; it is all sufficiently well documented not to need recounting here. The real lesson of the ANC's capitulation to the demands of international capital is that it is less a betrayal than a continuation of a process long in motion.

The era of 'realistic' politics in South Africa is under way.
The death of Rick Turner signalled the end of an era of resistance in South Africa. Most organisations of which he had been part or which had influenced him were either destroyed or so severely hammered by

repressive measures as to be rendered virtually unrecognisable. Ironically, this brutal repression of independent and non-violent opposition groups (which thrived in the absence of the African National Congress and the Communist Party) led to a resurgence of armed struggle and a recommitment to the banned ANC and SACP. By choosing to repress absolutely everything, the apartheid state breathed fresh life into its supposed worst nemesis.

In the years after Turner's death, the movement against apartheid grew generally much more powerful, but also more centralised, more 'united' and 'disciplined' under the leadership of the ANC, the Communist Party and the trade unions. In other words, the liberation struggle in South Africa came to be governed by more orthodox forms of organisation and leadership, as well as more orthodox and rigid ideas of socialism and revolution. The New Left (that is, an independent, transparent and idealistic radicalism), of which Turner is widely acknowledged as being a catalyst, eventually gave way to the Old Left politics of the authoritarian party liberating the masses.

The combination of a massive increase in trade union organisation, civic bodies, armed struggle and international solidarity succeeded in pressuring the government and the wealthy to accept that there was essentially no choice but to negotiate a transition to a parliamentary democracy with universal suffrage.

It is an impressive story; the stuff of myths, really.

South Africa is a good place for myth-making. Since the 1980s, at least, the country has been churning out images, songs and stories of the beautiful struggle of a righteous people overcoming at great odds an unjust system and replacing it with a 'rainbow nation', where everyone can live well.

The liberation struggle is used now to justify the status quo: power, privilege and poverty.

There is in South Africa the idea of 'struggle credentials'.

That is, in the growing story of the liberation of the country from apartheid, there are some people whose participation in the struggle supposedly made them deserving of unquestioned loyalty from the populace. Criticisms of politicians in power today can be neatly deflected by pointing to their service to the liberation of the country. In this way, national heroes are created in the mythology of the new nation and a political climate develops in which outside the party there is virtually no room for opposition and within the party the stifling of dissent is even more severe.

I want to spin the concept of 'struggle credentials' on its head.
There are two ways to think about how societies change. One can either focus on structures or on people, on power or on relationships. At one level, it is possible to analyse the broad dynamics that govern our lives: economic forces, ideologies we are socialised to believe in, political machinations, and so forth. I don't deny that this is a helpful way of thinking at times. But at the same time, it is vital to try to understand social change as a dynamic of human relationships: friendships and collaborations, shared projects and risks: drifting, distance and betrayal.

As it turns out, people made all the major, dramatic changes in the social systems of which we know.

Many of Rick Turner's peers have had long-lasting and fruitful careers as activists, trade unionists, professors and, eventually in the new South Africa, businessmen and government ministers. In tracing the trajectory of their lives, it is possible to see ourselves. In that early moment of constant opposition to the state, we want to recognise ourselves in their choices; we share their aspirations.

Then, with their more recent incarnations, we must face up to and try to unravel the slow drift, the unfolding in the direction of not only accepting, but justifying, a deeply compromised situation. At the core, there is the tremendous weight of rationality, the powerfully persuasive logic of pragmatism, of doing what can be done.

Rick Turner was overshadowed by the one-dimensional heroes of the revolution.
Already during Turner's lifetime, people who had once worked closely with him, and had been profoundly influenced by him, began moving away from his politics.

Is it enough to say that Turner's impact waned merely because of the banning order? Of course, this is a logical explanation. Not only could he not interact with people with ease after the banning, but it was also quite difficult for him to get his writing out to the public. Indeed, the answer appears obvious: he lost his prominence because he was banned.

State repression obviously had an effect on Turner's ability to influence people. But this answer is deceptively simple; it does not really explain why activists, people who opposed the state and were similarly repressed by it, would move away from Turner. Why would a man whom many acknowledge as an inspiring voice for a more radical politics lose his prominence so quickly?

There is an element of conscious choice that gets overlooked when all the emphasis is placed on state repression. People within the South African left stopped following Richard Turner's ideas because they wanted to, because they didn't believe in them, because they didn't think his approach would succeed. If people had found Turner's politics useful, they would have stayed committed to them, regardless of the state's decisions to ban and assassinate him. Placing the blame on the state is not dishonest, but it is irresponsible not to also interrogate the choices made within the struggle.

Marxism seems to be some kind of blueprint out of the quagmire of capitalism; but where does it lead?
The 1970s in South Africa were brutal, and many people wanted action, something clear that they could take hold of. Marxism seemed to offer the kind of programmatic politics that both justified people's aspirations towards leadership and explained how to build organisations of struggle. This form of coherent and comprehensive politics not only delivered a critique of the existing system, but also provided relatively clear instructions on how to intervene towards revolutionary change.

Many people claim that Marxism is a scientific ideology. For our purposes it is enough to realise that people *believe* that Marxism is scientific and all-encompassing (and that this belief provides them some comfort). In fact, scientific Marxism is only one of multiple strains within the socialist tradition. The Soviet Union was the clearest living example of the scientific approach to socialism. The Soviet government – and all of those throughout the world who proudly embraced Leninism and Stalinism – promulgated a cold and mechanistic Marxism. The grey tower

232

blocks of socialist states in Eastern Europe, for example, well captured the hard and crudely rational ethos of this world-view. For adherents of this politics, Marxism is merely a tool to organise large masses of people – to seize and exercise power.

Having adopted a mechanistic politics in order to build organisations to confront apartheid, many prominent Marxists since 1994 have found it seductively easy to settle into positions of power and privilege within the new political arrangement. Sadly, this means that many of the people who once faced grave risks in order to speak out in defence of social justice are now the authors of policies that maintain, and even harden, a profoundly unequal social and economic system.

How do we avoid following that slow drifting spiral of 'realism'?
To be sure, in comparison, Turner's politics were far less 'scientific' or 'coherent' than Soviet Marxism. Still, he was very much a socialist. His vision of socialism was an idealistic one, rooted in a profound sense of trust in human beings to be able to liberate themselves without having any rigid programme to follow and without any kind of vanguard to lead the way. Turner was extremely hopeful about the possibilities of human freedom. He refused to demand less, of himself, of his peers, of society as a whole, merely because the climate at the time was suffocating.

In fact, it is not surprising that Turner was unable to provide people with the kind of clear-cut answers that the Soviet-style Marxists promised. Quite simply, he didn't want to. Stubbornly, frustratingly to some, he would not help anyone go to war against apartheid, and would not recruit them to join any party or union; he simply encouraged discussion, and thoughtful action.[2]

Rather than offering a doctrine or a programme, Rick Turner espoused (and lived by, as much as he was able) a set of radical ethics. Turner's ethical choices remain resonant within the current political climate: place more value in people than things, and strive to share property as fully as possible; use dialogue to stimulate critical thought and change values; avoid, to the greatest extent possible, authoritarian and hierarchical methods of working together; and place a corresponding trust in 'the educative function of participation', the ability of people to develop the capacity to control their own lives through the act of collaboration.

Realistically, the pragmatists cannot possibly solve the fundamental problems that assail us.

In the increasingly popular account of the movement to end apartheid, there is a clean, linear progression from the social movements at the start of the 1970s straight through to the ferment of the 1980s and the end of apartheid in the 1990s. In this version of history, all the later developments took their inspiration from the radical notions put forward during the period in which Rick Turner was most active (this has come to be known as the Durban Moment).

There are a number of problems with this perspective, but all of them stem from the same root cause, which is a failure to recognise the unique qualities of the political developments of the early 1970s, which by necessity developed in counter-balance to the opposition politics that came before and after. While we must assume that people are genuine when they assert a logical congruency between the Durban Moment and the democratic transition, it is nonetheless a specious proposition, and seems to be made without any thorough investigation of the actual nature of the politics in either period.

While it may feel flattering for some to have their efforts in the early 1970s lumped together with the democratic transition two decades later, it is in fact a false compliment.

No one who would speak of him would go so far as to dismiss Richard Turner. No matter how strongly they disagree, people consistently attempt to give him credit for his contribution in one form or another. However, the ultimate erasure of Turner's ideas is to claim that they have been assimilated into the movements that developed after his death. As long as we believe that his vision was enthusiastically embraced by those who came after him, we will remain trapped within a deadening cul-de-sac. Ironically, if we can understand the extent to which Rick Turner was marginalised by the one-dimensional heroes of the liberation struggle, his ideas will have space to re-emerge as a viable alternative.

Rick Turner's way of thinking thrived within the political climate of the Durban Moment. It was precisely the absence of any institutionalised, hierarchical left that allowed his dialogic and utopian approach to gain prominence. People were ready to listen to someone who encouraged them to fundamentally re-examine their values, because there seemed to be so few concrete alternatives for opposing the status quo.

In the present moment, we are confronted with the opposite problem. Rather than the absence of an organised left, the organisations of the liberation struggle have gained so much power that nothing much else has room to breathe. Meanwhile, beneath the surface, people in all sectors of society are beginning to lose faith, as they can see that the ethos of the present system completely lacks a commitment to meeting human needs or providing for a meaningful life.

* * *

Choices. Our lives are made up of all the choices that we make, or do not make. Choices made visible, but not chosen. Choices made, but not understood, or not re-evaluated later, or regretted and carried like a weight.

These are, indeed, troublingly quiet times. It is tempting to drift into the numb comfort of cynicism. But simply naming the moral depravity of our times is not enough.

The only escape from cynicism, at this point, lies in utopian thought, in articulating and defending a vision of an 'ideally possible society'.

List of interviewees

Omar Badsha
Omar Badsha was raised in Durban, where he first met Rick Turner in 1970. The two collaborated on a number of projects, including ERA, Platform, the IIE, Phoenix farm, and the Wages Commission. Badsha was a photographer, a union organiser, and an activist within the Natal Indian Congress and the Black Consciousness Movement. He now lives in Cape Town, where he directs South African History Online.

Halton Cheadle
Halton Cheadle was a student of Rick Turner's for three years. During this time, he became involved in the Wages Commission at the University of Natal. Building on this involvement in labour politics, Halton became a trade union organiser, as a member of TUACC. After his banning in 1974, Cheadle studied law, and began a career as a lawyer, focusing primarily on labour issues. He was the principal architect of the 1995 Labour Relations Act. Cheadle now lives in Cape Town, and is director of the firm Cheadle Thompson & Haysom Attorneys.

John Clare
John Clare was a friend of Richard Turner from primary school. The two lived together during their years as undergraduate students at the University of Cape Town. Clare's early work as a journalist for *Drum* magazine earned him the unwanted attention of the apartheid state, and he was forced to go into exile in 1964. Clare made a name for himself as a journalist in the UK, where he worked for *The Times*, *The Observer*, *The Daily Telegraph*, ITN and BBC.

Andrew Colman
Andrew Colman met Turner in the student movement at the University of Cape Town in the 1960s. In 1969 Colman moved to Grahamstown, where he held a position as a psychology lecturer at Rhodes University. In 1970 he left South Africa for the UK, and became a professor of psychology at Leicester University.

John Copelyn

John Copelyn arrived in Durban in 1974, as a young graduate of Wits University, and quickly moved into a leadership position within TUACC. From 1980 to 1994, he was the general secretary of the Southern African Clothing and Textile Workers' Union. From 1994 to 1997, he was an ANC member of parliament. He is the CEO and executive director of Hosken Consolidated Investments Ltd, which owns the television company e.tv, and has served as director of numerous other companies.

Foszia Fisher (Turner-Stylianou)

Foszia Fisher married Rick Turner in 1971, and collaborated with him on his philosophical studies and political writing. She was also the director of the Institute for Industrial Education. After Rick's murder, she remarried, and moved to England, where she lives with her family in London. Though her new career is focused on personal development, she remains sharply aware of social justice issues, and continues to be committed to the ideals she shared with Turner.

Barbara Hubbard (Follett)

Barbara met Richard Turner at the age of 16, and married him a few years later. The newly-weds lived together in Paris while Turner was working on his doctorate at the Sorbonne. On returning to South Africa they ran the Turner family farm before separating in 1969. Barbara is the mother of Richard's two daughters, Jann and Kim. A few months after his assassination, Barbara and the young girls moved to England. She was a member of parliament in the UK for the Labour Party from 1997 to 2010. She is now married to the author Ken Follett.

Michael Hubbard

Michael Hubbard is the brother of Barbara Hubbard. A soft-spoken, gentle and warm-hearted man, his fondness for Turner is indisputable. In the years since Turner's death, Michael has diligently assembled an extensive personal archive of documents about Turner, including dozens of newspaper clippings, articles, photographs and his own notes about Turner's life and death. Since the early 1980s, Michael has lived in Birmingham, England, working as a professor, and raising a family.

Gerry Maré

Gerry Maré was a student at the University of Natal in the early 1970s, and lived with Rick Turner at his house in Dalton Avenue. Maré also assisted in the research for the book on the 1973 Durban strikes in which Turner was centrally involved. During Turner's banning, Maré was detained under the 90-day law, and interrogated about his connection with Turner. He went on to teach at the University of Natal (now the University of KwaZulu-Natal) from 1984, and later founded and directed the Centre for Critical Research on Race and Identity. He has published a critical account of the life and career of Mangosuthu Buthulezi, called *An Appetite for Power*.

Tony Morphet
Tony Morphet taught English at the University of Natal during Rick Turner's years in Durban, and the two developed a close friendship. After the assassination, Tony was asked to look after Turner's personal papers, and to write a biographical introduction to the 1980 reissue of *The Eye of the Needle*. Morphet had a long career as a professor at the universities of Natal and Cape Town, and was involved as well in a number of popular education projects. In retirement he enjoys a quiet life, reading and bird watching, interrupted often by younger people hoping to enjoy his keen intellect and sense of humour.

Dan O'Meara
Dan O'Meara met Rick Turner while working as a lecturer at the University of Natal, Durban, in 1972. A Marxist and member of the ANC, he later went into exile, in Mozambique, England, and finally Canada. His critical studies of Afrikaner nationalism, *Volkskapitalisme* and *Forty Lost Years*, are among the most important books on this topic. O'Meara now works as a professor at the University of Quebec at Montreal.

Lawrence Schlemmer
Lawrence Schlemmer was an academic involved in teaching sociology and in social science research. From 1972 to 1986 he worked at the University of Natal, where he became head of the Centre for Applied Social Sciences. Politically liberal, Schlemmer spent a considerable portion of his career with strong links to Mangosuthu Buthulezi. He was a consistently contrary and iconoclastic personality. Despite their divergent politics, Turner and Schlemmer became good friends during the last half-dozen years of Turner's life, collaborating on a number of projects, including the IIE. Schlemmer died in 2011.

Notes

INTRODUCTION

1 R. Turner, *The Eye of the Needle: Towards Participatory Democracy in South Africa* (Johannesburg: Ravan Press, 1980), p. 8.

2 The initial round of research and writing for this project was done towards the completion of a Master's degree at the University of the Western Cape, South Africa. Premesh Lalu taught the course described. The eventual thesis, 'Richard Turner's Contribution to a Socialist Political Culture in South Africa, 1968–1978', was awarded with honours.

3 'The Present as History' was initially a series of lectures that Turner presented to his political science class at the University of Natal.

4 Turner, *Eye of the Needle*, pp. 152–3.

5 It is important to note that the book became an illegal document from 1973 to 1978, during Turner's banning years. Despite the fact that Turner's writing had a considerable impact among a certain group of opponents to apartheid in the 1970s, his writing has become relatively obscure, quite hard to obtain, even in South Africa. *The Eye of the Needle* has not been reprinted since 1980 and is hard to find in most bookstores. (The book does exist online: http://www.scribd.com/doc/55744023/The-Eye-of-the-Needle-by-Richard-Turner.) The bulk of Turner's philosophical writings have never been published, and what copies exist are primarily within personal collections rather than public archives. A number of his shorter articles were published by journals at the time, and have been made available online (http://www.morethanthinking.wordpress.com), but still in general remain relatively obscure.

6 A. Nash, 'History and Consciousness in South Africa Today: An Essay on the Political Thought of Richard Turner' (Unpublished manuscript, n.d.), p. 4.

7 Fatima Meer passed away in 2010. Lawrence Schlemmer, one of Rick Turner's dearest friends, and a house-mate for a number of years, recently passed away as well, only a year or so after our interview.

8 Milan Kundera, *The Book of Laughter and Forgetting* (Faber, 1996), p. 223.

9 C.S. Rassool, 'The Individual, Auto/Biography and History in South Africa' (PhD, UWC, 2004), p. 28.

10 Tony Morphet, 'Why We Need Richard Turner', *South African Outlook* 108, 1024 (June 1978), p. 90.

CHAPTER 1
1 Rick Turner, 'Notes on Sartre's Political Theory, Chapter 5: Choice' pp. 20–35, Richard Turner Archive, University of KwaZulu-Natal, c.1977.
2 Tony Morphet, 'Introduction', Rick Turner, *The Eye of the Needle* (Johannesburg: Ravan, 1980), p. viii.
3 Named after Miss Welsh, Miss Carmichael and Miss Masters, who had started the tearoom business there before Jane and Paddy bought it.
4 Turner, 'Notes on Sartre's Political Theory, Chapter 5: Choice', pp. 20–35.
5 D. O'Meara, *Forty Lost Years: The Apartheid State and the Politics of the National Party* (Johannesburg: Ravan Press, 1996), p. 116.
6 The Hit Parade was a radio show that played the top songs of every week.
7 Turner, 'Notes on Sartre's Political Theory, Chapter 5: Choice', pp. 20–35.
8 Morphet, 'Introduction', p. xi.
9 As quoted in Morphet, 'Introduction', p. xii.
10 Turner, 'Notes on Sartre's Political Theory, Chapter 5: Choice', pp. 20–35.
11 Morphet, 'Introduction', p. xv.
12 Ibid., p. xiv.

CHAPTER 2
1 Morphet, 'Introduction', p. xv.
2 It was called 'Quelques implications de la phenomenologie existentielle', or 'Some Implications of Existentialist Phenomenology'.
3 Sartre's partner, Michelle Vian, describes Sartre and herself as people who 'were against everything that seemed a little for order. We hated that. As much as we could, we did whatever was forbidden, and prohibited.' Quoted in BBC's 1990 documentary 'Human, All Too Human'.
4   Annie Cohen-Solal, 'Sartre at his Centennial: Errant Master or Moral Compass?', *Theor Soc* 36 (2007), 223–30.
5 Annie Cohen-Solal, quoted in 'Human, All Too Human'.
6 Interview conducted by Michel Contat, 1975.
7 Turner, 'Notes on Sartre's Political Theory', Chapter 5: Choice'.
8 Ibid.
9 Ibid.
10 Ibid.
11 J.P. Sartre, *Being and Nothingness* (New York: Citadel Press, 1964), p. 463.
12 Turner, 'Notes on Sartre's Political Theory' Chapter 5: Choice'.
13 Ibid.
14 Ibid.
15 Sartre, *Being and Nothingness*, p. 352.
16 Turner's lecture to his political science class at the University of Natal, c.1971, recorded on cassette, Jann Turner personal collections.
17 Sartre, *Being and Nothingness*, p. 39.

18 Turner's lecture to his political science class at the University of Natal, c.1971.

19 Ibid.

20 Ibid.

21 Turner, 'Notes on Sartre's Political Theory, Chapter 5: Choice'.

22 Turner, *The Eye of the Needle*, p. 1.

23 Ibid., p. 1.

24 TV did not exist in South Africa until the 1970s. Turner maintained a subscription to *Les Temps Modernes* after he returned home to South Africa.

25 P. Gavi, J.-P. Sartre and P. Victor, *On a raison de se révolter* (Paris: Gallimard, 1974), translated by Mitch Abidor, January 2005, http://www.marxists.org/reference/archive/sartre/1972/compagnon.htm.

26 Morphet, 'Introduction', p. xvi.

CHAPTER 3

1 Turner, *The Eye of the Needle*, p. 102.

2 As quoted in Morphet, 'Introduction', p. xiii.

3 K.R. Hughes, 'Lessons of the Great UCT Sit-in of 1968'.

4 Ibid.

5 R. Erbmann, 'Conservative Revolutionaries: Anti-Apartheid Activism at the University of Cape Town 1963–1973', http://www.sahistory.org.za.

6 Ibid.

7 Ibid.

8 The speech is entitled 'Should South African Students Riot?', Richard Turner Archive, University of KwaZulu-Natal, Durban.

CHAPTER 4

1 Turner, *The Eye of the Needle*, p. 101.

2 S. Biko, *I Write What I Like* (London: Bowerdean, 1978), p. 20.

3 J.-P. Sartre, Preface to Frantz Fanon, *The Wretched of the Earth* (New York: Grove, 1991), pp. 1–2.

4 Biko, *I Write What I Like*, p. 29.

5 R. Turner, 'Black Consciousness and White Liberals', in T. Karis and G. Gerhart, *From Protest to Challenge* vol. 5: *Nadir and Resurgence, 1964–1979* (Bloomington: Indiana University Press, 1997), p. 429.

6 Biko, *I Write What I Like*, p. 69.

7 Ibid, p. 25.

8 Turner, 'Black Consciousness and White Liberals', p. 431.

9 1972 speech in Utrecht, as quoted in Peter Walshe, *Church vs State in South Africa* (London: C. Hurst, 1983), pp. 117–18.

10 I base this claim principally on a reading of the Spro-cas texts.

11 M. Nupen, 'Richard Turner on Dialectical Reason', Paper delivered at 15th Congress of the Philosophical Society of Southern Africa, UWC, January 1988, p. 15.

12 Turner, *Eye of the Needle*, pp. 152–3.

13 Ibid., pp. 143–4.

14 Ibid., p. 110.
15 Ibid., pp. 123–4.
16 Turner, 'Black Consciousness and White Liberals', p. 431.
17 Ibid., p. 427.
18 Interview with Omar Badsha, October 2009.
19 Morphet, 'Introduction', p. xix.

CHAPTER 5
1 Turner, *Eye of the Needle*, p. 67.
2 D. Greaves, 'Richard Turner and the Politics of Emancipation', *Theoria* 70 (August 1987), p. 33. Turner's own writing on the ideal role of the teacher echoes Greaves's idea of a facilitator.
3 Rick Turner, memo from the Education Reform Association teachers' workshop, Turner-Stylianou personal papers.
4 Morphet, 'Introduction', p. xvii.
5 Ibid.
6 Fatima Meer interview, April 2009.
7 Morphet, 'Introduction', p. xviii.
8 Turner, *Eye of the Needle*, p. 10.
9 Ibid., pp. 10–11.
10 Ibid., pp. 72–3.
11 Ibid., p. 74.
12 Situationist International, 'On the Poverty of Student Life', http://www.bopsecrets.org/SI/poverty.htm.
13 Turner, *Eye of the Needle*, pp. 79–80.
14 These ideas came to Turner through David Poynton, who had travelled to South America and met both Illich and Freire.
15 All the information I found on the ERA was derived from interviews (with Badsha, Morphet and Turner-Stylianou) or is contained in material in the Turner-Stylianou papers.

CHAPTER 6
1 Turner, *Eye of the Needle*, p. 1.
2 Ibid., p. 3.
3 Greaves, 'Richard Turner and the Politics of Emancipation', pp. 37–8.
4 Morphet, 'Introduction', p. vii.
5 Turner, *Eye of the Needle*, p. xxiii.
6 Spro-cas, *Power, Privilege and Poverty* (Johannesburg: Ravan Press, 1972), p. 6.
7 Turner, *Eye of the Needle*, p. 101.
8 Ibid., p. 19.
9 Ibid., p. 3.
10 Ibid., p. 44.
11 Ibid., p. 4.
12 From an unpublished manuscript, as quoted in A. Nash, 'History and Consciousness in South Africa Today: An Essay on the Political Thought of

Richard Turner' (Unpublished manuscript, n.d.), p. 28.

13 Turner, *Eye of the Needle*, p. 38.

14 Ibid., p. 91.

15 Ibid., p. 62.

16 Ibid., p. 61.

17 Ibid., p. 91.

18 Ibid., p. 42.

19 Ibid., p. 39.

20 Ibid., p. 39.

21 Ibid., pp. 9–4.

22 Spro-cas, A *Taste of Power* (Johannesburg: Ravan Press, 1973), p. 198.

CHAPTER 7

1 F. Fisher [R. Turner], 'Class Consciousness Among Colonised Workers in South Africa', in L. Schlemmer and E. Webster (eds.), *Change, Reform and Economic Growth in South Africa* (Johannesburg: Ravan Press, 1978), p. 198.

2 Republic of South Africa, 'Commission of Inquiry into Certain Organisations', 4th interim report, 12 August 1974, p. 558.

3 Turner, *Eye of the Needle*, p. 132.

4 'Poverty datum line' was the terminology used at the time, to convey the same meaning.

5 In my interviews I was unable to end the dispute about the level of Turner's involvement once and for all, but Cheadle, Badsha, Morphet, Schlemmer, Turner-Stylianou, O'Meara and Webster all spoke of Turner's involvement in the Wages Commission, stressing Turner's importance in the process to varying degrees.

6 M. Legassick, 'Aboveground Organisations and Activities, Part 2: NUSAS in the 1970s', in SADET, *The Road to Democracy*, vol. 2 (Pretoria: University of South Africa Press, 2006), p. 862.

7 D. Hemson, M. Legassick and N. Ulrich, 'White Activists and the Revival of the Workers' Movement', in SADET, *The Road to Democracy*, vol. 2, p. 256. Hemson and colleagues count the numbers based on the amount of workers on strike at any one time, citing that some days there were 20,000, and at the peak, 50,000 in one day. As there were dozens of strikes, and many of them short-lived, the number 100,000 is an estimate of the total numbers of strikers. This corresponds with J. Sithole, and S. Ndlovu, 'The Revival of the Labour Movement, 1970–1980', in SADET, *The Road to Democracy*, p. 187. The number 100,000 is also cited in IIE, *The Durban Strikes: Human Beings with Souls* (Johannesburg: Ravan Press, 1974).

8 In Fisher [Turner], 'Class Consciousness', p. 212.

9 Walshe, *Church vs State in South Africa*.

10 Fisher [Turner], 'Class Consciousness', pp. 213, 216.

11 Ibid., pp. 214–15.

12 IIE, *The Durban Strikes*. The book was a collaborative effort, with a number of people (including Foszia Fisher, Lawrence Schlemmer, Harriet Bolton, Gerry

Maré and David Hemson) crucially involved in the work. Primarily, assistance was needed during the research phase, although others helped with some of the writing and editing. Nonetheless, Turner was a central instigator for the project, and would have been listed as an author if his banning had not prevented this. My information on the collective authorship of *The Durban Strikes* is based on interviews with Maré, Turner-Stylianou and Morphet.

13 Workers were contacted with the help of Harriet Bolton, an unusually sympathetic organiser of black workers. Part of the question being investigated was whether the strikes were simply 'a black thing', or whether Indian workers were sympathetic to them.

14 Though Turner acknowledges the presence of Wages Commission activists and their contributions regarding a living wage, the overall finding is that agitators were *not* responsible. This is a position confirmed by Halton Cheadle (interview, 9 November 2009), one of the people who could have been seen as 'agitating' as a result of his work with the Wages Commission.

15 A random sample, as close to equal numbers of English and Afrikaans speakers as possible, was asked a series of questions by telephone.

16 Further, this section of the book was reprinted as 'The Case for African Trade Unions', *South African Labour Bulletin* 1, 1 (April 1974).

17 Of course, it is worth repeating that this text was collaboratively written, which may have affected the tone considerably.

18 IIE, *The Durban Strikes*, p. 155.

19 Ibid., pp. 176–7. 'Trade Union officials always dread strikes … Thus in societies where strikes are legal they are relatively rare occurrences, and in all societies workers and trade unionists dislike striking.'

20 According to David Lewis, the tragedy at Carletonville was not one of 'bloodier forms of protest' but rather of *the state* massacring innocents: 'In September 1973, police shot dead 11 black miners during a wage dispute at Western Deep Levels mine in Carletonville, west of Johannesburg.' D. Lewis, 'Black Workers and Trade Unions', in SADET, *The Road to Democracy in South Africa*, vol. 2, p. 205.

21 IIE, *The Durban Strikes*, p. 180.

22 Ibid., pp. 159–60.

23 Ibid., quoting Helen Suzman, p. 111.

24 Fisher [Turner], 'Class Consciousness', pp. 197–223.

25 Ibid., p. 200.

26 Ibid., p. 211.

27 Ibid., p. 216.

28 Ibid., pp. 215–16. 'It is worth stressing that in South Africa, managerial prerogative over African workers has traditionally been virtually absolute. Under these circumstances, all issues are issues of control, whether they concern the right of workers to negotiate for higher wages, or to have recognized trade unions, or to take away the managerial right to hire and fire at will. Because they are perceived by management as issues of control, they may at least come to be perceived in the same way by workers.'

29   Ibid., p. 220. Emphasis added.
30   Ibid., p. 213.
31   Ibid., p. 221.
32   Interview with Maré, November 2009.
33   David Hemson was a student activist at Natal, and later went into exile and joined the Marxist Workers' Tendency.
34   Interview with Halton Cheadle, 9 November 2009.

CHAPTER 8

1   D. Woods, *Biko* (New York: Paddington Press: New York, 1978), p. 83.
2   'The Testimony of Dr. R.A.D. Turner', Commission of Inquiry into Certain Organisations, pp. 552–63.
3   Nine members of the CI and four of SAIRR had charges pressed against them for refusing to testify. The director of the Christian Institute, Beyers Naudé, for example, was fined R50, which he refused to pay. He was then arrested, and held overnight, until someone from his church paid the fine for him, and he was released.
4   'The Testimony of Dr. R.A.D. Turner', Commission of Inquiry into Certain Organisations, pp. 552–63.
5   According to the Schlebusch Commission:
     1. *The Anti-Apartheid Movement* in London. (He has two friends) 2. *Spro-cas.* (He was a member of Politics and Economics Commission, and wrote *The Eye of the Needle*) 3. *Theatre Council of Natal* (Black Consciousness theatre that Turner attended a couple of times.) 4. *International Parliamentary Debating Society* in Durban. (Spoke once, or twice.) 5. *South African Institute of Racial Relations* (He is a member, and attends meetings) 6. *International Film Society* (He is a member; they do cultural, high class films) 7. *Citizens Action Group* (He is a member; Church leaders and academics) 8. *Economic Society of South Africa* (He addressed a meeting) 9. *Wilgespruit Ecumenical Centre* (He went once or twice) 10. *Young Christian Workers* (He gave a talk once) 11. *Methodist Youth Organisation* (He gave a talk once) 12. *The Coloured Labour Party* (He attended one or two meetings, and gave a talk) 13. *The Young Progressives* (He gave a talk on 'Mass Violence in South Africa') 14. *The Education Reform Association* (He initiated) 15. *The Natal Indian Congress* (He attended some of their meetings) 16. *The Committee for Clemency* (He was a member) 17. *The Union of Jewish Women* (He addressed a meeting) 18. *The Catholic Justice and Peace Commission* (He gave a talk) 19. *The University Christian Movement* (He gave a talk).
6   Ibid.
7   Woods, *Biko*, p. 84.
8   South African Police file, Ref. S.1/8242, signed Brigadier H.G..V. Cilliers, 8.6.1973, Jann Turner Papers.
9   Jann Turner's personal papers.
10   IIE, *The Durban Strikes*, p. 175.
11   IIE, 'The Worker in Society', lesson 4, p. 1, Turner-Stylianou papers.
12   Ibid., p. 15.

13 Again, it is important to point out that even as Turner was clearly the writer of the IIE workbooks, they should nonetheless be understood as collaborative documents, as Foszia Fisher was crucial for doing a great deal of work to get the books laid out and printed, and Nxasana was essential for translating into Zulu. Further, Alec Erwin speaks of his involvement in the writing process: 'Turner and I had long discussions. He would often write and I would read (as would others). We would sit there for hours, and argue and debate. For me, it was a tremendous learning experience.' Interview with Erwin, 3 May 2010.

14 IIE memorandum, signed Foszia Fisher (co-ordinator), 1974, p. 6, Turner-Stylianou Papers.

15 Ibid., p. 2.

CHAPTER 9

1 Letter from Turner to a friend, 1977, Turner-Stylianou personal papers.

2 Ibid.

3 Rick Turner was also very curious about and supportive of the new independent government in Mozambique, and even began studying Portuguese so that he could listen to radio broadcasts from there.

4 Interview with Lawrie Schlemmer, December 2009.

5 For more on the history of TUACC, see N. Ulrich, 'Only Workers Can Free the Workers: The Origin of the Workers' Control Tradition and the Trade Union Advisory Coordinating Committee (TUACC), 1970–1979' (PhD diss., University of the Witwatersrand, 2007).

6 IIE Report to TUACC, signed Foszia Fisher, 1975, Turner-Stylianou Papers.

7 According to John Copelyn, Nxasana 'was a guy who was involved in the Sactu union in the 1950s and had gone to jail for a year and came out. And the intention was to have him a secretary of the textile union. So he had been brought in by Halton along those lines. As they were about to form the union, the security branch got hold of him and said, "Listen here, you have to understand that if you had been convicted for a political crime, then you are not allowed to be involved in any organisation that's listed or scheduled" … and trade unions were listed or scheduled. So at the last minute they couldn't have him as a secretary of the union … By the time I got there he was already converted into a translator in the Institute for Industrial Education working with Foszia translating all the material. And translating by hand, typing in Zulu basically letter by letter, and he would have to scrutinise all that to see if it was correctly typed. There were no computers, so you couldn't just change the x into a w, you had to retype the page in order. So, the translation was unbearably slow.'

8 S. Friedman, *Building Tomorrow Today: African Workers in Trade Unions, 1970–1984* (Johannesburg: Ravan Press, 1987), p. 97.

9 Interview with Alec Erwin, 3 May 2010. Furthermore, Erwin stresses that the foundation of all education seminars needed to be discussion-based, and the workbooks would be offered as 'back-up' for those workers who expressed interest and had high enough levels of literacy.

10 Interview with Turner-Stylianou, 17 October 2009.

11 Ibid.

12 There are many ways to substantiate this claim. In particular, there is a great deal of discussion of the matter within 'The Present as History', postscript to *Eye of the Needle*.

13 Fisher [Turner], 'Class Consciousness', p. 210.

14 IIE, *The Durban Strikes*, p. 120.

15 According to Schlemmer, 'There was nothing formal about the community education curriculum. It was a method. This curriculum was never written down.' Interview with Schlemmer, 8 December 2009.

16 See G. Maré and G. Hamilton, *An Appetite for Power: Buthelezi's Inkatha and the Politics of 'Loyal Resistance'* (Johannesburg: Ravan Press, 1987).

17 J. Maree, 'Institute of Industrial Education and Worker Education', *South African Labour Bulletin* 9, 8 (July 1984), p. 81.

18 Ibid., p. 86.

19 Hemson, Legassick and Ulrich, 'White Activists', p. 271: 'Soon thereafter [Fisher's resignation] the IIE was targeted by the police, who arrested Eddie Webster in December 1975 on charges under the Suppression of Communism Act and Bheki Nxasana under Section 6 of the Terrorism Act.'

20 Maree, 'Institute of Industrial Education and Worker Education', p. 88.

21 Interview with Alec Erwin, 3 May 2010.

22 During this time, Turner also wrote an extensive essay on Althusser, and some introductory essays on Marxism, which were not precisely a part of his main project about Sartre.

23 From a letter to Johann Degenaar. Turner-Stylianou Papers.

24 Turner-Stylianou Papers.

25 The dean at the University of Natal did supply a letter to the Minister of Justice in support of Rick Turner's application to study abroad.

26 Letter to Johann Degenaar, 24 July 1976, Turner-Stylianou Papers.

27 Letter to the Minister of Justice, 1977, Turner-Stylianou Papers.

CHAPTER 10

1 Turner, *Eye of the Needle*, p. 99 and Steve Biko, *I Write What I Like* (San Francisco: Harper & Row, 1986), pp. 152–3.

2 Biko, *I Write What I Like*, p. 153. Steve Biko was detained on 21 August 1977. After a couple of weeks in detention, Biko was commanded to stand up during an interrogation. He repeatedly refused. Enraged, the officers picked him up and shoved him head-first into the concrete wall. On 11 September, four days after that brutal attack, the authorities decided that Biko was in need of medical treatment. In a semi-conscious state, Biko was driven – naked, in the back of a Land Rover – 1,200 kilometres to Pretoria. He never made it to a hospital; he died as a result of brain damage, on the floor of Pretoria Central Prison.

3 By 1976, the Christian Institute (the organisation that had created Spro-cas) had moved fully and openly towards a rejection of capitalism, calling for economic sanctions against the South African regime and direct support of southern African liberation organisations. Having once been relatively reluctant

collaborators with radicals such as Biko and Turner, the Institute had come quite a long way, to the point of virtually echoing them on many fundamental points.

4   Jane Turner's typed responses to the murder of her son, South African History Archives, University of the Witwatersrand, Johannesburg.

5   All of this from an interview I conducted with Foszia Fisher on 7 July 2011.

6   This statement is available in the original at the South African History Archives, University of the Witwatersrand, Johannesburg.

7   From her testimony to the Truth and Reconciliation Commission, 24 October 1996.

8   Interview conducted by Jann Turner, 1993. Transcripts of interviews conducted by Jann Turner for the making of the film 'My Father, Rick Turner' can be found at the South African History Archives, University of the Witwatersrand, Johannesburg.

9   Ibid.

10 Mtshali survived the shooting.

11 Jann Turner, from her testimony to the Truth and Reconciliation Commission, 24 October 1996.

12 From an interview conducted by Jann Turner, 1993. Transcripts of interviews conducted by Jann Turner for the making of the film 'My Father, Rick Turner' can be found at the South African History Archives, University of the Witwatersrand, Johannesburg.

13 Interview with Tony Morphet, October 2009.

14 From her testimony to the Truth and Reconciliation Commission, 24 October 1996.

15 Interview conducted by Jann Turner, 1993.

CONCLUSION

1   Rick Turner, *The Eye of the Needle*. p. 35.

2   Turner would often repeat statements like 'We've got to be able to think more clearly than the state allows', and 'Thinking, provided that it is done honestly and provided that one does something about one's thoughts, is far more revolutionary and dangerous than mere rioting'. Turner, 'Should South African Students Riot?', Rick Turner Archive, University of KwaZulu-Natal, Durban.

Index